"This book inspired me."

—Ted Turner, CNN founder, global visionary, and philanthropist

"I'm not one for spiritual reading, but I found Christina's journey fascinating and believable. As a matter of fact, I'm astral traveling my way to the bookstore right now."

—Chevy Chase

"A truly lovely and loving expression of life from a woman who is the absolute embodiment of her word. Thank you for being you, Christina."

—Rosario Dawson, actress and social and environmental entrepreneur

"A fascinating and inspiring story told with great honesty and lucidity."

—Duncan Campbell, correspondent for *The Guardian, The Observer,* and *The British Journalism Review*   .

"It's riveting! I was going to say mind-blowing, but I think mind-expanding is more accurate."

—Jayni Chase, founder of the Center for Environmental Education

*"The words and the teachings of Mother Teresa have greatly impacted my life for many years. As a young girl, it was her teachings that awakened my spirit and later sparked my interest to become a nun. Mother Teresa . . . has profoundly influenced my spiritual foundation and is my philosophy for living. Like me, you have been led by the greatest gift of all—love. I can now add **Love: The Saint and the Seeker** as a contributing tome to my spiritual evolution and growth."*

—Chaka Khan

love

love

THE SAINT AND THE SEEKER

CHRISTINA STEVENS

HAY HOUSE, INC.

Carlsbad, California • New York City
London • Sydney • Johannesburg
Vancouver • Hong Kong • New Delhi

Published and distributed in the United States by: Hay House, Inc.: www.hayhouse
.com® • *Published and distributed in Australia by:* Hay House Australia Pty. Ltd.: www
.hayhouse.com.au • *Published and distributed in the United Kingdom by:* Hay House
UK, Ltd.: www.hayhouse.co.uk • *Published and distributed in the Republic of South
Africa by:* Hay House SA (Pty), Ltd.: www.hayhouse.co.za • *Distributed in Canada by:*
Raincoast Books: www.raincoast.com • *Published in India by:* Hay House Publishers
India: www.hayhouse.co.in

Cover design: Amy Rose Grigoriou and Brian Sisco • *Interior design:* Pamela Homan

Library of Congress Cataloging-in-Publication Data

Stevens, Christina
  Love : the saint and the seeker / Christina Stevens. -- 1st edition.
    pages cm
  ISBN 978-1-4019-4591-6 (tradepaper : alk. paper) 1. Teresa, Mother, 1910-1997. 2.
Stevens, Christina. 3. Spiritual biography. I. Title.
  BX4406.5.Z8S76 2014
  271'.97--dc23
  [B]
                                           2014006401

Tradepaper ISBN: 978-1-4019-4591-6

10 9 8 7 6 5 4 3 2 1
1st edition, September 2014

Printed in the United States of America

To my parents,
who never knew the joy of their love for each other.

To the man on the motorcycle,
who try as he might and love as he must is still trying
to wrap his lips around those three simple words.
Unnecessary as they may be.

And for the one I cherish, who says again and again,
"It's true! I do. I do love everybody.
And it's a bright beautiful wonderful world..."

contents

Prelude to LOVE x

chapter one: Living a Privileged Life 1

chapter two: Emotionally Bankrupt 19

chapter three: When Destiny Calls 27

chapter four: You're Going to Have to Wing It 51

chapter five: Faith Is a Gift 71

chapter six: Money Always Comes. 85

chapter seven: Be Like a Pencil. 107

chapter eight: Love the Child 119

chapter nine: Heal the Invisible. 137

chapter ten: It's All in the Feeling. 171

chapter eleven: When You Wake the Tiger Inside 189

chapter twelve: The Wish Is Already Granted 209

chapter thirteen: Be the One 227

chapter fourteen: See Every Day as a Miracle. 241

chapter fifteen: Two Magic Words 257

chapter sixteen: Trust Love. 275

chapter seventeen: It's Why We Are Alive 287

One Last Thing. 315

A Thank-you Gift for You 325

About the Author 327

PRELUDE TO LOVE

Though it has taken me 20 years
to dig deep enough to tell you this story,
I do believe everything unfolds in divine right order.
We see now, clear evidence that you and I are at the tipping point
of a giant global shift. The natural quickening of our evolution;
the rush of technology, along with mankind's growing
footprint across the universe is impacting our daily lives,
our planet earth and all its species
in epic proportion.
The good news is, we find ourselves together, amid this
great awakening, collected in this moment of expanding
awareness, with every needed solution at our fingertips ~
to arise from polarity to unity consciousness.
To emerge out of the dark and into the light ~
seeking unity of the self inside the diversity of the whole.
The fact that we are still wantonly killing each other, often
with weapons in our children's hands, is a telling sign that
we human beings are still awaiting our transcendence.
As trite as it may sound ~ love is the answer.

I have not offered rules and tools
promising a life you have only dreamed of.
I am ill qualified to do that. And I don't presume to
think you may learn from my hiccups. Rather, I pray that
by leaping into my life adventure,
you may enrich and honor your own even more.

You are apt to wonder if a tale has been embellished
or a cloak of self-deception woven to deny an ugly truth.
Warts and all, I have done my best to keep the cryptic true.
Having grown up in the theater, my memory for dialogue is
reliable ~ my longing for drama, alive and kicking.
Timing though, is tricky.
I have dipped my pen into the timelessness of the soul.
In doing so, I found that life is a hologram of past, present,
and future, meshed intricately and endlessly, rather than
a lone linear journey that abruptly ends when we
fall off the edge of a flat world. So while this account of my time
with Mother Teresa covers only a few weeks,

it indeed embraces centuries.
For the purpose of expediency, some timelines
have been compressed.

There is also the consideration that so many people
participate in any adventure that to recount them all would
give you vertigo. There are those who are there in the room
beside us, and those who are there in the ether inside us ~ all
equally present and influential to our choices.
Separation is an illusion.
For clarity, certain characters are composite.
To preserve others' privacy ~ and even against their
wishes ~ I have changed several names.

As you might expect, God is referred to liberally, not as imposition
of a devout belief, but because God and Love are unifying elements
in all religions, indeed sometimes interchangeable. So I ask that you
interpret God, your creator, your source, your higher self, to be what
that holy essence means to you, in your heart.

The title is simply LOVE. Not because it involves a woman whose
utter simplicity of expression was her trademark. This narrative
reaches beyond time and space, and journeys into a realm
uncommon, where words are obsolete.

Love. Like a sweet fragrance from long ago
or a relished taste that remembers you home,
it has been my task to awaken those forgotten memories.
Love. Simply love.
To add anything more would limit the largesse
of the adventure you are about to take.

Many of the italicized quotes in this book were inspired by the
teachings of Mother Teresa, M.C.

CHAPTER ONE

LIVING A PRIVILEGED LIFE

Christina Stevens

*"When your heart speaks,
will you have the courage to listen?"*

Friday, September 5, 1997
Santa Paula, California

Every muscle in my body froze. I couldn't breathe. *This can't be happening.*

From the core of the earth I felt a loud roar. *Earthquake!* Immediately I gathered my senses. *What to do? Dive under the bed? Stand in the doorframe? Grab Maxi and get the heck outside?*

Before I could summon the courage to move I realized it wasn't an earthquake at all. Somewhere, deep inside my supposedly safe vehicle of flesh and bone I was being rocked off my core. There was a presence in the room and the rumbling was fear!

Oh God, help me! Help me lift my eyelids.

I slid a glance across the room. There was Maxi. Panting happily, tail swishing across the wood floor, and ears bobbing out in that happy way they do when she hasn't seen me all day. Her delight relaxed me until I saw her gaze was riveted all right, but not on me.

I opened my eyes wider, struck by a sense of impending doom as I beheld the foggy vision before me.

God? Is it you? Have you come to take me?

Suddenly the mist turned to light, glittering all around. It was alive, flitting here and there like lightning bugs. So alluring, so full of energy, so beautiful I wanted to give myself over to the light, become part of it, certain I would be engulfed in its ecstasy. Unable to resist it, I thought about nothing but the light and whoosh! I was in . . . in the midst of what seemed like a great gathering. Playing in a land of nothing, swimming in a sea of everything, I was outside my body and every other limitation known to man.

I don't know how long it was ~ perhaps it was the approach of morning and the hungry call of swallows outside my window that prompted the gathering to murmur, "When you write . . ."

Had I lost consciousness? Was that a voice talking?

Startled, I snapped back into my body and stirred under the covers.

"What did you say?" I bravely asked the glowing apparition hovering at the foot of my bed.

No response. Nothing.

"When you write!" the voice repeated ~ loudly this time.

For an instant I didn't know if I was awake or asleep. If I was in my body or out of it. Immediately I recognized her deep, guttural European accent.

It's her!

The gathering was complete, and the form became a presence I knew well, a holy, godly presence my senses recognized. And that was when all fear and confusion vanished. The familiar voice that began so sweetly, begging a question, suddenly took on a more urgent edge.

"When are you going to write?"

I bolted awake and sat up.

She was calling to me now, as if she were everywhere in the room at once, her small voice amplified by the chilling silence in which the beating of my heart was the only other sound. No longer was this the gentle, guiding phrase she had uttered four years earlier. No. This was an order. And with that order my very existence was shaken.

Propelled from my warm bed, the hardwood floor shocked me to attention. I shifted focus for a microsecond, and in that instant she was gone.

"Where did she go?" I looked to Maxi for a clue. She rolled over onto her back and pointed all fours up to heaven, her fluffy white tail happily swishing back and forth across the wood floor.

Here I have a visitation from one of the icons of our time and my sole witness is a blissed-out, 15-year-old mutt!

I wasn't sure what to think anymore.

Tell me: do you believe life rises up from death to call again to the living? Do you wonder if there is an unseen world, here and now beside us, simply waiting for us to lift the veil of our limited minds to see the bigger picture?

I paced the room, almost frantic with the need to understand and act on that understanding. And then I knew, as if my work, my seeking, had been preparing me all along.

In the half light I searched the silver jewelry box on my dressing table, but what I was looking for wasn't there. I dove into the top drawer of my lingerie chest, foraged around for the white silk jewelry pouch. Wasn't in there either.

Without warning, a sick, murky feeling landed in my stomach, sending a knowing truth to my heart. Years after I have gone, I will not be remembered. I have never married, I have no children, and I have done nothing significant for the human race.

But she, she had a heart so huge it touched almost every living person on earth. She was someone you would have reason to remember all the days of your life.

Of all the precious gifts to lose . . .

There was a small 18th-century cloisonné box nestled amid my sweaters, but it wasn't in there either. I took a deep breath and stilled myself. I visualized it, there in my hand, and going back in time, I retraced its journey.

3

Locating lost items is a rather wacky talent of mine and something I have always known how to do. *Yes. There it is.* I had been traveling when I last saw it. It had been four, almost five years ~ goodness, it could have been a million years for all I know ~ since she had presented that gift to me. I didn't keep it in any of the traditional places, because it wasn't that kind of thing. It was special.

Yes! Side drawer of my bedroom desk. I removed the leather passport wallet and felt for the bulge in the luggage ticket compartment. There it was. The silver ring, unusual to say the least, because it had a small raised effigy of Jesus on the cross standing on top of it. I held it to my heart as if it still possessed her and just by touch her energy could infuse mine.

From our religious beliefs to our lifestyles, there was absolutely nothing she and I had in common, yet there was a point in time when we connected, and something of what she wanted to give to the world, she gave to me.

She tore down the fortress around my heart, which I had been building for as long as I could recall. She cracked open the door to my soul ~ a door I never dreamed existed. And she brought meaning into my life that I had no right to expect. There was something remarkable in what she gave me that wasn't mine to keep ~ to keep secret, that is.

It happened in ways that went against everything she appeared to believe in, in ways I myself found hard to accept. Maybe that's why I waited so long to tell you the story.

Hesitation is nobody's ally.

"In nature, you find love in silence ~ the earth goes round
in silence. The sun, the moon, and the stars move in silence.
The trees and the grass and the flowers grow in silence."

I pushed open the french doors and stepped out onto the veranda. Maxi, rescued when she was but a handful in a box at the local feed store, flopped down under my dangling feet as I sank into the swing and looked up to the south mountain. Its jagged rock face shone like a towering cathedral in the evening blue. Angel, my

Australian shepherd, who at six weeks chose her job description as "outside sentinel," sat guard at the foot of the porch steps. Across the creek my two white Andalusian horses, feeling our presence, ambled to the fence and hung their heads in our direction. As if in cahoots, the frogs all at once launched into their soulful evening *ribbit,* soon joined by the owl's *hoo hoo* somewhere beyond the orchard. This was my world.

I lived alone on a 15-acre gentleman's ranch, behind a heavy electronic gate flanked by a wall of trees concealing an "if you climb this, you'd better have a damned good reason" barbed wire fence. And then what you couldn't see ~ the fortress around my heart.

I was an enigma in the small town of Santa Paula, having purchased the ranch from an equally reclusive human being ~ legendary icon and Hollywood King of Cool, Steve McQueen. The talk among the locals was I had been an actress who was now an aeronautical engineer, since I kept my antique plane in a hangar at Santa Paula Airport, the center point of this small, citrus-growing, oil-rich town.

When I heard this rumor I laughed. Appearances tell tall tales. Yes, I carry the burden of being born into a theatrical family and certainly was an actress in Australia in my teens. Equally, I entertain many aerodynamic interests ~ since as a pilot the pull of gravity holds little resistance for me. And some say I converse with the angels.

I laughed, but my laughter belied my shame. Flattered yet amused anyone would spend a minute considering my lone existence, that description was way too lofty, even for me.

Nobody knows the despair and isolation that live inside another's heart. My separation from those around me, that some would imagine as "being a snob" or presume I considered myself "better than," came from pain and fear and not knowing how to love. Summoning all the power within me, I sought to heal those deep wounds in my heart by encasing myself in beauty. Nature's creation and God's gift to man.

I lived with my three prolific chickens, Faith, Hope, and Charity; one rather obnoxious duck who in case her offspring reads this and will be wont to come nipping at my tail just as she did, will remain nameless; koi fish in the pond, but just try counting them; two speak-to-my-soul horses; the two most loyal doggies on the planet; and my ever-regal Queenie the goat. I worked in Hollywood as an executive producer in a commercial production company, but I couldn't live there. Where others commuted home to their wives and children, I journeyed home to my little creatures. They knew all there was to know about me. Indeed they were my solace. If I didn't have nature to commune with I would have curled up like a dry leaf long ago.

Nature has a way of nurturing the despair of aloneness. Every new day there is freshness, an aliveness that you and I in our mundane moments seem to forget. Even though every breath we take is emblematic of a new beginning, we tend to take it for granted.

A person, disconnected from other human beings, can get conveniently lost in the natural world. To me, loving another human requires a true act of heroism. Nature requires only that you honor it, work with it rather than against it, and if you do, all her power and breathtaking beauty is yours.

"Wear this ring, and God will write through you."

Those were almost the last private words she had spoken to me, and they took me by surprise. She knew me only as a woman with a film crew. Yet there was an assumption in her voice, a certainty that said I would understand her parting sentiment in a way no one else would.

"Why me?" I asked the crisp morning air. Years had passed since she had given me the silver ring with the cross on the end of it. Why would she come to me now, imploring me to write? *What is it she wants me to uncover? What is so important she would penetrate time and space to rouse me from my ennui?*

The sun was turning the blue glow to pink. Sunrise. When God flips the switch. The instant we are reminded: you are alive!

Suddenly I felt cold. I retreated back into the bedroom.

I slid onto the bed, gripping the ring she had given me so tightly its silver cross cut into my palm, causing one lonely tear to trickle down my cheek. To distract me from the emotions rising up, I grabbed the remote and turned on the TV. There was Mother Teresa's image framed next to Brian Williams, his woeful eyes almost moist as he said again, "For the second time in one week an internationally beloved woman has unexpectedly died."

Five days earlier, Princess Diana's tragic death shocked the world. Makeshift shrines overflowing with floral tributes, teddy bears, beloved toys, personal keepsakes, and a million lit candles popped up on street corners, embassy lawns, and palace grounds the world over. Regular business was put on hold, and the news media was awash with global mourning. Kings and queens, world dignitaries, political leaders, and citizens came together in a rare and peaceful way. News anchors reported around the clock, almost in a whisper. First from England and then, in the next breath, as if orchestrated by some higher conductor, there they were, en masse on their way to India.

In life, Mother Teresa and Princess Diana were friends. They shared a connection of compassion, and it seemed almost profound and certainly comforting these two friends passed over so close to each other.

I sat on the edge of the bed, immobile, willing the four wooden posts to shield me from that wretched memory. Isn't it bizarre how strong emotions can merge time like tears in the rain? I tamed the sensations rippling through me, and like a knee-jerk reaction the familiar fog of isolation shoved me aside like an inconsiderate lover.

Yes. It would cut me off from feeling, just as it had always done.

No. Not this time.

If my experience with her had taught me anything, it was that I could no longer ignore the messages screaming through my body. Time for me to stop being such a coward and deal with the pain rather than keep letting it morph and grow into who knows what inside me.

Like the last time, on that black summer night in 1984.

There I was, slumped on the same corner of the same bed ~ the only difference was I had the phone in my hand, holding it as far from my ear as I could in an effort to distance its vile message.

Stop! Take that back! Take back what you just said!

I didn't want to believe the words coming from 6,000 miles away in Sydney, Australia. My sister-in-law's father was yelling, to make sure I understood the harsh reality of what he was saying. My body was ice-cold, but my hands were hot and trembling uncontrollably.

"Your brother, Geoffrey, he's dead! Christina! Are you listening? Do you hear me?"

All I knew to do was scream. I sucked air but no sound came. Instead, I let the phone drop, never to forget the hollow echo it stirred in me as it crashed to the floor, proclaiming my fragile world shattered for good.

Struck by his timing ~ what are the odds that a son would pass a year to the day following his mother? For him, it was sudden. For me, it was searing. He was the only human I could turn to at a time like this.

"He's dead, Christina. Can you hear me? He's dead!" The old man spoke without compassion, without tenderness, of someone I loved, too much perhaps for propriety, but love him desperately I did.

For God's sake, why didn't my father call me? Does he even know he has lost his only son? Is he out in one of his fancy restaurants, wooing some strange woman?

Confusion and anger returned control to me. I retrieved the phone, collected myself, and icily demanded details.

"What happened? Where is Dad? Was Geoff in London?"

In two days, Geoffrey and I were to meet in New York.

He circumnavigated the globe often and never passed through American airspace without dropping down and checking up on me. Older brothers do that.

"Yes. In London," Bruce responded in a slightly more compassionate tone. And then it hit me. Here I am, wallowing in self-pity, and Geoffrey had a wife, Rosie, and four young children: Alexandra; Sophie; James, a three-year-old who will grow up without a father; and baby Jessica, just a few months old, who will never know she had one.

"Rosie's doing as well as can be expected," Bruce assured me. "We've told the children, but you know kids; life goes on."

Huh, life goes on. Are children the all-seeing ones? As yet unpressured by society's expectations, unintimidated by life's hopes and fears, and unschooled in the intellectual survival of the mundane? Of this world ~ not yet in it? Are they more closely aligned to their pure soul essence, with an instinctual knowledge of humankind's energetic continuum fresh in their minds?

I knew our earthbound Western notions of death being the end of our existence were limiting. I trusted Einstein was correct in saying energy lives on and cannot be destroyed. And though I could wax intellectually on any number of scenarios for the infinity of life ~ that death is a moment of piercing luminosity before the soul begins its journey to rebirth, or the light we are told to go to when we die is merely our emergence again from another vaginal canal ~ immortality remains a mystery. Wrench a loved one away from me and *The Tibetan Book of the Dead* is toast! Privately, I am as deplorably incapable as the next to cope with that kind of life-changing loss.

I was born into a family who concealed most everything: from the world, from one another ~ even from themselves. As a little peanut I learned well the art of hiding. Should you, on the other hand, wish to gain my love, you would have to prove your devotion to me. You would need to be a master seeker. Courageous and unrelenting in your quest to find my heart, pry it open, and make it yours. A Herculean challenge I was yet to find anyone up for.

Maturity gave me no learned reprieve. My divine test has always been to withhold my love, my pain, my caring, my heartache, my woes ~ my true self ~ from another. You could think this is more a cultural burden. Secretly I suspected it was where my God chip would be found.

To receive the gift of love in this life I would need to learn how to give it, bravely and unconditionally. Will I be standing at the pearly gates saying, I am sorry, God, I could not truly love another, other than my brother?

Geoffrey was the only person in the world I trusted enough to rescue me from that. And now he was gone.

love

> *"The greatest need in the world*
> *is not the want for food,*
> *it's the longing for love."*

When someone loves you unconditionally, they give you license to live fearlessly. Geoffrey did that for me. He was the keeper of all my dark and sacred secrets, just as I was his. I think that's why God gives us brothers and sisters.

To outsiders, our family appeared blessed with everything ~ beauty, wealth, intelligence, even talent. Peggy, my mother, was a child star. Australia's littlest comedienne! Adored by audiences from the age of three, she sang and danced her way around Australasia as the headliner in her mother's professional theater troupe ~ Baby Peggy and the Joybells.

When Peggy was 17, she had made two movies and was the darling of the international talent scouts, but war and love intervened. My father saw my mother on stage, and it was love at first sight. He figured out early on that "Madam," her mother, held the strings tightly on her daughter, so instead of courting her, he joined the theater company. It wasn't long before everyone discovered being an actor was neither his talent nor his interest. Against her mother's wishes and with the pressures of impending war, the pretty star chose love and married my father, William James Stevens . . . Bill. Bill was studying law while making a small fortune as an entrepreneur ~ but most of all, he was a charmer.

His deep velvet voice commanded the room the minute he entered it. When he laughed, women curled around him like sweet honey, leaving a bitter taste in Peggy's mouth. When war came, he gave up law and became a navigator with the Royal Australian Air Force, based in London, Cairo, Morocco, New Guinea, everywhere except home.

"Baby Peggy" had her prince, but it wasn't easy for her to go from the adulation across the footlights to a bed that felt vaster than the Bermuda Triangle, so she had a baby of her own. Their first child was a son, Geoffrey William James Stevens. He had to grow up fast to fill the gap of the big man who was never around and the applauding audiences who were long gone. When the war ended, Peggy thought she would have her husband back, but he merely exchanged his lieutenant's bars for Qantas wings.

Peggy had the kind of unsullied beauty that kept men at a distance, yet her hypnotic green eyes and unquenchable desire to entertain reeled them in like magnets. The blood that ran through her veins was English, Irish, and Italian. Born into a tribe of artists, eccentrics, and incurable romantics, she had no idea a line existed between fantasy and reality. For her, the scene never ended and the curtain never came down. In contrast, on my father's side, the strain was scientific and disciplined ~ German and Irish with a large dose of the wild Scot, to keep it interesting.

We Australians are the lovable mutts of the world.

When Bill finally made his home with us in Sydney, their love turned tumultuous. Money flowed like Niagara Falls and emotions erupted like Mount Vesuvius. That's when I made my entrance, stage left.

The way I saw it, my brother was the one God blessed. He inherited our mother's fiery eyes; dark, feathery lashes; and thick, curly locks that kissed those cherub cheeks. He was so yummy you just wanted to take a big bite of him. Though short lived, he arrived into a world of love, and as he grew older he did everything perfectly. It was no mistake ~ he had a touch of the genius. Brilliant at everything that interested him, he took top academic honors and was an accomplished pianist.

I, on the other hand, was born somewhat hideous. Praise the lord, I got "the eyes," but after that I was a string bean, with long, heavy, straight hair through which two big ears protruded. I was a sad child, a troubled teen, and a young rebel. Though I possessed a weirdly infallible memory for the spoken word, I was a dismal failure as a student, and the only thing that conformed to our family paradigm was my living, breathing dream of becoming a prima ballerina.

On a deeper level, we were children nobody had time for. Emotionally, we came from humble beginnings. Peggy had withdrawn into the numbing safety of an alcoholic haze while Bill found his consolation elsewhere ~ in his work and his women.

Geoff and I had no option but to resort to the alchemy of our survival. He was the maestro and I was the ballerina. Our favorite performance and the one most requested at family gatherings was Beethoven's *Moonlight Sonata.* While his fingers tripped over the ivories, I, in my silky white tutu, was the moon rising from her horizon, growing from new to full until I exploded into an orb of brilliance. Leaping onto my toes, fluttering my arms in the swirl of our energy, I transmitted my moonbeams into the audience, illuminating every shadowy nook and cranny until the whole world was bathed in light.

Those were our scant moments of bliss.

*"You do not need to fear
the perceived brevity of life.
Every religion believes in eternity and
science does not disprove it."*

You could tell in the way Geoffrey pounded the keyboard ~ hands lifting a clear eight inches off the keys, head bobbing, curly locks flying ~ he had a wildly passionate heart. It made him a noisy giant.

"Geoffrey had just finished signing the papers. Did you know he purchased the controlling interest of Cork?" Bruce queried, to be sure I was up on the latest news. "He left the boardroom to make a few phone calls and collapsed ~ right there in front of the secretary. They said he died almost immediately."

As I listened carefully to Bruce explaining as much as he could understand thirdhand from a dire transatlantic call, it dawned on me, Geoff's boisterous and transparent heart may also have killed him.

He had been helming the Dairy Industry in Australia, and now with this ownership of the Cork Corporation, it put him back on track to the fortune taken from him some years earlier. In those years, I was traveling the world and made it back to Australia only for special celebrations. Always concerned with my welfare, he told me nothing of the intense drama unfolding for him at home.

His downfall had been front-page news. Australia's youngest visionary investor, golden boy of the Sydney Stock Exchange, he had misappropriated a transaction ~ or so it appeared. A meteoric career incinerated in one headline. Years later he would be exonerated of all wrongdoing ~ in a two-inch, single column on the back page of the financial section. He had already given up his penthouse that gazed across the bay at the Sydney Opera House, sold his art collection and his Jaguar, and taken off his three-piece suit. To see his long, lean, fragile, lily-white body decked out in shorts and work boots, his elegant pianist's fingers wielding a sledgehammer, and his black curly hair dusted in mortar was a true testament to his inner strength. Shamed from his intended future at 29, his brilliance would not be diminished.

He was renovating old houses until one by one, he purchased them, eventually owning a percentage of an entire Sydney suburb. He moved on from the high-fashion models he was dating and married Rosie, a sweet country girl grown from good Aussie stock and educated in Europe as a Cordon Bleu cook. She took over the interior design of their investments, and when they were on solid ground, they went to work making babies.

Four babies later, he leveraged every asset he owned ~ cashed in his life insurance and all his stock, put every cent he possessed on the line, all the way down to his coveted wine collection ~ for a prize he would never get to take home.

Like him, I began with nothing. Worked my tail off 24/7 as a girl Friday in an advertising agency and moved quickly up to become a writer. I was 19, and my secretary was 35. My ticket to travel was a show reel of award-winning television campaigns. I joined an international advertising agency, making my home first in London, then New York, Hong Kong, and Paris. While in Paris, Geoffrey came to check in with me. His first daughter, Alexandra, had just been born, and he was financial advisor to one of the world's wealthiest men.

Picking him up from Charles de Gaulle I found him in an odd and serious state. When finally he relaxed, realizing it was me, his sister, the one with whom he shared all secrets, he regaled me with tales of global intrigue. The night before he had attended a trilateral meeting in London with the financial head of the Catholic Church, key people from Scotland Yard, the FBI, the CIA, and a few other players. What he spoke of spun my head.

For me to grasp anything, I need to be present in the room, not so much to hear the words spoken as to feel the intent. Gossip, no matter how elite it might be, has never been a favorite of mine.

In the days that followed we cruised through the Loire Valley in my Peugeot convertible, staying at country inns, meeting vintners, relishing their wine, accepting their gifts of grape seeds and vine cuttings, and dining *gastronomique*. We reminisced about our early years and enjoyed the "now" of where we were. There was no more mention of high-level clandestine meetings. Not until we were saying good-bye.

Geoffrey pulled two books from his briefcase, neatly covered in brown paper. "Don't read these in public, darling," he cautioned as he slid them into my purse.

When I laughed at the absurdity of his cloak-and-dagger activity, he fell quietly serious. "One of the authors was murdered. Just do as I say, or I won't give them to you."

I felt as if I had I just swallowed a brick.

"What was it? A heart attack?" I asked Bruce.

"We don't know, Teens."

"He wasn't sick?"

"No. They're going to do an autopsy and then we're flying his body back here."

My breath was heaving in shallow gasps. I almost couldn't take it.

After Paris, his trips to London became more frequent. But I moved to California, and as I was no longer in his flight path we saw less of each other. I was focused on my career and he on his flourishing family.

Out of mind, never out of heart.

I had to know how and why he died. I called London and spoke with his partner, his secretary, even the receptionist. Goodness, I probably even questioned the tea lady. I queried anyone who answered the phone. They revealed little, other than to assure me his body had been sent for autopsy to a hospital 80 miles outside London.

That didn't compute. There is the city morgue and countless hospitals in and around London proper. I asked for the doctor's name. I was told he would call me, but he didn't. I uncovered as much as I could from where I was, but in the years before the Internet, conducting a covert, global investigation was not easy. Nothing was coming up. The more I sought solace, the more it eluded me. I knew my brother as a straight shooter and undeniably not one for protracted conspiracies.

As they told it, he left the boardroom, his signature on the documents not yet dry. He went to his office and made two phone calls. One was to me, but I wasn't home. He left a message to be sure I would be there to meet him at his club in New York in a few days. Then he wrote one postcard. It was while handing this postcard to his secretary that he clutched his throat, gasping for air, and collapsed.

While traveling, it was his habit to send a souvenir postcard to each of his children every day he was away. They would trickle into their mailbox to squeals of delight, oftentimes even after he had returned home. The last postcard, addressed to his three-year-old son, James, arrived a month after his death.

It read simply, "Dear James, Your future is assured. Love, Daddy."

*"If we understood
that death was in fact
going home to God,
there would be no more fear."*

If I could feel any more wretched, I was haunted by a more private guilt. The last time Geoffrey and I were together, we argued. Disagreement was not unusual for us ~ the way we left it was.

As we grew older our alchemy did not diminish. Indeed our fervor for the larger issues of what fueled mankind and what would make the world a better place were fed by intellectual jostling.

Debate is an art, and Geoff painted inside the lines impeccably. He was calm, never emotionally attached, always willing to concede a valid point yet never willing to concede defeat. Victory was never stated nor assumed. When all arguments had been exhausted, we concluded with a kiss and an "I love you."

Then came the shift. We no longer chewed over weighty ideology. When I brought up the state of the world, he would shake his head as if carrying secrets that kept him awake at night. When I spoke of my life and my successes in America he would become visibly agitated.

"Don't worry about me," I assured him.

"I'm worried for us all," he murmured, his eyes glazing over. Withdrawing from the conversation, he was moving further and further out of reach.

When he chose to be present he dissected my decisions and doubted my choices. Doom and gloom's pessimism did not sit well with this Pollyanna who was having her first taste of material excess.

Nothing I did moved him. Upon learning I had been made the youngest senior VP ever in my company, he blinked. He was equally unimpressed when told I scored an almost perfect mark on my written exam for my pilot's license. When I purchased my airplane ~ a 1942 army rescue plane, he raised his eyebrows. That was it. No. Wow! Cool! Never thought you could fly your own plane! No. Just raised eyebrows. I could thrill him with a snap roll and delight him with the poetic weightlessness of a loop, compelling him to acknowledge that although his puny little sister hadn't achieved her dream of becoming a prima ballerina, she had pulled off something bigger! *Moonlight Sonata* in all her glory, I could pirouette him across the blooming sky! He remained nonplussed.

Our last eyeball-to-eyeball conversation left a black hole in my stomach. Mummy had just died, and for the first time ever he raised his voice to me. We said good-bye minus any assurances of love. I had committed the unimaginable. Without consulting my fiscally responsible older brother, I had just purchased a 15-acre horse ranch in Southern California, and the world was my oyster. Since I had never ridden a horse in my life, he considered this yet another notch in my ever-lengthening, frivolous belt.

Something deeper was troubling him. I made it my mission to dive in and talk about it the next time we met. I thought we'd laugh it off and hug it away when we came together in New York ~ but as you know, that was not to be.

One missed opportunity can herald a lifetime of regret. When will I learn? Never sleep on a disagreement. Never say good-bye without saying I love you. Never silence the urge of your heart.

Never postpone love.

CHAPTER TWO

EMOTIONALLY BANKRUPT

Richard James

*"You cannot give
to the outside
what you do not have
on the inside."*

Why do we always look outside ourselves for that which can only be supplied from within? Perhaps it is because each time we do, we find a clue. And that clue is a reflection from the outer world to you.

Most times, when someone of stature dies suddenly, news of their demise cycles newsrooms for a day or so and then they're gone with the wind. It was almost day three, and talk of Mother Teresa's passing was still saturating the airwaves. A producer from KCET in Santa Barbara, hot on her game, called me to request an interview. *What would I say?*

"You could tell us what it was like to be near her," she offered.

"There are countless books out there," I responded. "You can create a nice piece without me. I will give you my footage and you can use whatever you would like."

"If you are available at three o'clock tomorrow I would like to book you for an on-camera interview," she insisted. "You could tell us what inspired you to go to India."

Whatever I may say, no one will understand. Not one moment in her presence was what you would call "normal," or even "in the slipstream" of this world. They will certify me, I thought.

"How many hours do you have?" I chuckled. "I don't know if I can condense it into anything intelligible."

Goodness, I would need to go back to the time before we met. I would need to talk about how my life was selfish and empty and without purpose. And I would have to speak of other things I am hardly proud of.

"The filmmaker's journey . . . ," she added, not giving up.

There was a long pause.

"Like I said, how many hours do you have?"

I could hear her breathing. I cut it with a friendly yet nervous chuckle.

"Being in her presence was like being bathed in truth. No, even better . . . it was like swimming in love."

Ah! There, I gave her a sound bite. And I didn't have to give up anything of myself.

Mirroring. Universal law 101. Whatever you send out will come back to you.

This producer was stubborn, just like me.

"I saw an interview you did last year with Steve Edwards on *Good Day LA* that was quite in-depth."

Oh. Yes. I almost gave my game away then.

Unwittingly I had let slip that this tough-little-cookie producer/ director broke down and cried when Mother Teresa said "No," refusing my cameras in her presence. A crafty interviewer, Steve perhaps sensed I had opened a floodgate and he wrapped it up before I could confess it was an anomaly. I never cried. Didn't believe in crying.

Most of my life tears have been an unattainable depth of feeling for me, unless of course, a performance called for it. Coming from a long heritage of stage actors, comedy or tragedy, I knew easily how to conjure enough emotional manna to prod an audience way back in the bleachers to reach for their hankies. But nothing in life could touch me deeply enough to burn tears. Goodness, I was so out of touch, I could watch the orchestra on the *Titanic* play on as they slowly went down into fatal waters ~ and sing along.

I glanced over at the ring on my desk. *Everything leading up to her gift had been so deeply personal, yet so remarkably universal ~ how could I share what I learned in an interview of sound bites?* My heart raced. There was so much to recall, and my memory was growing faint like a morning mist evaporating in sunlight. All I knew was I couldn't let it go.

I stepped over a snoring Maxi and padded across to the bedroom chaise. In the soft morning light I riffled through my photo albums, scattered by my emotions of the night before. In the last few years my stack of family mementos had found a new spot ~ within easy reach on a sleepless night. I had been in search of one particular photograph. One image that spoke to me, so indelibly of love. I didn't find it and had run out of options of where to look. So I did what always works. I dropped onto the chaise and, resting my head on a pillow, traced back to where I had last seen it. Reversing my memory screen, I visualized all the way to Sydney and Geoffrey's memorial service.

Rosie was in the front row, cradling pretty baby Jessica, flanked by her three other little ones, with my father bookending her, clutching little James's hand. From where I stood at the lectern they all looked so terribly lost. The chapel was packed. Mourners lined the walls. The doors had to be opened and speakers mounted outside for those who could not make it in, to stand in the street and listen. I gave the first eulogy. I chose not to choke on the tragedy before us and instead told stories from our childhood ~ since everything Geoff pursued later in life, he beta tested on me.

His passion for high finance began with me.

Friday and Saturday nights our parents went nightclubbing. Often, we were left home alone to fend for ourselves. No sooner had their car left the driveway than Geoffrey dove into Mummy's closet hiding place for our piggy banks, having figured out how to undetectably break into them. Under the guise of "counting our money" and having already polished his pennies and dulled my two shillings, his agenda was to trade his beautiful, shiny copper pennies for his little sister's dull and ugly silver two-shilling pieces.

At that age I couldn't add two and two. One penny? Two shillings? Copper? Silver? What? But I sensed the hunger in his eyes and the significance of my silver coins. So I played the game, coquettishly dangling uncertainty to his trade until he had almost matched the value in shiny pennies. The money was inconsequential to me. I was simply over the moon I had something my big brother wanted.

Money has never meant much to me. Time, I find, is a far more valuable commodity ~ and from the year dot he gave me that in abundance.

Of my many stories that spoke of his generosity, I chose to share from the pulpit the earliest. I hoped in the telling I could elicit a chuckle or at the very least, a light smile from my dour audience. I knew the last thing he wanted was for them to be sad.

The picture projected on the chapel wall said it all.

I was three and his much adored baby sister queen. He took it upon himself to be my manservant, and he built me a chariot for my journeys in this world. Though resources were limited, Geoff was able to scrounge up two wooden fruit crates, one set of wheels, some rope, some very delicate lace that I think he extracted from a kindly neighbor, and hanging crystals that I gathered were unhooked from a family chandelier. One crate he laid lengthways, wedging on two wheels at one end. The other crate he propped up and slipped inside the first, to shelter Queen Christina from the harsh elements of the lower world and to frame her being in crystal elegance. The carriage itself was makeshift, in contrast to the lace and hanging crystals he spent days fashioning. When done, it beautifully encased Her Highness for the moments she chose to peer out from her royal vehicle to wave to her constituents as he dutifully dragged her from place to place ~ which he did selflessly, endlessly, and tirelessly, before school, after school, day in, and day out.

I am pained to report there was one serious flaw with his construction ~ the absence of back wheels. Without wheels, the splintery wooden slats of the chariot hit the ground, as did I. While darling Geoffrey dragged his beloved sovereign hither and yon, over hill, over dale, across dirt and pavement, down stairs and up gravel driveways, my bottom became progressively bruised and splintered, rubbed raw and bloody from the gaps in the slats. Still, in royal British fashion, I never revealed the silent agony I endured. I smiled and waved and all appeared well in our kingdom.

As I reminisced to the hundreds of captive faces looking up at the projection of Geoffrey with his freckle-faced grin minus two front teeth, standing proudly at attention beside my chariot, this story was more poignant for me than for them. In that moment I was enduring immense agony. Yet being a girl of the empire, stiff upper lip, warrior woman and all that, the world would not see me falter. Amid great pain, I swallowed my emotions and found my way to the end of the eulogy with many deep gulps, sans tears.

When it is upon you to sum up a life, there is really only one word that suffices. Whatever has lived in our hearts, whatever fruit has grown from our actions, whatever service we have given or place in the world we have earned, we are humbly, inextricably, universally connected to one endless, timeless, priceless thing. We have spent our lives either shining light upon or deeply in search of ~ love.

"When you nurture your inner world
as much as you do your outer world,
your life will take an unexpected turn."

I reached over for the ring, pressing the silver cross into my palm, the way Mother had when she gave it to me. I thought it would prompt a recollection. But it didn't. I couldn't play back what I saw and heard the first time it imprinted my hand because for some reason, my elephant memory of those last minutes with her had temporarily deserted me. The brilliant retention I always relied upon had abandoned me. I couldn't understand it. *What was happening?*

God will write through you, she said.

I squeezed it tighter, praying it would work its magic. *Who is this God she speaks of? Is her God now the keeper of my recollections?*

"Beam me up, Scotty," I whispered to the ring. "Take me home," I implored, as if click, click, it was Dorothy's red slippers. Maybe if I rubbed it a genie would appear to grant my wishes?

Oh silly girl, I said to myself. *Reaching for some mythic trick of illusion.*

I opened my palm and offered it to the heavens.

Will white doves flap their wings wildly, lifting my magic carpet from the confines of earth and carry me through time at will? And will I return to you with the wisdom of the heavens?

Without another mundane consideration I slipped the ring onto my finger and took a deep, relaxing breath.

An unusual energy washed through my veins, tension drained from my pores, and when at last all mindful thought had gone, I lifted out of my body. In a flash I was no longer sitting at my desk, fingertips poised upon keys of physicality. I released my earthbound grip and rocketed high through cloudy mists, into the starry blue, effortlessly, as if carried on the wings of angels.

Ahh! Freedom at last.

Soaring through time and space I looked for something familiar.

There she is. The blue planet, Mother Earth.

I dipped down and the moistness of the clouds gave way to salty ocean air. Now I was moving fast, over isles and a continent, to the other side of the globe. Drawn nearer to earth by the resonance of human voices, I wanted to swoop down and explore.

The pilot in me took over. *Reduce power. Shift attitude. Get the airspeed down to 90 miles per hour. Don't want to rush it.*

Land ahead! Around and around we spiraled, leaving the starry blue above. I leveled out and picked up speed again.

As if my thoughts were an act of creation, I let the updrafts lift me high with the hills and low with the valleys, gently tracing the terrain, inching us closer to terra firma. As much as I loved my lone journey, one vital aspect was missing.

People. Where are the people?

In the twinkle of an eye, a cluster of sari-clad women appeared upon the rainbow fields that blanketed the provinces. They were picking flowers and singing.

I have been here before.

India. Exotic fragrances, intricate patterns, vibrant, living color pulled me even closer. Amber-skinned children squealed and giggled as they worked alongside their mothers ~ collecting baskets of blooms and carrying them to oxen waiting by the roadside. I moved with them, tracing the colorful bales as they swayed back and forth, along the pastoral dirt roads to the river's edge where the oxen turned their bounty over to boats.

Floating free now, I tracked the bright baskets' graceful path down the Hooghly River, which feeds into the Ganges Delta, to their destination ~ the flower market at the steps of the Howrah Bridge. Men, women, and children, all with their own unique sleight of hand, were weaving intricately fragrant posies, stringing colorful leis, creating wreaths and bouquets so painstakingly ornate it was clear they were preparing for a very special celebration: to honor their beloved goddess.

Ahh, Calcutta has never smelled so sweet.

Oh, but I am getting ahead of myself. I do that all the time. I race ahead because to sit here in the moment of "now" can be so damn uncomfortable. Surpassed only by the discomfort of digging up ghosts buried long ago.

I turned the ring over in my hand. *God will write?*

Was she referring to some omniscient being who would take hold of my hand and play it like a puppeteer, or pull at my ear, whispering sagacious thoughts? And if so, what was her celestial vision for me? I was wont to be somewhat imaginative, fantastical, bordering at times on otherworldly. She indeed lived in the real rough-and-tumble world. So you might wonder, what's someone like me doing, entertaining visitations from one of the revered Catholic saints-to-be of our time, a woman to whom no less than three miracles have been certified? And why would she implore me to write about it for you?

To begin I need to take you back some years, to a time when I had barely heard of Calcutta's "vision of the streets," to a chapter rife with material excess and superficialities masking my extreme emptiness and personal confusion.

CHAPTER THREE

WHEN DESTINY CALLS

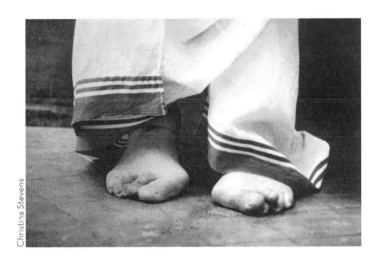

Christina Stevens

"Get your head out of the clouds.
You and I are here for a reason.
You have come to bring something to this world ~
don't leave before you have done so."

Five years earlier . . .
Monday, June 22, 1992
The sky over Santa Paula, California

At what altitude will I lose consciousness? I wondered as I advanced the throttle and nosed my plane upward. *Will I wake on the spiral down? Can I be sure I will bull's-eye my own property?* The last thing *I want to do is splatter myself all over a neighbor's land or take out an innocent bystander. I just want it done. Over. Ended.*

Sorrow, depression, whatever you want to call it, will take you down, swirling freely in its fragility, picking up speed as it goes. In aeronautical terms we call it the "graveyard spiral." All a pilot needs to do to get out of trouble and stop the momentum is to perform a specific yet counterintuitive set of actions, or to be more accurate ~ to resist knee-jerk reactions.

Indeed in life, in order to rescue ourselves from a destined outcome, we simply need to replace learned habits. When caught in a maelstrom of melancholy, though it may take superhuman strength, we are advised not to go with the flow but to reach to feel the opposite from what we are feeling. When all around is dark, seek the light. Replace a thought of fear with an emotion of love. Pretend, even, if we have to. Change our thoughts and we change our feelings. Change our feelings and we will change our future.

Is it that simple?

Reconsidering my destination, I altered our heading for a less populated space, continuing to climb until we were over the ocean.

I checked the wingtips to be sure they were angled up just right. Not too far that she would stall out and cause me to fight a messy demise ~ but hanging with that precise attitude where we could hover delicately on the edge of grace, maintaining control until I lost consciousness.

I eyeballed the altitude indicator ~ 6,000 feet and blissfully quiet. At 7,000 the wood propeller would get sluggish, unable to gain traction in the thinning air.

Eyes fixed on my watery grave, I swallowed hard and inched the stick back toward my belly. Like a paper cut slicing the silence, the pocket of my leather jacket rustled. It was Geoff's last letter. Its aged, curling corners divulged the years I had been carrying it close to my heart. It wasn't his words that meant so much. It was that, for as little free time as he'd had in life, to actually take up a pen and write to me spoke volumes.

Paper rustling was the only sound, other than the pounding of my heart. Dead as a hollow volcano a moment ago, it was now erupting in my throat, and in a few more feet it would reach my dizzying head.

The last fateful rays of the setting sun popped bloodred from behind the clouds, and in that nanosecond an arc of gold shimmered across the heavens. As if it emerged just for me, it lit up the cockpit, blessing me with incandescent illumination. Clarity at last! Euphoria danced around my mind like a flutter of butterflies.

Where have you been? I asked the light, loosening my grip on the stick between my legs. *I had such resolve a moment ago.*

The beauty of God's last kiss upon a day of darkness ripped that resolve right out of me. I had been testing the almighty all my life, and once again my God source showed up.

Geoffrey's letter rustled again, punctuation upon my cowardice of *"To be or not to be . . ."* The crack had begun to show. Through all regrettable affairs of the heart, I had been able to patch it over. But he was the foundation of my life. And the scaffolding I had built around my precious reality, in an effort to do a little structural repair was so poorly assembled it was now breaking apart.

I yanked the stick back into my belly, and at the vertical point, my heart dropped into my head, infusing it with clarity. Over we went.

I emptied the throttle, and featherlike we completed a perfect loop.

Perhaps you have had a minute like that and told no one.

Perhaps you have found yourself in a dark place looking for a bit of light. Wanting to be a better person and yet tired of fighting the pretense. Secretly hoping reincarnation actually does exist, so you could come back and try again.

Adrenaline tingled through my body. I advanced the throttle, pushed the stick of my military rescue plane as far to the left as it would go, and with a little encouragement from the rudder, we languidly circled down to 3,000 feet before I fixed on the heading for home.

*"You will know when the greater reason
for your creation has arrived. Your feet will leave the earth,
never to touch down again quite the same."*

love

The next day
Production Offices, Hollywood, California

There are friends we make in life who are so tuned in to us, we are certain we loved them before we knew them. Blessed with impeccable timing, they seem to intuit what we need, precisely when we need it. One word from them can open up a universe of possibilities or just as easily dash the same. Those friends are our beacons of light.

I could tell it was Sam hugging me from behind because he had this unmistakable whistle when breathing through his nose. And he was so tall, his hug always scooped me up, lifting my feet off the ground.

You would recognize Sam Bottoms for his roles as the hippie gunrunner with the painted face in Francis Ford Coppola's *Apocalypse Now,* and the young cowboy bedding down beside Clint Eastwood in *The Outlaw Josey Wales,* or even his first movie role at 15, as the backward mute who was run down while sweeping dust outside *The Last Picture Show,* which starred his brother Timothy. That's what Sam was to me, a brother. He had a deep and complex soul and of the four Bottoms brothers, actors all of them, Sam was the most gentle. He was fascinated with the world, particularly the state of the environment and the evolution of the human spirit, and we couldn't get enough of each other. But like many dedicated actors in L.A., Sam was forever broke. Every penny he made he gave to his ex-wife and their two girls. He lived separately from his family yet spent all his free time doing repairs on their house. He was a stand-up guy, and we brought him in whenever a role called for a handsome dude in his mid-30s. Mark, my business partner, loved him, too, and sometimes we deliberately wrote him into the script.

"You didn't need to come in for the audition. The client has seen all your movies. He loves you already," I assured Sam as he ushered me into my office.

"That's not why I'm here, darlin'. I have a project you're going to love." Sam was always coming up with ideas, oodles of them, forever ingenious and bighearted, which made it easy to get sucked into his whirlpool of enthusiasm.

"I just got word from my friend Gregg at the Climate Summit in Rio. Ted Turner has committed to air an Earth Day television special called *Planet Live.* They're going to transmit live music from all over the world, like the Rolling Stones from London and the Bee Gees from Australia, Ravi Shankar in India. Just imagine, we're all going to stand together and acknowledge what we must do to protect the planet."

"It's never been done before ~ not on this scale," I enthused.

"They've asked me to help. And then I thought of you. You film all over the world, and I don't know anyone who loves the earth more than you."

"I have filmed rock videos, but I've never done a live concert. I'm not sure what I could . . ." I was trying to hop on Sam's train of thought.

"They have the music covered," he said. "But we were thinking, why just have hours and hours of wall-to-wall music?"

"Needs some substance," I agreed.

"Why not also have messages from some of the world's great—"

"Hearts and minds," we said in unison. "Live!"

"It's everything we've been talking about," he added. "You know a lot of these people, and you should direct them. And I'll do everything I can to help you with the production."

Coordination would be mind-boggling. But I loved the reach of the idea.

Immediately my energy was pulsing a mile a minute. *This is just what I need,* I said to myself, in light of how I had been feeling lately. *Something real. Something that will make me want to get up in the morning. Something that will make a difference.*

I leaped from my chair and like an octopus dove into my files.

In contrast to me, just as he did when studying a script, Sam gently gathered himself. He sat his lean torso politely on my couch, crossed his long legs, and quietly put pen to paper. "We should draw up a list."

"Yes. We can come at this from all angles," I said, pacing the floor. "Amory Lovins. He can address climate change, and Steve Jobs, technology. Uh . . . the list here in the US is long. In the UK there's Stephen Hawking. Then we'll drop down to South Africa and get

Nelson Mandela and Desmond Tutu, Jane Goodall, Arthur C. Clarke, he lives in Sri Lanka . . . I have a great crew in Hong Kong. There's Dr. Helen Caldicott in Australia. Oh dear, what a pity Krishnamurti has already passed . . ." I was tripping over myself.

Out of the corner of my eye I noticed Sam had not yet written one name down.

"Mother Teresa," he said with such uncharacteristic force it cut clean through my chatter.

"Who?"

"You know who Mother Teresa is," Sam retorted, somewhat incredulous. "The living saint," he added with such solemnity I felt rather embarrassed.

"Of course I have *heard* of her," I came back defensively.

What I knew about Mother Teresa you could pour into a teacup. Granted, she was an icon. Her name was mentioned everywhere from therapists' offices to water coolers to courtrooms and a plethora of movies in between. It was hard to escape reference to her.

I knew she lived in a place called Calcutta ~ "the black hole of the world," as it was mysteriously referred to in my childhood. I knew she was a nun who wore a white sari and took care of poor people. Still, I couldn't have been more ignorant about this saintly woman, as my lifestyle couldn't have been more diametrically opposed to hers. She was synonymous with piety, compassion, service, and sacrifice. Attributes that, I am ashamed to say, could not describe any part of me.

"But she's a religious . . ."

Sam caught me stumbling. "Loving the earth is embedded in every religion," he murmured in his soft, tender manner, returning to his wide grin and notepad. "If we can get her, it will be a coup!"

With the little I knew of Mother Teresa, one thing was clear ~ she understood that we could never care about the earth and the water and the trees and the air and all the little animals, while we were still struggling with our love for ourselves and one another?

And boy, I am the perfect audience for that.

"Yes," I agreed. "Mother Teresa should be the first."

In the ensuing week, while my assistant, Gilly, was on vacation, Sam did indeed move into my office, roll up his sleeves, and dive into production. Documents went flying back and forth from folks in Atlanta and New York to us in L.A. I put crews on hold, pulled together a budget, and on our list of proposed speakers Mother Teresa held her place, right on top. I heard a resounding "yes" from everyone ~ even my out-of-this-world conversation with the computerized voice that was the remarkable Stephen Hawking got a thumbs-up. But every journalist and producer we talked to in search of the nun's contact information told us this saint of the streets explicitly, and they emphasized explicitly, "refuses to give interviews."

Day five. As if the air had suddenly been sucked out of the room, everything came to a screeching halt. Calls went unanswered and messages no longer returned. We were still searching for Mother Teresa's phone number when we were finally told why ~ Ted Turner had pulled the plug.

Puzzling. Even as an enormously astute businessman, Mr. Turner intuitively listened to his heart when making programming decisions, and his passion and generosity for an environmental cause were legendary. Jacques Cousteau would never have educated us about the wondrous world under the waves without Ted supporting him. *National Geographic Specials* owed their very beginnings to funding from Mr. Turner and TBS. But it was over. We, a small satellite operation in L.A., were not given a reason. Devastating as it was, death before birth was something we media dreamers were all too familiar with.

Sam was offered a movie role in Thailand. He was to play the head of a drug cartel. The character didn't suit him at all. But he needed the payday. Reluctantly Sam accepted it and left immediately.

I went home to lick my wounds and to ponder again the graveyard spiral.

If only I possessed the powers of prediction. I would have found comfort in knowing that in a matter of months, a greater destiny was set to unfold.

"When providence takes your hand,
you are meant to let go.
And let God."

love

Tuesday, January 26, 1993
Santa Paula, California

I find the first time you meet someone is the truest moment of a relationship. The energy between you is pure, untainted by human error or worldly influence.

I daresay if my first connection with Mother Teresa hadn't been such a surreal, almost preordained event, I may never have given what was to follow the authority needed to hang in when all heck broke loose.

Before dawn, I emerged from my meditation somewhere between heaven and earth. I meditate early and sometimes it can be so deep I seem to drift back into dreamtime. I shook myself awake and opened my eyes, stunned, shaken, almost moved to tears. It was pitch-dark except for the one brilliant beam of light streaming in through the open window. I sat up and looked out at the full moon sitting on the mountain ridge, reaching into the recesses of my mind in an attempt to hold on to as many details of the quickly dissolving images as I could.

Now I realize many who meditate do it by emptying all thought and chatter from their mind, replacing it with mantras or positive affirmations to ultimately enter a state of relaxation and complete peace. I am a visual person. For some reason I can slip deeply into meditation, and it becomes like a waking-dream experience, where I go to feast on soul food. I open all chakras, and if there is something I need to know or a place I need to go, a solution I need to find or a friend in need of guidance, I close my eyes and the doors of perception open wide.

Some people don't believe in the value of this. For me, it's a tool that connects me to the untapped 88 percent of my consciousness. I am transported to a realm not of this world, and there resides all I will ever need. I have found what I see and hear in this dreamlike state always has a purpose. With my hand clutching my heart, I know this did.

There I was, standing in what appeared to be a natural utopia ~ a technically perfect, interconnected, parallel world. Instinctively, I knew the environment well, almost as if a part of me lived there. I had been there before.

I was inside a magnificent domed structure, where the walls were made of glass. Sunlight streamed in, bringing its godlike illumination. I looked out the windowed walls to emerald rolling hills that led to a meadow beyond. There, all kinds of animals were grazing. Birds and butterflies played in the air, and in the distance a river flowed. The light all around didn't just shine, it glowed. And there was something else that was unusual ~ it was the rocks at the river's edge. They weren't dense as most boulders are. Instead they appeared to illuminate and shimmer from within, reflecting the river itself as if they, too, were living and breathing.

Something told me moving in this world would be effortless, that making contact with the ground was gentler, the air lighter, and if I wanted to run, the wind would carry me. I wanted to test it out ~ run down to the water ~ but an inner guide stopped me.

Instead, my attention was drawn inside. I turned. What came first into focus was an inner dividing glass wall reaching high with what was the treasure of this place ~ knowledge. Fashioned into the glass walls were slots containing crystal sheets ~ and each sheet contained information. I was inside a massive library of books! Books written centuries ago and books yet to be conceived. There was a timeless quality about this akashic place and everything in it that I couldn't quite grasp. All form was movement, shapes changing at lightning speed around me until what had been random particles in the air transmuted themselves into a human form.

What emerged was a lady sitting quietly upon an old wooden bench.

The first thing I noticed was her bare feet. White cracks around her heels and misshapen toes told me those feet had walked a million miles.

Colors and shapes shifted until they became a palette of loosely woven white fabric, edged with blue. I followed the folds of material. Resting on her lap were her hands ~ soft ripples of skin enveloping strong, generous, highly capable, beautiful hands.

She noticed my presence and stood to greet me. A glow of white surrounded her diminutive frame. My eyes were drawn to her face. A sublimely peaceful and loving expression beckoned me to come closer.

She reached out and took my hands in hers. I was magnetized by her power. She looked deeply into my eyes and said quite clearly, "If you wish to film me, I will let you." And then her gaze and her touch electrified my being as she cautioned, "But you must come soon."

Her warning stopped me for a moment.

Then she looked deep into my eyes and lightened the moment by playfully lifting my hands up and down as two children would when repetitiously chanting words they don't want to forget.

Then, all too quickly, she was gone. And the vision evaporated.

I burst through from that wondrous place empowered by a sense of urgency and by an odd mystical shove.

What just happened? The illumined emptiness before me had no answer other than a hollow echo that had been the benchmark of my life. As is my way, without another thought, I sprang into action. I jumped up, my bare feet welcoming the shock of the cold floor. My fingertips, my arms, all the way down to my toes vibrated heat from her touch. I had transported a physical sensation from that world into the real, corporeal world. Though I knew so little about her, I knew I had just met the icon of love, Mother Teresa.

I didn't realize it at the time, but I had been called.

"God will call each of us in a different way,
on a different day, and with a different voice.
Just know, you will not be left out."

The invitation to dive into the purest depths of ourselves can beckon at any age, from 3 to 93, disguised in a brush with death, shrouded in the wretched loss of a loved one, or just as mysteriously, appearing in an unexpected piece of good fortune. It's hard to know what illusion lifts us out of the mundane and propels us into our own personal destiny. One thing I do know ~ nothing is as it seems.

The crisp, salty air flared my nostrils, and the heavy *thunk* of the Range Rover door jolted me out of my musings as it closed behind me. I was in postproduction for a music video, prepping two million-dollar television campaigns and bidding three more, and I had no time for dreamy escapades.

I wanted to shut out that "fuzzy feeling," but as I sped south along Pacific Coast Highway to work out with Jackson, my trainer, Mother Teresa's vision flittered around me like the wispy beckoning of a butterfly.

Normally, my workout with Jackson was at 8:30 A.M., but my meditation had gripped me so early I called and booked the 6:30 time slot. Pierce Brosnan, in those, his pre-Bond days, had 7:30 A.M. permanently reserved. My adrenaline was rushing. I was uncharacteristically eager for my sweat session, anxious to get through it and relieved when Pierce arrived early.

You get to know a lot about someone when you observe them day in and day out, even if it's just a nod, a smile, an observation at a dinner party, or a brief exchange of pleasantries you share. Pierce had lost his beloved wife, Cassandra, an Australian like me, two years earlier, and although he appeared to have the whole world in his hands and was the most jovial of dinner guests, there was an unmistakable sadness in him that was harshly apparent early in the morning.

We human beings are such accomplished actors, juggling our shadows and light with such creativity, rarely does another know the colors pulsing inside our hearts, unless, of course, those shades mimic our own.

Jackson suggested I join him and Pierce on a run through the mustard fields that trailed down to the ocean. At that time of year, the maze of willowy yellow flowers towered high above our heads and swayed with the sea breeze, showering down their tiny golden petals like confetti. I would have loved to let my guard down and sprint like a happy child. How I would have enjoyed that release! But I was unable to shake the physical effects of my dream. I knew I had something "to be" or "to do." I was succumbing to the pull of the day ahead. I declined, showered, jumped back into my car, and headed into Hollywood. With the Pacific Ocean to my right, I turned off talk radio and made an attempt to gather my thoughts.

Out of the clear blue a low red sports car cut across my lane. Instinctively I pushed my foot onto the brake and steered onto the median, missing a collision by a hair. Snapped to attention for the second time since the moon rose, I white-knuckled the steering wheel back into the fast lane and thanked my shaky stars.

They say our entire life passes before us when we face the prospect of death. I knew it was not time for me to leave yet. I had come to a crossroads of sorts. Inside me, something was missing. I sensed there was a promise I had made that had not yet been fulfilled. I was fairly sure if I died tomorrow, God would throw me back, saying, "Sorry, you're not ready. You haven't done anything worthy."

The thought of a wasted life turned my stomach. You don't get it back. Though I sometimes felt like an odd duck in my snake pit of a business environment, particularly after a harrowing corporate meeting, I wondered and many times hoped I was being prepared for something else.

Precisely what, I did not know.

The second my stilettoes hit the marble floor it was clear I was on a mission. No ordinary mission.

"Get me every book, article, and film you can find on Mother Teresa and see if you can find a contact number for her."

Gilly, my trusty right hand, seldom blinked at my sometimes oddball requests, yet I felt her snap to attention on this one. We were preparing for two back-to-back shoots, first to sunny Florida and then high into the Grand Tetons of Wyoming.

Gilly simply turned another page in her notebook.

Born in the south part of London, clever little minx Gilly wiggles around in the tiniest skirts that barely cover the prettiest legs and everything is toodle pip, toodle pop, and toodle-oo! What makes her perfect is that she gaily runs on an even keel. She calms my anxieties, cools my excitement, and keeps me together when funds run low, as they so often do in the film business.

"Mother Teresa," she said, drawing her next breath in through slightly clenched teeth. "Right."

We've been together long enough for me to hear the aside of that sigh ~ "Please don't tell me we're doing another 'love' job. We haven't received final payment on the last two contracts, you've maxed out the credit cards, and it always falls to me to keep everybody happy."

Gilly has been with me since I was senior vice president, creative director at Ogilvy & Mather, one of the world's largest advertising agencies. Now, with my partner, Mark, we have a production company: traveling the world, conceiving and producing television commercials ~ the rather spectacular, expensive kind. We also made public service announcements for various institutions and music videos for starving musicians ~ neither of which paid the bills.

"You worked out without me," Mark observed, spotting my gym bag and my endorphin glow.

"Yeah," I snapped, unwilling to explain. I didn't need to. He knew why. It could be Milan, Paris, Bangkok, wherever ~ we would head out, morning or evening, and jog around the city together, exploring locations, formulating ideas while staying healthy. But then he, being the so-called stronger sex, got into the habit of streaking ahead of me, leaving me to huff and puff behind, begging him to slow down. I heard myself stepping out of character, turning into a don't-go-so-fast, weepy whiner, when one day I whined too much and he went too far. We were filming in San Francisco ~ his hometown. It was dusk, the mist had turned chilly, and we were jogging through the Presidio. The fog was thick in the air and our conversation was equally dense. I was losing steam, and he just took off. Up the hill, around the bend, through the trees, and he was gone. He knew his way home and he knew my sense of direction is absurdly foggy. And he just left me ~ stranded ~ in the dark. It took me two and a half hours to find my way back to my hotel. We never went jogging together again.

Aside from me, Mark is the most contradictory being I know. He can be mean one day and uber-compassionate the next. Some days, I think he is a genius, and other days I am convinced he's a fraud. He can be generous to a fault ~ his Christmas gifts are over-the-top outrageous, but come January first he can be downright stingy.

He's the tall, handsome, laconic mystery man every new female assistant we hire hovers over, batting her lashes, vying for a date, until she realizes Mark is too entwined in his own world to notice. He does notice, to our amusement, that his belly is expanding and his hairline receding. He remembers every phone number he has ever dialed, but he forgets where he parked his car. He can do complex math in his head but can't count the dollars in his wallet. Reluctantly, Gilly and I have been forced to embrace his incongruities ~ and as driven to distraction as we are by them, we smile because we love him anyway.

Mark wanted me to love him in a different way. However, as you have probably guessed by now, I'm not what good girlfriends are made of ~ too independent, too passionate, too idealistic, and too headstrong. Those attributes make me a better business partner.

As you have perhaps also guessed, flying was my amour. To soar up into the sky lifted me higher than most anything I could name. The fulfillment of a childhood wish ~ to rocket through the heavens dispensing precious gifts to all on planet Earth. I knew the little girl in me was the truest part of my spirit, with an acceptance as big as the sky ~ touching the joy.

In between film projects, I piloted antique planes: the white scarf, leather helmet kind ~ the poetic essence of flight. It's the dancer in me who loves to fly aerobatics. Lifting up onto my toes and leaping 3,000 feet in the air, to pirouette through the atmosphere, beyond the capacity of a mortal body; to turn myself upside down and inside out, laugh at gravity and reach across space to touch the hand . . .

Up there was where I learned to take my hands off the steering wheel of my life. Up there was where I saw how the twists and turns of life can all at once appear beautiful and ugly, cruel and kind, just and unfair. Up there was where I was able to let go and let God.

Flying reminded me ~ God's plan for us is invariably truer and bluer than our own.

"Love begets love.
Peace begets peace.
War begets war.
I don't know why, its just contagious that way."

Friday, February 26, 1993
Gainesville, Florida

This was to be no ordinary day, although it began like every other that week, with a 3 A.M. wake-up call, to shower and put on the layers, to be in the van downstairs by 3:45. The van then delivered us promptly at 4:15 to the film set on the end of runway 22 at the Gainesville Regional Airport.

In the pitch black, smells, sounds, and dots of lights were our guides. Craft service was set up beside the camera truck, and that was naturally where we all gathered until the aroma of Bunsen burners was eventually snuffed out by coffee and breakfast burritos. Mark and I quickly shook off our dreamtime cobwebs and went over the morning's shots with the assistant director and the pilots, while the cameramen and their assistants built the cameras, loaded film, and made sure all their equipment would work faultlessly at 1,500 feet.

We had been filming a campaign for USAir for two weeks and were now prepping the second-to-last shot: a complex dance from earth to heaven, between a man and his son and a Boeing 757. We were filming from the ground and remotely from a helicopter that zigzagged between them. Mike Dewey, famous in the industry for his daredevil flying in every Hollywood flying film made since I have been alive and, I am honored to say, my personal aerobatic flight instructor, was our ground-to-air liaison for this shoot.

Mike was checking the flight crew and tower walkie-talkies and his open channel emergency phones as the first rays of sunlight appeared. Before we knew it the 757 was airborne, the helicopter was warming up, and the crew was in position and raring to go. But someone was missing. The assistant director breathlessly tugged at my jacket and pulled me aside, whispering, "I just found out. Sam didn't get his wake-up call. Don't worry; he's coming now, just as he is."

Our star was beyond late. The sun would be up and a half day of filming would be wasted if Sam didn't make it in 15 minutes. I didn't need to ponder the math; I knew this little snafu could cost us "the shot" and well over $100,000.

Panicking is as useless as worrying. Besides, Sam Bottoms was a pro.

"Don't tell anyone Sam isn't here," I cautioned the assistant director. "Stand in for him and pretend he's still in makeup."

No one noticed our smoke and mirrors. Granted, it was still dark out, but nobody raised the alarm that our lead actor was not on his mark. In true form, without any hoopla, sandy hair pointing straight to heaven as if he had just lifted his head off the pillow, Sam was in front of the camera in 11 minutes.

A half-hour drive in 11 minutes? Hey, I wasn't going to question it.

Some days are like that. From sunrise to sunset, nothing makes sense, yet everything falls into place. Near disasters are miraculously averted at the last minute. And then there are those other days, when the sky falls.

When the clock struck noon, directly north of us, in New York City, one disaster was not about to be averted. For a handful of innocent bystanders, the sky fell.

High noon in Manhattan

A rented yellow Ford Econoline van cruised along Liberty Street, turned right onto West Street, and veered down into the parking basement of number One World Trade Center.

Leaving the van on the south side of the North Tower, a handful of men crawled out and calmly lost themselves in the bustling lunchtime crowd.

Moments later, the van exploded and two of the tallest structures in the world were hit with what the FBI described at the time as "the largest improvised explosive device" in the history of American crime.

Tremendous damage was done throughout the confines of the garage. Five men and one woman, who happened to be a few yards away in the basement, were killed instantly. A thousand other innocents were injured. Dense, toxic smoke flooded through the entire ten million square feet of office space, all the way up to and beyond the Windows on the World restaurant on the 106th floor. Electricity failed. Backup generators shorted out. With no public address system, no emergency communications, and the fire stairwells narrow and unlit, evacuation of the thousands who inhabited the mighty colossus that rose majestically above New York Harbor took ten slow hours.

Steadfast and structurally unharmed, the sister skyscrapers remained the world's tallest imposing "edifices of capitalism." But a warning shot had been fired. The fearful hand of terrorism had reached out and touched the home of the brave, in the land of the free.

We, an insignificant film crew in Florida, insulated in the alchemy of our art, would not have heard this news until the end of day, except for the fact that Mike caught it on his open-channel radio.

I was in the wardrobe trailer when I overheard Mike click in over the walkie-talkie.

"Hey, guys. Just heard on the radio, someone bombed the Twin Towers in New York."

Red with rage I grabbed a PA's walkie. I wanted to comment but had no idea what to say.

At any given time there are no less than 60 wars being waged in pockets all over the world. We in the West are simply not informed. Our awakening to this we owe to Ted Turner and his creation of CNN, the world's first 24-hour live news network. It was his intent to begin a dialogue, to bring the world closer. And in an unexpectedly painful way, he did.

Snapped out of ambivalence when the United States bombed Baghdad in 1991, we awoke in our beds and into consciousness to see, for the first time, real-time, live war.

That morning while dressing, I had been watching CNN as they covered the US bombers striking civilians in Baghdad. Momentarily I imagined myself inside my TV. I was not flying the plane that was dropping the bombs. I was there, in the home of an innocent person whose world was being torn in two. Having climbed into the safety of my bed and put my head on my pillow the night before, believing I would wake to a new dawn and a new day, I was woken by my world in flames and my future dreams exploding. Someone I had never met was carving out a new reality for me.

Seeing human carnage play out right before my eyes, like it was the Fourth of July, doused my energetic morning regime. Simply putting one foot in front of the other became a chore. I chose a black and white dress that day because the world had lost all color for me. I recall being uncertain which shoes to wear. Black or white? Which side would I choose? When someone wins and someone loses, no one wins. No war ends in peace. Later at work, while walking down the corridor to a meeting, a voice called out, "Hey, Christina! Are you trying to set a new fashion trend or something?" I stopped in my tracks, mystified. "Do you know you're wearing one white shoe and one black one?"

I had become slightly unhinged from my usual "together" self. Suddenly we, who had been so coddled, were bearing witness to innocents dying.

It is two years later and once again we are shaken awake to the knowledge that there is also the war we don't see. The innocent bystander, the beloved is hit, only this time it is on our shores. I could hear walkie-talkies crackling, but there were no comments to Mike's news.

I thought my head was going to burst. Silence condones.

I opened the channel. "If anybody can tell me why someone wants to blow up the World Trade Center please go to channel two."

I switched to channel two, not expecting a response.

"Terrorists," Mike clicked on. Filmmakers, ever the global travelers, we were all savvy to the growing threat of terrorism.

"Terrorists? Who?"

"They're the bad guys," clicked on the AD.

That comment sounded remarkably like I was listening to a comment from a 1950s cowboys and Indians movie.

"We're all the good guys and we're all the bad guys," I snapped back. "It just depends what side you're on."

Empty. The airwaves were empty.

"Look," I chimed in to whoever might be listening. "Let's say you were walking down the street and this guy, someone you've never even met, just comes up from behind and whacks you over the head. Wouldn't you turn around and say, 'Hey, what did you do that for?' Wouldn't you want to sit this guy down and find out what his problem was?"

A vacant silence on channel two.

"Shouldn't we be trying to understand one another?"

Suddenly Mark's voice broke in.

"Oh. Don't worry. Be happy," he sang lightly, upending my soapbox.

Airwaves crackled.

"What's that saying?" I called into the walkie, not knowing if anybody was even listening anymore. "'Evil happens when enough good men do nothing.'"

I heard a mumble here, a mumble there ~ sounding distinctly like heads toppling into sand until all that was left was dead air.

I felt alone, foolish in my upset.

Doesn't anybody care?

It wasn't that nobody cared. It was that nobody had an answer.

For the following hour the crew kept their distance from me as I wandered the tall grass at the end of the runway and kicked up sand. Then Mike sent Sam ~ of course, the only one brave enough to speak to me ~ in a golf cart, with instructions to deliver me midfield, where the 757 jet sat.

My outburst had been noticed. Someone had cooked up a little scheme to soothe and distract me from my anxiety. They had no clue it would actually spark a passion in me and ignite a decision from which there would be no turning back.

I would be reminded of that passion when those same towers turned to rubble eight years later. It would begin a transformation that resonated around the globe, bringing us to our knees, illuminating one truth ~ in the heroic act of love we humans are the most glorious of all animals.

*"Sometimes the most implausible,
unlikely moment in your life turns out to be
your moment of truth."*

It was early afternoon. Rehearsed and ready for our final scene, we had three hours to kill before magic hour, that 20-minute window that occurs every day when the canvas of the world is converted into a lucid glow of shadows and light only Mother Nature (and maybe Maxfield Parrish) could paint.

Mike greeted me with Captain Steve under his wing. Both of them had a twinkle in their eye. Captain Steve invited me to do the "walk around" checklist with him while he gave me a crash course on 757 safety. How exciting to discover a Boeing 757 and the single rotary engine aircraft I flew were the same. Screws and cotter pins. Rudder, ailerons, lift, and drag.

"We need to fly a few touch-and-gos. Burn some fuel. Lighten the load before the afternoon shoot. And you're coming with us," Steve said as he tugged at my arm.

Climbing into the jet, I immediately sensed some kind of mischief afoot. To give the jet surer maneuverability, we had drained all water from the plane and removed all seats in coach and business classes. For balance, we left the front seats intact. First class was full of beaming faces; Sam was front and center grinning like he had just swallowed the Cheshire cat. Our six clients, most of our production ground crew, minus Mark, were sitting, strapped in and smiling expectantly. Mike took my hand as if he was about to kiss it and guided me into the cockpit. The captain motioned for me to sit. Right-hand seat. Co-pilot!

I looked over to Mike. He was privy to some information that nobody else knew. In the last few months we had been filming all around the world, and I had little room for my passion in the sky. Each time I opened my hangar door, I noticed more and more dust creeping onto her fabric wings, and I no longer felt one with my beloved machine. It wasn't that I was rusty or anything ~ like riding a bicycle, you never forget. But for lack of attention, there's a connection you feel, a bond you share with a machine that gives you joy like a lover that will dissipate and desert you if it isn't nurtured. In terms of safety, there is an attitude you must assume, an edge of "being" you must possess, a form of "taking control" of everything in your world and taking responsibility for the world outside you that piloting demands. My plane, once owned by Steve McQueen, was a hot property, and in a weakened moment I accepted an offer I couldn't refuse. It was a sad day for my spirit. My angel in the sky was mine no more.

My passion for flying would never die. Piloting is a rush that cleans you out from head to toe. I can't say it's better than sex, but it comes mighty close. Sex isn't as dangerous as dangling from the sky. Or is it?

Talking me through the controls and the cockpit layout, Captain Steve showed me how familiar it felt, only more and bigger. For me, there's nothing like flying to make sense of everything. When faced with problems, difficult choices, or life's everyday confusion, nothing compares with the perspective a few thousand feet can provide to reduce everything to its proper proportion.

Captain Steve fired up the engines, put them through his checklist, nodded to me, and lifted his hands high from the controls. That's the signal for the co-pilot to take over.

The moment my right hand wrapped around the yoke I recalled my first aerobatic lesson with Mike. What he murmured through my earphones while I had us hanging upside down on top of a loop would remain with me. "Hold her like she's an egg in your hand. Don't grip tight ~ gently hold her firm. Feel your way with her." This advice could be applied to most things in life.

My left hand pushed the throttle forward, and 1,000 revelations awoke inside me. Power surged us forth and at my tugging, we lifted featherlike from the ground. As we gathered altitude, I was faith. I was poetry. I was the sky. I was an almighty vessel, in league with the wind, out to accomplish the impossible.

In a lightning moment the altimeter shot past 3,000 feet, and I flashed on what a 757 performing a loop would feel like. Glancing over to my left, I noticed Captain Steve's hands, resting loosely in his lap. Looking outside I scanned for aircraft in the vicinity.

I advanced the throttle firmly, yanked the yoke back hard, and we nosed straight up to heaven. Our happy passengers sucked in their breaths as if they were on a roller coaster. The assistant director who was standing beside Mark safely on the ground hollered through his walkie, "Holy s***!"

I imagined Mark, sprouting roots, fretting desperately that we would crash and burn ~ before he got his last shot. From the corner of my eye I caught Captain Steve grinning. Relieved he knew as I did that we were fine, I eased the nose over and pulled back power and resumed the agreed-upon flight plan.

As I turned onto base leg of the landing, naughty girl that I am, I wanted to give my captive audience one more thrill. From straight and level, I pushed the nose down 90 degrees, accompanied by more gasps from first class and sound activation from the cockpit computer.

"Obstacles ahead! Obstacles at one hundred feet."

Time to risk it all. Time to listen to my heart. It seemed the world was spinning faster, time was accelerating, and mankind was getting uprooted in the midst. More and more disagreements dotted the globe. The land of the free wasn't feeling as free anymore. Children were wielding weapons. Pollution in the air and chemicals in our systems were birthing babies with deformities. There were fewer fish we could eat, fewer rivers we could swim in, less water we could drink, and so on and so on. Human nature was not in tune with Mother Nature. I had consulted my navel long enough. I was hearing a higher calling and that voice would no longer be silenced.

"Gain altitude. Climb. Climb," the automated cockpit voice proclaimed. That was it. I lifted the nose. We rose in the sky and leveled out, to relieved *ahhs* from my passengers.

The sense of control was empowering. Just as a child tests their boundaries with a parent, I was testing the boundaries of the jetliner. And Captain Steve knew it. We circled the airfield three times, and each time I became even more daring in the sensations I metered out to all and sundry.

Cheers rang out when our wheels touched ground for the last time, and I became again that little girl who was a fearless being. Fearless in a manner most people aren't. I had faith the universe would take me only when I was needed elsewhere. But as humiliating as it was to admit, I was terrified of one very natural, basic emotion. I was petrified of something most people seek out and effortlessly fall into every day. Love.

Gently I eased back the throttle, and Captain Steve wrapped his hands over mine, joining me in guiding it back. His touch was lovely. In that moment I could have turned to him and fallen into his sky-blue eyes and been lost forever. But almost by rote, I slipped my hand out from under his.

When I climbed out of the cockpit and hit the tarmac, the cobwebs around my heart had been blown away. My next steps were galvanized.

Willing to run into the fire rather than away from it, eager to confront my fears rather than ignore them, I was one person in a world of ones. Whatever may come, we as a civilization must answer the resounding call of the spirit.

It occurred to me then, if I were to do this, it would be necessary, no matter how painful, to go on a journey of purification, to exorcize the unhappy ghosts of my soul. In order to reset a new true north on my personal compass and come face-to-face with a "living saint," I had to remove everything in my heart that wasn't love.

Where to begin?

I knew one true thing. Love has no flight path and no estimated time of arrival. Love is not a destination. Love is there, no matter where we are.

Love is the air.

CHAPTER FOUR

YOU'RE GOING TO HAVE TO WING IT

Christina Stevens

"Yesterday is history.
Tomorrow, a mystery.
We have only today ~ this moment. Now.
Let us begin . . ."

That night

Downstairs in the bar, the wrap party was in full swing. Captain Steve, no doubt with Sam egging him on, had called twice, giving his best to convince me to leave the solace of my room and join them. I was tempted.

"I told him not to take it personally," Gilly confessed when she appeared with my flight ticket for the morning. "I said, 'She doesn't come to the wrap parties. She pays for them, but she never shows up.' And then Mark chimed in and told him you used to be the life of the party. Poor blighter didn't know if he was coming or going."

"Mark was right." I hated to admit it. I am Australian and aw mite, ow wee luv a-good pardy!

I planned our wrap parties from the live band down to the toothpicks. Often we were joined by a celebrity who was filming nearby or dating one of our crew, and sometimes we made it a dress-up theme party. I always made them special events. Never first to arrive, I was always last to leave. Then wham! As if a silver bullet had punctured my party-girl heart, I moved on.

Gilly handed me my itinerary for our next location and my Amex card. I gave her a hug. She was always thinking ahead for me, and I cherished her for that. "Thank you for everything you do. The things I know about and the things I don't."

"Look. I don't want to . . . I mean, I know it's not my place . . . but you're always alone . . . and . . ." Gilly was hedging. "You've been looking especially beautiful lately," she said.

It was only the second time anyone had ever referred to me as beautiful. When I discovered boys were different from girls, I begged my brother to just give in and admit that I, his beloved sister, was the most beautiful of them all! Truthfully? I believed I was ugly. I promised I would leave him alone if he would just fess up and tell me how exquisite I was. Though he adored me more than his record player, I could never budge him, "Well, Christina, you're different!" Uh, I was right.

Gilly blinked in my face. "You are beautiful, you know; you just don't seem to know it." She laughed lightly. "I watch you. You don't ever notice when someone fancies you. I swear that captain's feet leave the ground every time you go near him, and you don't even give him a blink. He's handsome and he likes you. And you would like him. I got the scoop. He's single, he has a house on the beach in North Carolina, and he loves his mum."

"Ahh, he's perfect." I was flattered, but after today, I was not to be moved. "There is something I need to do right now." It was a pathetic excuse for not engaging in life's great mystery; however, once again, a deeper passion was taking precedence.

I had fallen, head over heels, more than once, in love with men, unavailable or at varying stages of loving someone else, romantically lost, emotionally damaged, or just like me, paralyzed with fear. They were exactly what I desired. But panic always hit when the games ended and they set their sights on me. *Move over, Scarlett O'Hara. Tomorrow really is another day.*

I knew I was overdue for a new love paradigm, yet grateful Gilly didn't take the conversation any further.

"Oh, yeah, I almost forgot." Gilly pulled a folded note out of her jeans pocket and passed it to me. "You wouldn't believe, I had to turn myself into a . . . what is it Americans love so much, yeah, a pretzel, I had to bend like a pretzel to get this for you."

The note read: "Missionaries of Charity, Calcutta" ~ with a very long telephone number beside it. Perfect timing.

"So." Gilly hovered from one foot to the other. "Tomorrow morning you and Mark are on the seven forty-five. I'm taking the earlier flight, and I will meet you on the mountain." We hugged again. "I've got to go rescue my beer," Gilly added as she danced off down the corridor. "Maybe you should pop down for a wee nightcap?"

"Uh, maybe," I responded. We both knew I wouldn't go.

*"Follow your dream. It speaks to you alone ~
in a language only your soul can understand."*

9:30 P.M.

I calculated it to be early morning in Calcutta. I took a deep breath, cleared away the debris of the day, and sent focus and energy to my heart. Summoning the pure energy of mother earth, to soar from its depths and land in my heart, empowering my intention with clarity, so I may speak to a mother of heaven. Scientists and sages agree ~ the organ of the heart is infinitely more powerful than the mind.

If ever I needed to be present, it was now. Here! Now! I know that seems like a natural state of being, but for me particularly, it wasn't. I have lived an extraordinarily successful life, taking care of business with one hand tied behind my back ~ partially present in my body and partially out. Half asleep, so to speak. With my head in the past and myself on autopilot, drifting into some false and dreamy future. I, like so many I know, am masterful at concealing my state of presence.

I dialed the Missionaries of Charity. Doing what one would do when falling into meditation. Relaxing every muscle, from the top of my head to the tip of my toes and beyond, to the very core of the earth and the very ceiling of the heavens. I stretched my fingers, wiggled my toes, and exhaled. *Yeah, I'm awake all right.*

"Hullo?" Her voice was unmistakable.

"Yes. Hullo. May I speak with Mother Teresa please?" In my heart I knew to whom I was speaking, but I needed to borrow a moment to compose myself.

"Yes, God bless." Goodness. Mother Teresa answered the phone herself.

The conscious part of me was dumbfounded. Every other part of me simply wanted to continue the conversation.

"Oh. God bless you, too, Mother Teresa."

I swallowed and caught my breath. Silence. I had to speak.

"Firstly, I want to tell you, Mother Teresa, you are an example to us all. Your compassion. Your commitment . . ." Clumsily, I listed all the attributes my scant knowledge of her recalled, peppered with ums, ahs, and dumb, awestruck silences.

Each time, she filled in the gaps with a kindly "Yes, God bless."

"The world needs to hear your message. I am coming to film you."

"Come and see. Come work with us, in our homes. There are many who come from all over the world to do God's work."

Brilliantly elusive, she was proving the rumors circulating in the press corps true. Mother Teresa did not and would not grant interviews. She had an aversion to cameras, believing they make celebrities out of simple people, and her nuns were to be the simplest of the simple, tending to the poorest of the poor. She was supremely polite and kind in the way she ricocheted my requests.

"I wish to come and film and show the world your work, Mother. That is the work God has laid out for me."

"Yes, God bless," she responded with more blessing than agreement.

"I am working on a series I call *Voices from the Heart.* They are messages from the great hearts and minds of our time. And yours will be the first."

"Yes, God bless," she answered, but again, clearly, it was not agreement.

"I will bring you into their homes, to see your face and hear your words. You can speak to families all over the world. Everyone will at last understand what love is."

"My Missionaries of Charity are all over the world. Come see the work, the beautiful work the Sisters do."

"Yes, I will come to Calcutta and film you in your home."

"Come and work in our homes here. It would be good for a girl like you."

Her invitation, no matter how obtuse and nonresponsive to my request, was a first step. Her English was excellent, and I was certain she understood everything I said. Don't mock me, but I felt as if she was speaking not just from Calcutta, India, but from a world of higher consciousness, a different reality.

I white-knuckled the receiver, sorting through her every utterance, reaching for a sliver of hope, a ray of reassurance, one word of encouragement. For in the cold light of day, there was nothing in what she had said to me that I could hold on to.

As Mother Teresa repeated one last time, "Yes, God bless," I could feel under my skin that she had answered the phone for a reason and that I had already stepped over into her world. And something else was at work here. Something that I, in my present conscious state, could not comprehend. Like love at first sight, in one transmuting moment, life is changed forever. I could no longer go back. In the annals of time I could not erase the exchange that had just happened.

In my heart I was the one who had said yes.

In my soul I had given my word. Come heck or high water, I would leave the safety of my world to be present, in spirit and in the flesh, in hers.

Inconclusively and in a shower of "God blesses," we disconnected. I heard Mother Teresa clearly. She had not said no. She had not said yes, and yet if I listened between the lines, she rained down on me a flood of yeses.

I didn't appreciate it then, but I had already pushed away from the shore, and rudderless and without a paddle, begun my adventure into the unknown. Assurances, a map, maybe even a companion or two would have been helpful, but this kind of journey is a soul one, and on that trek we must all go solo, clinging against all odds to one incandescent thought . . . there is nothing to fear.

♡♡♡

"There may always be a voice in the dark,
a disbeliever seeking the wisdom of your light.
Have no fear. That voice is a blessing,
come to test your resolve."

Monday, March 8, 1993
Jackson Hole, Wyoming

Gilly had set up our production office in a corner suite on the top floor of our hotel, which squinted out onto the Teton peaks. She had arranged all the desks around hers so she could keep an eye and ear on every crisis from every department as it unfolded. The grand majesty of the mountain range and the oncoming blizzard were imprinting their influence into the room. To add to the drama, she had the television on 24/7, muted, and always tuned to CNN.

Mark and I shared an adjoining suite with an even more spectacular and imposing view of the Tetons, with its necessary conference table; cork wall on which to pin up storyboards, schedules, and cast; desks for our laptops and phones; a couple of televisions; and the fall-about-area of couches. Even before technology sequestered us all and gave us its wonderfully false illusion of connectivity and empowerment, it has been beneficial for me to have a locale in my office where everyone can sit around and relax together. I have found it breaks down barriers and freely encourages the creative spirit to express itself, and for me, that's what business is all about.

We had completed two days of a seven-day shooting schedule when the blizzard became the star and production ceased. This was actually a godsend because half the crew, most of the actors, and our number one camera were suffering from various high altitude and cold weather maladies. The delay gave everyone time to acclimate and me time to focus on my heart's call.

"I'm going to India to film Mother Teresa's message to the world."

"You're kidding," Gilly responded, sans smile. She knew I was preoccupied with something, for I had not been bothering her the way I usually did with requests every five minutes.

"May I inquire as to where this Mother Teresa fixation came from?" she asked.

"She came to me in a vision."

"I hate it when that happens," Gilly tossed lightly. I ignored her silly humor because we both knew she thought meditation was boring. She dropped it. "No. No. Tell me, I must know. What happened?"

"She told me if I wanted to film her, she would let me, but she said I must come soon."

"Do you think she's getting ready to die?" Gilly threw her hands to her lips in an effort to quell any further outbursts.

"Maybe it's me who is getting ready to die," I countered lightly, though wondering if my words were prophetic. There was a discomforting silence between us, so I broke it. "Do you think I'm crazy?"

"Yes." Gilly blinked and smiled. "But you know me, I busted Santa Claus at the age of two. Honestly, if anyone else had told me this, I would think I had better go looking for another job. But you, if you really feel you should do this, then you must. And I'm beside you, behind you, wherever you want me, I'm there."

"Good. Because I have a couple of things I need you to do."

I handed Gilly two letters. One was addressed to Mother Teresa and one to His Holiness the Dalai Lama. They explained the project in detail ~ I was offering to film their simple messages to the world, the first international public service annoucements ~ adding that I would arrive in Calcutta at the beginning of April and then travel to the upper regions of India to film His Holiness two weeks later.

"And I've put together these presentations that I need hand-delivered immediately."

With raised eyebrows Gilly leafed through the colorful proposals outlining a new concept of goodwill messages from Nobel Peace Prize winners, brought to you by some of the world's largest corporations.

Gilly gulped. "Do you really think they will pay for this?"

"The way I see it, these multinationals sell their products everywhere. They drink Coca-Cola in Iran. They eat McDonald's in France. They have American Express offices in Pakistan. Corporations are made up of people. Who says they won't be the ones to bring us world peace?" Albeit, we both knew I was being particularly idealistic and hopeful.

Gilly smiled sweetly and thrust her fist to heaven, proclaiming in her lilting Cockney accent, "By the people! For the people! We the people!" She clicked. "Oh, I almost forgot. You have to watch this." She squealed while pulling out of her production bag a video about Mother Teresa. "My friend Jessica sent it over for you. Do you remember her? She used to work for ICM, and while she was there she told me someone came in to see her boss, Ed Limato. You know him, he's Richard Gere's agent. Anyway . . ."

At times, Gilly has this nutty way of taking you on a vast journey before she makes her point. "Jessica told me about these two women who made this documentary on Mother Teresa, and, well ~ you're not going to like this tidbit of information ~ it took them five years to get permission!"

"Five years?" I had to sit down on that one.

"Yes. And Mother Teresa made them go all the way to the Vatican for the final blessing."

While I was privately reeling over this information, Mark stepped into the fray, fresh from the gym and raring to rock and roll.

"Who are we tracking down now?"

"Mother Teresa," Gilly blurted out.

Mark looked at Gilly. Gilly looked at me. The energy in the room screeched to a halt.

"Christina is going to Calcutta to film her," Gilly added.

The hair on Mark's chest bristled. This wasn't the way I wanted to break the news to him.

"I spoke with her," I said, hoping that disclosure would legitimize the blow.

"You talked to her? In person?" Mark asked, unusually impressed.

"Jessica said if Mother Teresa says no, she means no," Gilly chimed in.

"Did she say no?" Mark asked.

"No."

"Did she say yes?"

"No. But she will."

"What makes you so sure?" I could tell this conversation was heading in completely the wrong direction.

"She came to me in meditation."

"Uh-oh, here we go." There were volumes of judgment in Mark's comment and the facial expressions that followed. He had a built-in reluctance to my intuitive messages, my feelings, my hunches, my visions and dreams, even though he paid deft attention to them, had benefited enormously from them, and indeed taken them to the bank. He was never willing to admit it.

He swiveled on his heels, adding as he made his exit, "Christina. I love you dearly, but you're broke. All hell has broken loose up here and you want to go film the most impossible person you could think of, in the most god-awful place in the world."

He slammed the door behind him, not allowing any response. But even behind a closed door, we heard him add, "And what makes you think anyone would want to go with you?"

I felt deflated and humiliated.

Gilly rolled her eyes and let a silent "Sorry" fall from her lips.

A moment passed, and then a voice emerged from behind a wingback chair.

"I'll go to India with you, darlin'."

He stood, revealing himself, and winked. It was our director of photography, Conrad Hall. The famous Conrad Hall. He wasn't a young man in terms of years, yet he was more charismatic, vital, and focused than most people half his age. Connie owned an island in the South Pacific and was more globally aware than most. He had already won an Academy Award for cinematography and in the coming years was destined to win another two. His schedule was always booked tight for any foreseeable future.

"Sounds like a good idea," Connie said. "I'd like to help. If we can do it right after this shoot you can count me in." Without missing a beat, Connie instructed Gilly to call Panavision and have them book his regular package plus some other lenses we talked about and backup equipment. Then he got on the phone himself to be sure they gave it to us, for free!

Sometimes all you need is just one other person believing in you.

With renewed vigor, Gilly got to it and started the paperwork. Visas, tickets, equipment carnet, and appointments for inoculations.

Mark was right, though. How I was going to pay for all this, I knew not. Corporate sponsorship was a long shot.

For the next week the weather hung over us threateningly, like an ever-present cloud, and it wasn't alone.

"Christina, you've got to hear this!" Gilly called as she turned up the sound on her television. The story was almost over, but the gist was painfully clear. The pernicious hand of terrorism had struck again. This time, India was making headlines. Bombay bombed! What timing!

We were contending with Mother Nature in the mountains, but human nature was taking its toll elsewhere, and the news was growing even worse.

Calcutta was in civil turmoil. Two hundred people, caught in a Hindu–Muslim uprising, had been injured in an explosion in a downtown shopping complex.

The following day the State Department issued an advisory that Americans should not travel to India at this time.

"Afraid I have more bad news" was Gilly's greeting to me the following day. "Civil war is not a favorite of the insurance companies. Afraid you have no insurance. They won't cover the crew or any of the equipment. I did my best kissy-kiss sweet talk, but I can't budge them."

We knew that without insurance, Panavision would not allow their cameras out the door, let alone out of the country. Conrad, darling

Conrad, mild-mannered, never-to-be-thrown Conrad, was confident we could pick up our equipment in India. "After all, Bollywood is home to the largest film industry in the world."

We were not prepared for the disclosure that there were only two 35mm sound cameras on the entire continent and both were antiquated, unreliable, and unavailable. After further investigation I discovered that with more than 80 different dialects, all of India's movies are made MOS, "mit out sound," and dubbed later. It didn't end there. With the news of civil unrest, my key crew begged off. Couldn't blame them. They all had children. Then, with our weather getting worse and our shoot being extended and the start date for Connie's next movie moved up a week, it crushed him, but Conrad had to beg off. While the trouble in India remained in the headlines, one by one the rest of my crew backed out. Overnight, my perfectly buttoned-up production had fallen down around my ankles.

Still, I hung in there. I followed up on my corporate presentations. I made calls to Atlanta, New York, Seattle, and Chicago. I got through to corporate heads who normally decline talking with anybody, let alone a filmmaker from California. I took it as a sign. God was on my side. And though I got my foot in the door, their responses were unanimous. An honorable effort, but let's face it, how many cases of Coca-Cola could a Nobel Prize winner move off the shelves?

Goodwill; you can't buy it, and jokes aside, it's damn hard to sell.

I felt defeated. I felt foolish at how easily my grandiose plans had crumbled. Mark's faith in the universe, finite and empty as he knew it, was restored. My faith, and I still had some, was stirred ~ not shaken.

Studying many religions, seeking the points where they intersect and agree, I have found there is an underlying principle that emerges in beliefs all over the world; it is a pursuit that links one person to another, as we travel to its divine destination. The quest for the Holy Grail, the conquest of Medusa, the slaying of the dragon, seeking the paradise of the 72 virgins, the journey to Nirvana ~ all pilgrimages lead to a "promised land," whatever we may imagine that to be. To succeed in our pursuit of the spiritually blessed life requires one simple thing ~ that we turn our backs on fear and embrace love.

love

Consciously or unconsciously, we are all on that blessed journey, where every step is governed by faith. Faith that is asking us to bravely open our hearts ~ to release all limiting thoughts ~ luring us into the unknown, demanding we fear not its many tests.

To succeed in this, my small quest would prove to be no different.

♡♡♡

"Before you open your mouth,
remember your words will fall on deaf ears
unless they come from within.
Say less and mean more."

After three grueling weeks of Wyoming winter, grabbing shots when and where we could, our 60-plus crew limped home to Hollywood, suffering from altitude sickness, near frostbite, and fatigue.

It happened with regularity that on an extreme shoot like that, I can hold it together, working 18 to 20 hours a day, until I make it home. Then I will go down for three days with some mysterious malady. Sure enough, I was knocked out by a bad cold, and I lost my voice.

A filmmaker with a mission but without a voice can be ineffectual and overridingly dangerous.

I had not received a response to my letter to Mother Teresa. In a normal world this would be exactly the clue to tell me ~ Give it up, baby. No crew. No Mother Teresa. No shame. Save your money, Teeny. Stay here and make a bundle. Even my own sometimes lopsided logic could rationalize it was "not meant to be." However, the intensity of Mother Teresa's touch would not lessen. I had fallen completely under her spell.

I needed to speak with her. But my cold had lodged itself deep in my throat, and I couldn't squeak out two syllables. Now I know I should have listened to the very clear signal my own body was sending. When I could at least manage a husky whisper, I called Calcutta. This time I came up against the infamous fallibility of the Indian phone system. Did this deter me? Nope. For days I drifted in and out of sleep with the phone poised on the pillow beside me without having even gotten a dial tone to Calcutta.

Under normal circumstances, this, too, I should have noticed as a deterring sign.

I know we hear those clichés of "go with the flow" and "roll with the punches"; however, in truth, and in small things, there is a lot to be said for waiting for the universe to join in and take over.

I am a great believer in timing. It's a subtle yet valid partner to success; however, I was without subtlety at this point. I was not going to wait for the right time. I was going to muscle my way in and create the right time. Big mistake. My dogged persistence paid off and the phone rang through and wouldn't you know ~ Mother Teresa answered.

"Yes, God bless."

I detected a thickness in her voice this time, and I asked if she had a cold.

"Yes, God bless," she responded.

How curious. We both have a cold, I thought.

"I'm sorry you're not feeling well, Mother Teresa."

"Yes. Thank you," she answered.

My thinking was fuzzy. I was nervous, so nervous, and I knew I should make this short and to the point. I didn't quite know how to begin, because I didn't want to hear her say no. Then I would have to honor her wishes. So I spoke quickly before my voice disappeared again, giving her no room to disagree.

"I am coming next week to film you, and I need to be certain you will be there." There was silence at the other end of the line. *Pushing, I was pushing.* I was going about it all wrong. Reeling with insecurity, my faith was slipping, and she could feel it. Worse, in her silence and the lack of sweet "Yes, God bless," I could feel her disappointment in me rising.

"I need to be certain you're going to be in Calcutta."

"There was a film made a long time ago," she retorted rather briskly. "You can use that."

"Yes. And it is a beautiful film, Mother. It tells your story, but it isn't you speaking."

I wanted to say, "We must go further than to simply talk about you and show what you do. There's trouble in the world. It's not getting better, and it will get worse. We need understanding! We need love. We need to look deep into your eyes and meet your soul. And understand what real love requires." But I couldn't.

I was clenching the phone so tightly the blood had left my hand and my arm was prickling. I knew the film I envisioned didn't exist. But I was tense, and I wasn't expressing myself clearly. I wasn't feeling well, and my temperature was rising. So I blurted out an anxious, desperately abbreviated version.

"It isn't the same. You must speak to the people."

There was a murmur and then, in the next breath, the line went dead.

In that instant I felt a toughness in her that I would later learn was necessary to run more than 600 homes in more than 126 countries, across five continents and to fearlessly run them on faith and unsolicited donations.

I had pushed too far. She was human, too, and she wasn't well. I scolded myself for having forced her to become irritated when I knew that was not her nature.

Conventional wisdom, at this point, would say, give it up! Let it go! But in ordinary hours, I am neither conventional nor wise.

Where was that child in me who would make me great? A child believes in "thy will" whereas an adult believes in "my will." I needed to find my innocence again.

My friend the Reverend Michael Beckwith has a saying that comes in handy in times like this: "When everything looks like it's falling apart is actually when it's coming together."

You will never truly know the unseen forces out there, working on your behalf. Neither will I. Rest assured, they are there. I know that now. I didn't then.

Something will always tell you when it's time.

Time to let go and let God.

"Its all in how you look at it.
A stumbling block may be nothing more than
a rock you can step on."

I received a fax from His Holiness the Dalai Lama, and it was his acceptance of my request giving me an actual date, place, and time. However, the expense of filming in such a remote area only made sense if I could also film Mother Teresa on the same trip.

Was the curtain on Act III of my Greek tragedy about to rise? I clung fiercely to the hope that my intuition had not been warped by wishful thinking. It took everything I had to hold tight to the shreds of my calling, when all I needed to do was let go and accept that "little me" was not in control of any of this. When I did, something profound happened.

An invisible force was taking over, and it was destined to unequivocally topple my belief of how the universe actually functioned and how we conduct business in it. Details unfolded in simple, logical fashion.

"I think one of my countrymen is on the phone for you," Gilly said with a confused yet curious twinkle in her eye. "Guess I've been away too long 'cause I can't understand a flippin' word he's saying. He gave me his name twice. It sounds like 'I smile.'"

It was Ismail Merchant, partner of famed director James Ivory and head of Merchant Ivory Productions in Bombay. Merchant Ivory won an Academy Award almost every time they made a movie. I had contacted their New York office some weeks earlier searching for a location scout in Calcutta and with perfect diction Ismail confirmed yet another discouraging rumor.

"All filming in Calcutta is banned!"

He went on to explain that a few years earlier, the Indian government had imposed a moratorium on filming after the movie *City of Joy*, shot on location in Calcutta, was released. There had been numerous problems with the film, the worst of which, from the government's perspective, was that the movie had shown the city in a bad light, depicting poverty and corruption rather than also showing its beauty. Of course, the film's artistic integrity required realism but it left a chip on the government's shoulder. The city remained off-limits, closed, locked out to any further film crews, especially foreign entities.

"No permits! Consequently, no work! Resulting in no location scouts."

"What about shooting without permits?" I asked Ismail, knowing this outlaw style is professionally discouraged.

"Ah, well . . ."

Having been the producer of features such as *Howards End* and *A Room with a View,* Ismail knew how to solve a problem, so I reined in my need to control, shut up, and gave him the space to do his thing.

"I think it would be wise to fly your crew in from elsewhere," he said, sounding for all intents and purposes like an English lord. He went on to describe to me how, for true and valuable compensation, this lawbreaking could be accomplished.

Ismail had, by chance, just wrapped a feature and the camera had not yet been returned to England, and his sound engineer (who had his own equipment) was chillin' on holiday on an island in southern India. Ismail was confident that for sufficient "incentive" I could convince him to hang out a while longer. Following that, Ismail stated that, for the right price, he could put together a first-class crew I would be happy with.

We agreed I would first land in Bombay to meet Ismail's nephew Nayeem, who was to be my production manager. We would discuss my vision, and he would show me cinematographers' reels. I could interview them and meet more members of Ismail's family who were to be my crew. I wanted to ask how much all this might cost me. Can I get into the country with my raw stock? Could I get out of the country with the negative? Could we be arrested? But I held my tongue and appreciated the fact that from the other side of the world and by all outward signs, my mission had been rescued.

After Ismail and I disconnected, I sat staring at the phone for the longest time.

Green light. This is the point in a production where a producer turns into a machine, making calls, choosing crew, checking everything from the extended local weather to the size of the camera truck to the blend of the coffee. Briefing wardrobe, casting, locations . . . on and on, getting the vision communicated to everyone involved and setting the stage for the magic to show up. Instead I fell into an unusual calm. I surrendered. Someone greater than me was pulling the strings here and taking a cue from someone I hoped to meet soon.

I merely had to say, Yes, God bless.

♡♡♡

*"When you are finally committed,
moving in the direction of your dream,
there comes a sign to cheer you on."*

Tuesday, March 30, 1993
Hollywood, California

My bags were packed. Every penny in my bank account had been transferred to traveler's checks, and my leather valise was heavy with all the books Gilly had gathered on Mother Teresa, along with the videotape I had not yet watched. Under advice from a dear friend, J.T., another acclaimed cinematographer, I purchased two rather expensive Pro-Mist filters. J.T. and Conrad had used them on everyone from Elizabeth Taylor to Mel Gibson. They soften the craggy edges and smooth the lines of a face in a way all the makeup in the world could not accomplish. Mother Teresa's beauty would shine through.

Gilly was folding 1,000-foot rolls of Kodak negative in Bubble Wrap and packing them into lead-lined protective bags.

"So. You're really going," Mark stated in a surly but resigned manner. Take your pick: after six years we were like an old married couple or two kids playing in a sandbox. This portended one of those times where he kicked the sand in my face. I knew as sure as I knew him, I would pay dearly for this public display of independence.

"You're making a career choice, you know," he said with a threatening scowl. "We've got a two-million-dollar job coming in and you're leaving. It doesn't look good."

"I've replaced myself with the best people in the business. You're the only one who doesn't seem to understand I'm doing something I have to do."

"No. What you have to do is be here with me, instead of chasing some harebrained idea."

"Limo is here," Gilly called out.

Mark shook his head disapprovingly and withdrew into his office.

I waited for the "toodle pip" that always followed when Gilly wanted me gone. Instead she clung to the doorframe of my office, looking as if she had just swallowed poison.

"I have a fax I don't think you're going to want to read."

My heart raced.

The moment this news had left her pert British lips, Gilly relaxed and returned to her old self. There it was. A tilt of the head, a raise of the brow, a shrug of the shoulder, and a wiggle of her tartan skirt always informed me that all news is open to interpretation.

"Then why don't you read it to me?" I said, collecting myself for bad news.

"It's from the Missionaries of Charity in Calcutta. It says, 'Dear Ms. Stevens. Thank you' . . . mmm . . . 'As Mother has already explained to you on the phone, she has not been giving permission to others to do any filming, and therefore will not give you the permission either . . .'" Gilly frowned, not wanting to go any further. But, sensing my impatience, her eyes dropped again to the page.

"Okay. Bottom line. It says, don't come; don't bring your film crew; Mother will not allow filming under any circumstances. However, I wish you well with your project . . . yada yada yada."

Before I could utter a response, Mark's voice burst through the crack in his office door.

"You see! You're going all the way over there and you won't even get to meet her."

I didn't respond. Instead, I became quite still.

Gilly blinked, tilted her head down, and peered at me as if over some invisible wall.

"The film is already packed and ready," she said meekly.

I listened to the pregnant silence. And I heard again an inner chant that had been my mantra for some time. *Don't give up the dream. Don't give up the dream.*

"Who signed that fax?" I asked.

"Sister Priscilla."

One attribute the illusive film business brings out in a person is the flair to seize that one ray of hope, to reach for that one dangling golden thread and hold on tight. Without missing a beat I resumed my packing.

"Since Mother Teresa didn't personally write that letter and I could have already left when it arrived, I am going to act as if I didn't receive it."

"Right you are!" Gilly smiled and shoved the paper into her notebook, out of sight. Spinning around, she left, adding, "And that wouldn't be a lie."

I do believe in faith. Not blind faith, mind you ~ faith with a purpose and a pure heart. I felt no guilt ignoring that fax.

I was carrying six heavy cans of film stock, and I knew that would alter the extent of my usual carry-on items. I locked away my normal collection of techno-toys and instead slipped an old-fashioned diary into my coat pocket and crawled into the limo.

"Hold on. I'm coming with you!" Gilly leaped in beside me with papers and checks in her hand for signing.

Mark was right behind her, leaning in as he gently closed the door. "I can't help it. I love you anyway. Even if you are a little weird." Then he waved us away, calling, "Just don't go buying golden Buddhas for everyone. We can't afford it."

Speeding along the coastline to LAX, I changed from my business suit into comfy slacks and a sweater. Toodle pip! Heading clear out of my comfort zone.

"It's a sign!" Gilly squealed with delight. "No. Better. It's an omen!" she added. With half her body hanging out the window, her eyes popping at a school of dolphins leaping southward with us, she waved. "They have come to bid you farewell."

We both watched the dolphins as far as we could, and that's when it hit us. I was actually leaving. Together we stared into space for a bit.

"Are you sure you're going to be all right?" Gilly asked with the first pale of concern I had ever seen cross her face.

"I've traveled the world a hundred times." I laughed nervously.

"But not alone like this," she retorted, concerned. "You're used to being taken care of. You live in a bubble. You're Hollywood soft now, you know. Blimey, things can happen. It could be dangerous."

love

    I had no inkling I was beginning a journey that would forever remove me from my lulling armchair lifestyle. No hint I was about to stare death, life, and immortality in the face. I thought I was going off to make a film when instead I was going off to make a memory, one that would transform my life and the many lives of those around me. I was going to find courage I never knew I had and see worlds I never realized existed. I was about to shatter time and space and enter India's vast labyrinth of myth and magic. I had no notion I was stepping into a timeless land where eternity reigns. No, I had no clue.

    With the dolphins' blessing, I rolled down the window, thrust my face into the moist foggy evening, inhaled my last familiar fragrance of Pacific Ocean air, and called to the architect of our veiled destiny.

    "I'm ready. Bring it on."

CHAPTER FIVE

FAITH IS A GIFT

Richard James

*"Love and faith are inseparable.
One completes the other."*

Wednesday, March 31, 1993
Somewhere between Hollywood and fantasyland

"Do you realize the shell of a plane is less than three inches thick?" Mark would routinely announce to one and all within hearing distance every time our wheels left the runway. Then, taking his thumb and first digit and holding them an eighth of an inch apart, he would add perilously, "Doesn't it worry you that we're about to spend the next ten hours this close to disaster?"

Mark's phobia of flying knows no bounds. Habitually he will fly, only first class, insisting on the window seat so he can white-knuckle the edge of the porthole as he watches for other aircraft in the vicinity. Indeed, he could identify the make, model, weight, fuel, and passenger capacity of every commercial aircraft in service.

I, on the other hand, am giddy. The planes I fly are fabric wrapped over a wood frame. Featherlight. Open cockpit. You strap on your parachute before you strap on your seat belt. You eat clouds. And when it rains, you get wet.

I relish losing contact with the ground. Only then am I reminded of the infinite promise given to our mortal journey here on earth. As a dreamy youth I believed that with wings I could soar upward in my evolution. I imagined my spirit connecting heaven to earth ~ as if creating this union was a soul path of mine. For me, being a passenger on a jetliner is like hanging out in God's palm. I am on vacation. Along for the ride. Content that someone other than myself is affirming ~ science is indeed capable of achieving the angelic.

I would normally choose to listen to music and let the clouds swallow me for the entire trip, but I hadn't had one night of sound sleep since I had felt Mother Teresa calling me.

The more I wanted to nod off the harder my seat became. At first I squirmed, searching for a soft spot, and then I thought to simply relax, to sink down and lose myself. It was a physical sensation of falling through the rabbit hole that brought a smile to my face and took me back to a time when I was on the brink of discovering for myself that our universe is indeed one of infinite possibilities. I was a lone traveler then, just as now.

It was the night before my initial departure from my home, Sydney, Australia, my first transatlantic flight. When I was 11 years old I announced to one and all that I would be going to America to live. Everyone laughed and commented on what a funny little girl I was. From that moment on, it seems I counted the years, months, and days in anticipation. Then one day, it was down to hours.

I went to bed exhilarated, with butterflies in my tummy. I lay there in the moonlight trying to get those butterflies to fly in formation, but they refused to be contained. I looked at my bags, rimmed in the moonlight. My entire physical world was zipped up into those two brown leather valises. I got up and turned on the light and looked again at my BOAC ticket. Sydney, Bali, Cairo, London. And then New York.

I remember thinking, *I may never sleep in this bed again. I won't be here tomorrow night, or the night after that, or the night after that.* If I was scared of heading out into the unknown world by myself, sheer excitement erased any trepidation.

You know that space between waking and sleeping, where you're totally relaxed, hovering on the edge of consciousness? I know you've felt it, maybe not often, but I know you have. And it's sublime. That's where I was.

It was a familiar feeling. Tipping onto the verge of sleep, I felt I was a little girl lying across a giant boulder, toasty warm from the sun. The cozy rock, though hard and jagged, was soft and comfortable. I felt tinier than a baby and the rock was huge and safe. It cupped my body like two giant hands and then as consciousness released its grip, my body let go of its boundaries and the warm stone absorbed me. Somewhere between waking and sleeping, I fell, in, in, in.

Suddenly the door to my bedroom flew open. With a start, I sat up. There in the doorway was the most brilliant light I had ever seen ~ white, yet reflecting a kaleidoscope of colors. The light started flashing and began to take form. It was my uncle Ben! He and his wife, my auntie Bon, though not without their own challenges, had been a touchstone of peace and sanity in my early years. Uncle Ben, at that time, was the only member of my family who had passed over to the other side.

He reached his hand toward me, and I was delighted to see him. Eagerly I leaped out of bed and went to him, my arms outstretched. I was so looking forward to his lively hug, and I had so much to say to him. He had died so suddenly . . .

And then it hit me.

He's dead! What is he doing here?

I was almost touching him when his image left the open doorway. I turned to follow his light. Immediately he was standing in the garden, outside my bedroom window. I ran to the window. Uncle Ben was standing right there straddling the wisteria, brighter than day. He smiled at me and his mustache crinkled and his eyes lit up. He lifted his arm and pointed toward the bed. I didn't want to turn away from him, but out of the corner of my eye I saw something. Then I felt impelled to turn and look directly at what he wanted me to see. It gave me such a start that I literally hit the ceiling.

It was me! I was there ~ in bed! But I was also on the ceiling, looking down at myself ~ in bed sleeping. And less than a second earlier I had been at the window? Vaguely, I could see a fainter light connecting me to the body in bed. So I came down to take a closer look at her. It was me, all right. I looked out the window. Ben was gone. His light had left, and I felt a shivering coldness. I sucked in my energy. I think I got frightened. Like lightning I was back in the body. I opened my eyes and sat up.

The room was dark, but through the moonlight I could see shadows of the wood carving in the door. It was closed. I was certain he had been there and equally certain I had seen the door open. I pulled myself out of bed and went to the door, letting my fingers run over the carved wooden panels.

I had to feel if it was real.

In that moment I asked myself a question that would forever haunt me. It was a question for which I would find my answer, if only for my own truth. What is real?

No doubt we often leave our bodies when we sleep, and I wondered then if I was simply discovering what everyone else already knew to be true but nobody talked about ~ that the body is a vessel for the spirit, and with just a slightly different focus, the spirit can travel the entire universe, unfettered and at will.

I was 20 and off on the quest of a lifetime. I wanted to return to this miraculous experience and explore the invisible realm more courageously. I wanted to leave my body again and learn how to astral travel to destinations unknown. But the physical world is an adventurous place, and in my waking moments there was always something else and somewhere else. Nevertheless, every day that followed, when putting my head on my pillow and falling off to sleep, I considered my astral adventure. Up, up, and away.

The cabin of an aircraft is probably no place for this kind of out-of-body dream walking, so I stirred myself awake.

I glanced over to a fellow traveler: snoring, legs sprawled, completely out of it. I saw another, curled into a ball, snoozing quietly.

I spotted another passenger and another, each off on their own cloistered island and yet at any moment lightning could strike and in that instant our destinies would be fused for all time. In one act, our individuation would merge into one. How unique and separately we live our lives, yet how completely alike and unified we are.

I was reminded again that there is no separation between us. Whatever I do for you, I do for myself. Whatever I discover, someplace in you learns it, too. And the journey I take right now, inside the pages of this book, you take, too.

Was this Jesus's message when he suggested we turn the other cheek?

As we dig deeper into mankind's frame-breaking unity, scientists and sages once again agree ~ when man gives up his need to be special, we as a species will move closer to realizing our universality. Our oneness. We have left the world of polarity consciousness and have entered the realization of unity consciousness.

Stepping onto Indian soil it was as if the earth reached up and infused me with a new notion . . .

Nothing that divides us is real.

"How do you know if a decision is right?
When your belly flutters
reminiscent of a brush with love."

I have heard it said that India forces you to come face-to-face with yourself, to confront the life you have led so far, to return home never the same again.

Our plane landed in Bombay around midday, and our connection with one another as passengers inside the silver sky capsule dissipated, and we went our separate ways.

I headed immediately to Merchant Ivory's office to meet Nayeem, look at cameramen's reels, and order equipment.

Everything was pretty much as we had arranged except for one small item on which Nayeem could not negotiate. It would put me over budget, representing my initial plunge into debt.

"It is the only lens in this entire country that can accomplish what you wish. Fortunate we are that it just happens to be available right now, which is rare indeed," Nayeem politely informed me.

"But, Nayeem, I don't understand why I have to pay to fly a man thousands of miles, whose sole job it is to carry the thing on his lap. I have never hired a guardian for a lens before."

I had been in India for a few hours, and I didn't entirely appreciate that I had come from a place of material abundance to a land where mere everyday conveniences were in short supply. I wanted, nay needed, this long lens because it would ensure we could capture someone intimately from a great distance. I knew without permits to film in Calcutta, our massive camera may need to be skulking under the radar, far from the public eye. I also love the look a long lens puts on film. I was selecting equipment intuitively since I didn't have a storyboard, a shot list, or even an idea of what I would encounter in Calcutta, just some art book references and a vision of how I wanted the film to look and feel.

My ability to anticipate meant everything.

In film production, some days can be like heading out to war, with a script to conquer and an army to lead. Certainly no risk to life and limb, yet I knew it was vital for me to approach it with that sort of military discipline, and there were two things I needed to be sure of ~ my tools and my intuition.

I checked my intuitive button on how I felt about this choice, for a decision made from fear is never a good decision.

Though it was absurdly extravagant, my inner voice told me absolutely, without question, yes yes yes, I had to have that lens, whatever the cost.

"Okay," I surrendered enthusiastically. "That's one more man, one more airfare, and one more hotel room."

"Listening to that which no one else hears
can be a sign of madness
or a whisper from God."

Nayeem was standing politely at attention in the foyer of the Taj Mahal Palace, Bombay, waiting for his date. Looking to be in his early 20s, he had a perfectly chiseled face, skin like soft caramel, a mop of curly black hair, and teeth as shiny as pearls. I swept down the giant staircase, and he moved like a gazelle toward me, offering his arm. We stepped out into the early evening, with the moon rising over the bay as the fragrance of incense and spices wafted through streets teeming with life.

Ismail Merchant had just that morning departed for Los Angeles for the Academy Awards ceremony in Hollywood (yeah, they were about to win yet another) and so Nayeem, being a gracious stand-in, insisted on taking me to dinner.

We strolled just a few blocks from my hotel to a most unusual restaurant. It was dimly lit yet rich with color and alive with wall hangings and curtains that undulated to the wake of a fan and the music of a sitar. Carved wooden beds and poofy cushions encouraged diners to lie together and decadently feed each other with their fingers. We chose a table that sat low to the floor, where we each had our own individual chaise.

Indeed even more unusual was the live entertainment. Going from table to table, palm and tarot readers, numerologists and astrologers, and psychic seers stopped by and for a few rupees entertained patrons with their visions and predictions. Nayeem, intent on talking business, waved away all comers, and we enjoyed a lavish six-course feast, uninterrupted.

Then, just as jet lag and the overly stuffed chaise were about to swallow me completely, a man, looking more ancient than anyone I had lately seen, placed his small stool firmly beside me. Squatting on it, he gently took my hand in his and turned it palm up.

Cocking his head slightly as if listening to a child's whisper, he waved his free hand in the air, beckoning the discussion.

"You will travel to many dangerous places in your life. Be assured, you are protected," he said, without even a hello, how-do-you-do.

Nayeem rose from his seat to protest, but the old man ignored him and moved closer, focusing intently on my face, speaking softly.

"You are here on a very important mission." Helpless but intrigued, I glanced over to Nayeem and then back to the stranger as he added, "You will find the love you seek." The old man looked at me, searching for some sort of acknowledgment to continue.

I didn't respond. I realized that, of course, this is entertainment. This prophet thinks I am a romantic explorer from the Western world.

Nayeem brushed a dark curl from his handsome brow and blushed a little.

"Uh, I don't think so," I murmured quietly.

"Ahh. Yes," said the sage, nodding enthusiastically as if suddenly all the chips had fallen into place. "You are working for the government."

Both Nayeem and I chuckled at the absurdity of his assertion, well aware of what we were covertly planning.

"Love and government together?" Nayeem chuckled.

"Yes. She is working for the government," the sage repeated.

"I don't think so," I managed to say through my snickering.

Not only had I flown in under government red tape on a tourist visa, I was planning to film one of India's most beloved residents, who had not given her permission, and to top it off, minus all film permits. Working for the government? I think not.

Once again, Nayeem moved to pull the seer off his stool, but the old fellow dug in and Nayeem immediately retreated.

Distinctly I noticed a certain deference and respect given to metaphysicians in the East that are not proffered in the West. I could see, too, that Nayeem was torn between wanting to hear what the old sage had to say and wanting to protect me, should I be offended or displeased with his message.

I smiled to put him at ease. The old man, unfazed by my negative response, let his unusual eyes trace the lines of my palm.

"You indeed have the permission of the government," he repeated.

"Oh no. You're absolutely wrong there." I roared with laughter, pulling my hand away, adding, "In fact, if the government had known what I was planning, the embassy would have refused my visa."

The old man stared hard into my eyes, and I saw his brown peepers had the most unusual specks of gold, almost as if there were suns spinning inside them.

"You do not understand," he protested. "I am not speaking of the people's government. I am speaking of the spiritual government. That is who you work with."

That statement shut me up. And I felt Nayeem snap to attention.

The old man cracked a smile. At last he had gotten through. "That is your protection. You will be happy to know everything you wish for will be granted." With that said, the old man straightened his crooked body and rose to leave.

I wanted him to stay and tell me more, but he was clearly finished. When I dipped into my purse for some rupees, he waved my offer away yet leaned in close to murmur one more thing.

"Your journey here is most auspicious."

That said, he evaporated into the evening.

"Who was he?" I asked Nayeem, who seemed equally curious. He went over to the owner, who clearly he knew well. They spoke briefly and Nayeem returned shrugging. "He has never seen him here before."

As we walked back to my hotel in the soft moonlight, the lightness in Nayeem's step exposed the fact that he was elated by the old man's words.

"Spiritual government. I've never heard of that," I said to Nayeem. He nodded but didn't respond, so I added, "As on earth likewise in heaven?"

Nayeem stopped and threw his hands up. "You Westerners have such absurd ideas of a heaven."

"What do you mean?"

"You think God is an old man with a white beard, and you see angels with flowing robes."

"Oh, those impressions came from the art of our ancestors. We do know that we don't know. For myself, I think our creator is right here, with us and in us ~ invisible to our earthly eyes yet always present. And I believe all good things come from God. And I am comfortable with that."

"Very good. We have an understanding," Nayeem said jovially, and we continued our walk in a consensus of subject dropped.

love

> *"Listening is an art.*
> *Hearing is a gift."*

The fragrance of nag champa incense was thick in my room. No chocolate on my pillow ~ instead a card from the hotel manager graciously offering the gift of a complimentary astrology reading.

I pushed open the french doors onto my balcony, slid onto the chaise, and gazed out at the moon hanging like a lantern over the bay. I don't know about you, but I have always felt magic in moonlight. Science has yet to confirm the hypothesis that full moons make for crazy times, though the word *lunatic* has its basis there. Law enforcement will tell you they become very busy on a full-moon night. Lunar cycles affect the tides of the oceans and since man is biologically made up of 98 percent water, it naturally impacts our human ebb and flow. This moon was not yet full but was lulling me away.

A gust of wind swept across the balcony and whisked the gift card away with it. No matter. Long ago when I was 17, before I left Australia, I had seen an astrologer who had the same ageless composure and the same confidence in his words as the Indian tonight.

Australia is Shangri-la, inhabited by the most authentic, fun people on earth and offering a lifestyle few nations can match. But I felt I had something to do, a mission of sorts on the other side of the world. I needed to speak to someone who had nothing to gain or lose from my continued presence in my paradise home.

His address was on Phillip Street, in downtown Sydney. Surprisingly he wasn't listed on the tenant directory. I followed specific directions up a back staircase to the third floor. The corridor was chilly and dank. As I passed glass-paneled offices that showed no signs of life, I felt as if I had been transported into a film noir, expecting Humphrey Bogart and a leggy blonde to appear at any minute.

It was spooky all right, and under any other circumstances I would have turned on my heels and run home. But home held no growth, no light, no air, and no sustenance. I was dying.

I knocked on the last door, marked Private, and heard a faint shuffle. In the next instance I was gazing into the face of an ancient.

No way to tell his age through his white beard and his well-worn though respectable three-piece suit.

"Hi, I'm Chris . . ." He waved away my introduction, shuffled back behind his desk, and motioned for me to sit. His office was a clutter of books. The air was dusty and yet the books, though old, shone with use.

It is said the only things certain in life are death and taxes. But there is something else more reliable and true: the celestial movement of the heavens. Hurtling at speeds beyond our comprehension, those trusty tomes filled with numbers and symbols, graphs and charts, predict where the stars and planets have been and will be throughout time. To the educated eye those mathematical computations extend man's reach to encompass the footprint of the galaxy.

The old man said nothing as he pulled out a file and opened it. Inside were two sheets of paper. One with my name, exact date, hour, and minute of my birth and some kind of code scrawled beneath. The other, a pie chart, sliced into 12 pieces, with colored lines and symbols and degrees written by hand connected by even more lines. He reminded me that an astrological chart is a valuable portrait of one's soul in time, a scientific measure older than the sundial, and as they had done for centuries for kings and queens, they reveal unique opportunities and aspects to help guide our actions. Ahh! I had come to the right place. I was reaching for help and he was offering saintly support from the universe.

His craggy face squinted, examining me in a most deliberate manner. After the longest time, he spoke.

"This is the most powerful chart I have ever seen . . . in fact, there was only one other . . ." He drifted for a second and then returned. "There isn't a lot I can tell you, except encourage you to travel."

"Where?" I leaned forward.

"Oh, you know where you're going," he responded confidently, peering into my eyes for acknowledgment.

Yes, I knew where I was going.

I sat on the edge of the worn leather easy chair and held my mouth shut while he, in a remote and businesslike tone reviewed my life so far, almost as if he had lived it with me. He knew there was unhappiness and turmoil. He touched on violence, pinpointing exact dates and years and events nobody but I could have known. He looked upon it with a content detachment, almost as if it were all going perfectly to plan. He encouraged me to look at my life with a different pair of eyes. It was akin to a healing for as he spoke I could feel the strings that connected me to my early life unraveling, gently releasing me from the shackles of judgment and shame.

He pointed to a combination of numbers and frowned a little. My father, he said, in regards to me was an extreme disciplinarian. He coughed a little and tried to make light of his statement by adding that he was "making up for a time when he wasn't at home," yet that, too, he added, is perfect, because he could see I had the strength to move beyond it and use it to great benefit.

"The mother is very strong for you. She will have great influence in your life."

Oh. No. Ever since I could remember, I, together with my brother, had been my mother's caretaker. I grunted disagreement. "That's not right."

The old man cocked his head and raised his hand.

"I say it is the influence of the mother. If it is not the person who is your mother now, there will be a woman who will represent that to you, and she is extremely powerful."

He kept on about the destiny in my chart, all the time looking at the page in front of him and glancing occasionally to the various neatly placed open books. Then in midsentence he closed the folder, leaned back, and then forward.

"Tell me, do you ever feel different?" His eyes scanned me. "Does something . . . unusual ever happen to you? Do you ever feel, er . . ."

I shook my head. "No."

His look became even more penetrating, if that was possible, and he said, "You mean you have no awareness?" And then he squinted.

Awareness? The word triggered something.

As if he saw recognition in my face, he fell quiet. He cocked his head again, listening for me to speak.

"Well, I do have these times where my hearing gets weird," I said cautiously. "I hear a high-pitched tone like a phone is ringing." He nodded in compliance and let me continue. "When that happens every other sound becomes almost lifeless, I mean, it's all a soft monotone. It's strange. I mean, I can be walking down a busy street, or even in the midst of a performance at the theater, or someone can be talking to me, and I can hear them, but I can't distinguish any highs or lows, no emotion in their voices. The sounds of this world are on one level but it, it sounds like, I have to listen to another. When I speak I hear my voice, but it's in that same monotone just like everything else. And then I get the strangest sensation. I feel as if I have stepped outside of myself, and I am outside, looking in. I am just observing."

The old man nodded and blinked in agreement.

"It happened a lot when I was younger," I added. "I know no one else had spells like this because I used to ask. But no one knew what I was talking about, so I stopped asking."

He settled back into his chair. "And it doesn't scare you?"

I shook my head. "I don't think I'm going deaf. Actually it feels sort of pleasant."

For the first time, he smiled, and a new energy sprang into his voice. "Good. You're aware of it." He sighed, satisfied.

But I wasn't. I wanted to know more. "What? What is it?"

He waved away my curiosity. "That's not important right now," he said. "You'll know in time. Just be patient. The door is opening for you. The important thing is you aren't afraid of it." He stood. Whereas moments ago his presence had been like a giant balloon filling the entire room, I suddenly realized how small and frail he was.

"That's why you came to see me today," he murmured assuredly. When I quizzically drew in my brow, he added, "To hear that." He seemed to glide through the air, and instantly the door was open. "You have a lot of work to do, young lady. Don't let anybody hold you back."

It didn't occur to me until I was halfway home that I had forgotten to pay him. I wanted to call him, but somehow I had misplaced his number. A few days later, I went back to the building on Phillip Street. His door was locked. I worried that he might be sick, so I checked with the building superintendent. He'd never heard of him.

I left that day wondering if I had imagined him. Or if perhaps he had been an angel sent to earth to help me. The old man didn't exist, and yet I would never forget him.

Decades later, on the other side of the world, I left the balcony, the three-quarter moon, with Venus and Mars and Mercury and Saturn sending down their light, and slid into bed.

To listen to the silence.

The hearing episodes of my childhood returned in my adulthood. The difference being that after years of meditation and teaching, I had learned to listen. I could take myself to that same place where I would hear a voice. Not random, misguided mutterings, but clear statements. Not a voice from my mind that I could process, but an awareness, an instantaneous "knowing." I would be informed and enlightened, more often for the benefit of another. The information seemed to come from the same source as my intuition, and when I became still and listened, insight and clarity were the rewards. In time there were no more voices. Like a bolt of lightning, there was just the "knowing."

Perhaps I had been infused with the energy of the evening, but as I sank deeper in the pillow, my many probing conversations with scientists came back, confirming that as our species moves onward in our evolution, time, technology, and our changing environment will open wide those doors of perception for everyone.

Whether we know it or not ~ we are all in the knowing.

CHAPTER SIX

MONEY ALWAYS COMES

Christina Stevens

"Right there inside you
is your endless supply.
Just waiting for you to realize it."

Friday, April 2, 1993
Bombay, India

Nayeem and I boldly strode out of the American Express office armed with two big brown paper shopping bags filled to the brim with cash. Colorful rupee cash. Nayeem couldn't quite understand how or why I was paying for this myself. "Ah! You are married to a wealthy American!" he said victoriously as if he had just cracked the code.

"Not at all," I assured him. "I am single, and I work for a living. Believe me, normally, I could never have afforded to do this. But, you could say, God provided me with an unexpected windfall."

Nayeem's ears pricked up when I explained I had been on location filming an advertising campaign for Texaco when our work screeched to a halt under six days of torrential downpour. We were filming Formula 1 racecars and their famed drivers in Arizona, where at that time of year you would expect no rain at all. The client insisted our bid be a fixed price. I knew rain would stop us dead on the track and I had crew in from out of town, so the downtime, equipment rental, per-diem, hotels, and salaries would have buried us seriously in the red. Intuitively I purchased weather insurance ahead of time and it was expensive ~ insuring against an act of God always is. On the same instinct I negotiated rain-or-shine flat deals with the crew. My heaven-sent hunch turned a potential loss into a huge profit. My bonus check arrived the day after Ismail called.

"Fitting, don't you think, that oil company profits are paying for this? The first environmental public service announcements in the world."

Nayeem nodded happily and went on to reassure me what a "good transaction" I was enjoying. If I had known how many years it would take me to pay off the debts I was about to incur, I might have hesitated, but hesitation was not an option. Almost everyone I knew would question my present folly, to spend so much on a film that possibly no one would see. All I could say was my heart signed the checks and for that, the ink was overflowing.

Nayeem and I returned to his office, and he took possession of my bags of rupees for equipment, crew payroll, hotel expenses, and miscellaneous bribery. I gave him my Amex card to purchase seven nonrefundable air tickets, and we agreed he would bring the crew and equipment to Calcutta in ten days, ready to shoot.

I was handing over hard-earned cash on faith, though I must say at every step, whatever I needed, God provided.

We had not yet fully entered the impervious digital age, and the exquisiteness of 35mm film is only matched by its sensitivity. I needed to bring 6,000 feet of film into the country, in lead bags that could not be tampered with, X-rayed, or opened. And so it happened that the second message in the series *Voices from the Heart* was to come from His Holiness the Dalai Lama. And while Mother Teresa's office sent a letter of rejection, His Holiness's office sent an official letter of acceptance that once presented to customs gave airport security permission to wave my film through, without question. While Mother Teresa's message would be about creating a revolution of love, His Holiness's message would be about finding inner peace, the kind we create ourselves through our own intention. Something the Dalai Lama, through his lifetime of tribulations and challenges, had mastered.

Immediately after Calcutta we were to trek up to the foothills of the Himalayas, to Sikkim, on the border of Tibet. We were given a window to film His Holiness at the end of a weeklong annual ceremony called the Kalachakra ~ the ceremony that spoke of life's impermanence. He was then to immediately leave the country.

Our schedule was ironclad. Everything had to unfold in perfect timing.

"Relax. There is always a grander plan at work.
Once the train has left the station, you are on your way.
Sit back and enjoy the ride."

I thought it wise to immerse myself gently in this strange land. So instead of flying, I opted to cross India on the Rajdhani Express. Sounds exotic, right? Yes, I thought so, too.

Ah, to see the land, in style and comfort.

Bravely, I had chosen to take care of those travel arrangements myself. I had gone to Victoria Terminus but the ticket office was closed. Instead, taped to the door was a map and barely legible handwritten directions guiding me to a most unusual travel office in the basement of a restaurant behind the meat market, four blocks from the train depot.

However temporary his place of business appeared, the travel agent assured me my trip would be "positively regal, m'lady. You are very lucky. Normally, our members of Parliament travel in your car."

love

The high cost of my ticket and the travel agent's flowery description confirmed my anticipation. For a moment I flashed on dear Geoffrey's chariot ride, built for his queen.

I saw myself passing through picturesque Bengali provinces chasing the setting sun, while sipping Champagne from a crystal goblet, dining on roast lamb and tiny herb-encrusted potatoes. Later, nestled in my ebony-paneled stateroom, my attendant would pour chamomile tea from fine bone china. Ah yes, and following that I would rest my weary body between crisp linen sheets while my attendant freshened my outfit for our early morning arrival into Calcutta. It was to be my first delicious adventure in this exotic land.

Doing my best not to panic, I dragged my large bag, trailing Nayeem, who was hauling my heavy box of raw film stock, while my other smaller bags balanced precariously on the heads of two paid Indian porters.

"I think my train is over there," I called out to Nayeem, certain we were racing toward the wrong platform. He was incapable of hearing me over the indigenous hubbub and his own rush to please me. I had no choice but to follow him, plunging headlong into the human chaos.

By the time I caught up to them, the cabin attendant was shaking his head, motioning that my train was the one blowing its whistle and about to leave ~ on the other track!

Immediately a discussion ensued that I couldn't comprehend. But I did follow the actions and their intent. The porters dropped my bags as if they were rice. The taller one thrust out his hand to me.

Nayeem stepped in, refusing to pay until the job was complete. He motioned for them to pick up my bags and carry them over the bridge. More words were exchanged that I could not understand, but for some reason they stood their ground. Desperate, though praying I would not diminish Nayeem's intent, I shoved a wad of rupees into the smaller porter's hands. Wouldn't you know . . . in a blink they and my rupees were gone ~ leaving the five feet five inches of me and the slim-built, five feet eight and not particularly buff Nayeem to haul everything over the bridge and down onto the other track.

"The trouble is you should be taking the plane," Nayeem frustratingly stated in his very proper English.

Oh, but I could already feel myself lost in the feathery down pillows. And please, my mouth was already watering to taste the succulent lamb . . . But let's get back to the battle at hand.

Nayeem bent down and loaded onto his back everything hands couldn't hold and with the strength of an elephant I picked up the rest and man, we ran!

The whistle blew again, the engine was puffing life into the giant lungs of the iron snake as we stumbled and dragged ourselves up the stairs, over the bridge, and down again, collecting a sympathetic onlooker for assistance. Nayeem practically had to hurl my bags and film on board, and I held my breath and leaped as the locomotive rolled out of the station.

The attendant checked my ticket, picked up my bags, and escorted me down the moving corridor. Handwritten: "Private stateroom. Premium class."

I looked again at the compartment number and the four men sitting contentedly on the four well-worn leather seats inside my cabin.

"I think there is a mistake here," I stated as politely as possible. But they didn't seem to understand me.

"I am looking for a private stateroom," I said, to which they all nodded enthusiastically and motioned me in.

"Do you have your tickets?" I asked, waving mine in the air. The youngest of the gentlemen appeared to comprehend and encouraged the others to dig deep into their pockets.

Their tickets were the same. Actually, all five tickets had identical information, except their tickets were printed, more like the real thing. Mine was handwritten.

Feeling guilty that I may be the interloper and in an effort to beg their pardon, I explained my encounter with the travel agent. I gushed with friendliness, certain they didn't understand a word. When I was finished, they huddled among themselves, the youngest occasionally glancing in my direction, flashing me his bright white smile. The four men politely nodded and happily made room for me to join them. Seems I was the only one concerned by the oddity of our situation. A 15-hour train trip. Five people, four beds. Four men, one woman.

I deduced from their clothing and makeshift carry-on bags that they were not members of Parliament. I took a deep breath and found myself delighted to be sharing space with four most accommodating individuals.

I nodded to each of them with my attitude of gratitude.

The attendant asked for our dinner orders, and since I didn't comprehend a word he said, I held my smile and motioned I would be content to have exactly what the others ordered.

Settling in for the duration, we each maintained our smiles for as long as we could. I pulled out my books to read while they all simply turned their gazes out the window to take in God's canvas, rich in simple treasures.

Sorting through my books on Mother Teresa, it occurred to me we learn much about ourselves when we look inside another, especially one whose inner discipline and determination had built steel-hard muscles over her human frailties. I, for one, could do with an inner workout. Chugging through the countryside would give me the space and time to piece together what it was that had transformed a normal, mischievous little girl into someone many were referring to as a "living saint."

I don't know how you feel, but I have always felt deep in that unfathomable part of me there is a grander plan to our individual existence; that we are not merely a random experiment on the face of an indiscriminately revolving planet, only to explode into life and burn out just as quickly. I have imagined each of us possesses a destiny, written before we were born into earthly time and that it was our hand, resting in God's, that fashioned the script. And in that co-authorship, with the scope of higher consciousness we cast our parents, as we do our friends ~ to play their roles in our life saga.

As I unfurled the books before me I felt an odd presence. Not only did words and phrases start leaping off pages; the rhythmic clatter of the locomotive became a metronome lulling me deeper into visual fragments of Mother Teresa's childhood. I was hearing a voice, a deep, guttural murmur coming from within me, and yet it wasn't me. At moments it emerged like narration to scenes from a movie tugging at my heart, giving me comprehension and understanding, empathic to a life journey that clearly bore no resemblance to mine.

It appeared Mother Teresa had indeed selected the perfect parents. Challenged and strengthened as she was by their presence and by their absence, they provided her with the foundation needed to help mold her character and the experiences to guide her choices.

Her childhood was quite ordinary except for one tragic turning point.

She was born Agnes Bojaxhiu in the year 1910, youngest daughter of Nikolle and Drana, a wealthy and politically active family in Skopje, which at the time was in Albania, now Yugoslav Macedonia. The oldest child was her sister, Aga, next came her brother, Lazzaro, and finally Agnes. Closely resembling her mother, Agnes was very pretty, known to be a gay and mischievous little girl who loved to sing and dance yet who lapsed into moments of deep seriousness. Inside, she had her mother's religious strength, balanced with her father's intelligence and her own tongue-in-cheek sense of humor.

Skopje was where East and West met, a cacophony of cultures, religions, and peoples. She was almost four years old when Europe's shaky balance of power was toppled by a teenager with a handgun. Archduke Franz Ferdinand, heir to the Austrian throne, and his wife, Sophie, were assassinated by a militant Bosnian student, and in a matter of months, the world was at war.

Though surrounded on all sides by unrest, the Bojaxhiu family enjoyed and understood true abundance. They loved one another with a deep devotion and shared all they had with anyone in need. Their home was known as a place to go for sustenance and warmth, spirited conversation, gales of laughter, and music from dawn to dusk. They were so happy they didn't know they were happy, until one fine day tragedy came to stay.

Her father, Nikolle, spoke many languages and traveled often to distant shores, trading goods and purchasing materials and equipment for his construction business. When he was gone the children spent their evenings taking turns reading the Bible aloud while their mother sewed.

I loved books. If I could have only two books it would be my Bible and the world atlas. The atlas was filled with maps and pictures that showed me how people were separated, what made them different. And the Bible was filled with stories of how people were brought together and what made us all alike.

I was no longer in a compartment of the Rajdhani Express; I was watching little Agnes's early years unfold before my eyes while her soft voice spoke in my ear.

When my father was home, we had a special ritual. I would sit on his lap and he would open his atlas and carry me off on a magic carpet of colorful stories about his adventures with all the different peoples on earth.

Abruptly, the cabin attendant lured me out of Agnes's world as he offered my dinner tray. The only food item I recognized was one overripe banana, which I immediately peeled and ate. I was ravenous. Gingerly I tasted the currylike dish. Whatever it was, it wasn't for me. I sipped my soda and fondled the single flower bud on my tray. Suddenly a hand put another banana on my tray. I looked up and the youngest of the Indian men, the lean, cute one, I might add, nodded and smiled. I offered him my curry dish in return, but he graciously declined.

Agnes was seven years old, World War I was raging through Europe, and her father had just begun to explain to her the revolution that was unfolding in Russia, when overnight, revolution entered her life. Nikolle had to go away on important business in the south. Three weeks had passed and excitement bubbled through their house. He was to return on the morning train.

My mother moved very fast to prepare for my father's arrival. We didn't understand and we teased her. What a tremendous, delicate love she had for him. It didn't matter what happened. She was always there, with a smile to meet him. But that day a messenger came instead and told us he had collapsed on the train and had been rushed to the hospital. At once, my mother left for the hospital. We were all told to stay at home.

There before me was little Agnes, her feet not even touching the floor as she sat on a chair by the door, waiting for her papa to come home. In all things she was obedient, but this one time she disobeyed.

I ran all the way to the hospital, but they would not let me see him, she said quietly.

It was a time of danger and turmoil not just for Serbia but also for many of the neighboring nations, and Agnes's father was a politically powerful and outspoken man.

There was talk he had been poisoned."

Such things a little child could hardly comprehend. Rumor and innuendo, even direct discussion confused her desperate longing. As the evenings multiplied and her precious atlas bookmarked at Russia gathered dust, she slowly grasped the terrible outcome. *I would never see my father again.*

The Bojaxhius had enjoyed great wealth and abundance, but without Nikolle, their future lay in question. Agnes's mother was a gentlewoman, a woman of spiritual strength and trusting love, not a businesswoman. There were debts to pay, and equipment, houses, and land to be sold, and they were easy pickings for a greedy and corrupt business partner. He took control of the estate. Titles and documents went missing, and after all the books were balanced the only thing left was the roof over their heads.

Many nations, especially in Europe, were experiencing economic hardship leading up to the Great Depression in America. For this little family of four, their greatest loss was their beloved father and his death dealt them another blow; it plunged the once wealthy Bojaxhiu family into a life of poverty.

*"There will always be poverty
when we don't share."*

Something indelible happens to a child when they lose a parent. The gap creates space for a mighty inner echo of influence to expand

and live. For better or worse, shaping growth then rests with the surviving parent. What was worse for the four Bojaxhius was they had lost all their outward trappings of wealth.

We would always share what little we had with anyone who reached our door. To be able to share meant having to balance frugality with generosity, a more than challenging paradigm for a family who had nothing.

The children called their mother "Nana Loke," meaning mother of my soul, and it was her strength and belief in God that provided core beliefs for her children. To survive without relaxing her integrity, she required her children to always be mindful of every *leke* they spent and every service they consumed. While her mother meted out discipline, a virtue Nana Loke had in abundance, Agnes used that example as a building block for her own indomitable spirit.

Many days Nana Loke did not know where she would find sustenance for her brood, and when someone came to the door needing food or clothing, she and the children would each take the better portion from their own plate or the most favorite sweater from their own back and share happily. Tough lessons for a little girl but in those moments she learned well the warm, joyous feeling of love received when what she offered was gratefully accepted. Compassion for the poor was Agnes's birthright.

She grew into a classically pretty teenager with big bright eyes and a finely chiseled face. She laughed and sang and yet there was always a certain seriousness about her ~ she was never without a book in her hands. Always learning. Not yet ready to open up to her true purpose in life and her role in the world. And perhaps that is why her middle name, "Gonxha," meaning flower bud, was particularly fitting.

In time, Nana Loke turned adversity into industry with her own embroidery business. At night, Agnes would sit in front of the fire helping her mother with her sewing while longingly casting her eyes over the books on her father's shelf ~ books about the origins of the world, its buildings, its bridges, and its beliefs. There, at the end, in its own special spot, was her beloved atlas.

There was a world out there, calling to little flower bud, beckoning her to peel open her petals and spread her blossoms, to expand her joy of sharing beyond her home and hearth. But as with most of us, change and growth are not always easy.

Agnes was barely 17 when she fell deathly ill with malaria. Nana Loke prayed and prayed, and God's response was that she must scrape together every leke she could and take her youngest away to a better climate. It was the only thing she could do if she wished to save her littlest child. In truth, she was on the verge of losing her youngest daughter, but not to malaria.

When the body is weak, the spirit becomes strong.

The long train trip was arduous, and Agnes's fever was high. However, it was in this most critical time of her life that Agnes heard the words spoken aloud that she had always heard in her heart.

"Follow me. I am the Way. I am the Light." It was Agnes's first call from God. From that moment on she merely needed to listen to know where her feet should step. And she was listening, because like Joan of Arc, she was being called from the highest order.

A resounding "yes" vibrated throughout her entire being and her recovery was swift. A year later, she set out for the Loreto Abbey near Dublin, to enter the Irish Order and to study English.

She was beginning her travels in the world for which her father, in his wisdom and maybe in his vision, had prepared her so well. Her beloved mother and sister traveled with her as far as Zagreb.

My eyes were trying to focus on her words, but the book became blurry. I heard her speak and felt a deep sadness in my heart as I watched their farewell play out like a movie before me.

We spent a few days together, celebrating our joy and our love for each other. When we hugged and kissed good-bye it was big, as if we would never see each other again.

Fate was at play here because in fact, they would never see one another again. Could this be the "suffering" for love that Mother Teresa so often referred to?

When we parted, my mother said to me, "Put your hand in His and walk all alone with Jesus."

Suddenly, before me, a hand was offering a white flower. I looked up. The loud slurping sounds that had come from my cabin mates' gastronomic enjoyment had ceased. The four who had said very little since dinner arrived had inhaled every morsel on their trays.

The youngest of the group, the handsome one with the black curl that kept falling over his right eye, placed the flower from his tray upon my book, and I accepted it gratefully. It warmed my heart. Little did he know I would choose a roomful of flowers over an armload of diamonds.

We smiled back and forth until realizing we could not enter into any valued verbal exchange, and then I dove back into my reading.

"Flower bud" was opening. Upon taking her vows she chose the name, Teresa, after St. Thérèse of Lisieux, known as "the little flower," who had dedicated her life to "an unconditional surrender to love." St. Thérèse experienced a lifetime in such abject pain and was so frail she could not travel. Young Sister Teresa's health, too, would never be strong, but she would not let that hold her back from her calling.

As a novice, it was known by one and all, even the bishop, that Sister Teresa could become quite exhausted and faint simply from the task of lighting the many candles for Mass. In later years it would be noted by many close to her that she "walked on the delicate side."

She was perceived as a rather ordinary Sister, definitely not one capable of embarking upon an exceptional and exhausting path. Yet as the sun of God shone upon his little flower, one by one her petals expanded to embrace a destiny few on this planet would ever walk.

At St. Mary's in Calcutta she taught a subject close to her heart ~ geography. Of course! She showed her students the landscape upon which human beings explored life, and then she went deeper, revealing to them the secrets inside the heart and soul of mankind. Her passion for the world created a gifted teacher, much adored by her students.

The devotion of those around me was made clear one particular day. I had been appointed headmistress of St. Mary's. The students and teachers were gathered in the dining room awaiting my arrival, but I was unwell that morning and could not rise.

The malaria had returned as so often it did, without warning and without respect for her work.

Gradually they realized I must be malade and immediately, miraculously, as one, they knew what must be done. Gathering outside my room and along the corridor, wherever they could, branching out even into other rooms, they assembled. They knew in their unity, in their spiritual oneness they would bring me healing. And then, in unison, they began. Sweet, clear voices, straight from the heart, raised in the healing prayer of song.

I considered for a moment the images Mother Teresa was revealing to me. I sensed a tiny clue, a hint of something important she wished me to know. But for the life of me, I couldn't quite wrap my mind around it. As if sensing my quandary she said it again, in slightly different words.

I was being serenaded by those I loved. It was the salve that elevated my soul, lifting me to a place where my body's limitations were no longer a concern.

When the Sisters sang, even the debilitating disease that continued to threaten her life was held at bay. Singing was her tonic. And yet she was telling me something way larger than I yet had the knowledge to grasp.

Even the inestimable joy of her loved ones' healing music was not quite enough to prevent a new illness.

Mother Teresa had been at St. Mary's for 20 years when she was diagnosed with tuberculosis. She would no longer be able to teach. Through this illness, Mother Teresa's life was about to encounter another revolution.

The clatter of the track we rode on shifted an octave and became hollow. I glanced out the window. No longer winding through mountains, we were on a long wooden bridge crossing a river. The water reflected like glass the fading amber light, and the flames being lit inside shanties dotted the river's edge like stars coming out.

Stretching my legs felt like a much-needed thing to do, so I put my book down, left my cabin, and took a stroll through the moving car. As I snuck sideways glances I spotted large families crowded into other so-called private, first-class staterooms. I entertained briefly what it would have been like if I'd had my fantasy train ride, sipping tea, alone in my stateroom. Lady Muck, having all her needs tended to, yet frightfully alone.

Turning on my toes, that observation made me want to be back with my dear cabin mates.

While I was gone the attendant had retrieved our trays and leftovers. There, sitting on my book, were three pretty white orchids, from the others' trays. Flower power.

I squealed with delight at my floral gifts, mimed a little dance of ecstasy for them, twirled around, bowed deeply in gratitude for their sweet thoughts, and placed them with the other two in my water cup.

My cabin mates talked among themselves, looked over to me, and broke out in hilarious laughter. The young one had a loud, cute giggle that curled itself into my ears. The older one sitting next to me ~ his laughter seemed to emanate from his toes and express itself through his big shaky belly, reminiscent of a wobbly, generous hug. As for the other two, their joy wasn't as distinct; still, the energy of their enjoyment was contagious. So much so that try as I might to stifle it, I began to laugh, though I had no idea what I was laughing about. The air between and around us was light and lyrical, and I felt unusually safe and content in my company of strangers.

I settled back into my seat, trying to recall where I had left the young nun ~ ah, yes. The onset of a new illness heralding a necessary shift in the course of Sister Teresa's life. Clearly she had reached a turning point. She could no longer teach. Perhaps it was time for her to retire into the catacombs of prayer.

Change comes upon us all, and often. Sometimes it arrives uninvited, out of our control and not necessarily with the appearance of good; but good, bad, or otherwise, change itself is inevitable, and one thing we may indeed rely upon.

"Embrace change. It is a miracle unfolding," I heard a voice say. Though I was no longer sure whose voice it was.

September 10, 1946. A date that would celebrate a historical moment for the Missionaries of Charity. A date when confusion became clarity. It was time for Sister Teresa's annual retreat to Darjeeling, and she dearly needed the respite in order to recover from the tuberculosis and the silence for contemplation.

No one would have been surprised if the little flower had dried up and fallen from the stem. She had given her all. She'd had a good run. She could retire with pride and ease, into the sanctity of her church. With her head held high she could have whiled away her days, reading, contemplating, living her life out as a faithful and contented bride of Jesus.

Yet she was about to hear something of even greater joy to her than her Sisters' voices raised in song; a new calling was but a whisper away.

God, as always, had another plan.

The train ride to Darjeeling was long. Eighteen hours. The locomotive wove through the foothills of the Himalayas, and for the second time on the train ride, Sister Teresa heard a call from God. As she described it, this was "the call within the call."

She was sure it was God's voice she heard, certain, in fact. And the message was clear and definite. There could be no mistaking what God was asking of her. But it was a most surprising and challenging task for one in such frail health. She was told that she must leave the safe harbor of her convent and go out into the streets of Calcutta, to live as the poor, among the poorest of the poor, and give her unconditional love to them. This was a mission more rigorous and more dangerous than anything she had ever tackled.

I took a deep breath. Incredulous for a moment. What person in perfect health would even consider doing this?

Sister Teresa was called to begin her own work, to show the world what real love is and to shine the example of compassion into every corner of the globe. If she must leave the Church to accomplish this then she would comply. Whatever was asked of her, she would do.

love

When she returned to the convent, she had two pages of a written plan. Without hesitation she requested permission to leave the order and begin her own Missionaries of Charity, from the streets of Calcutta. She was determined to leave the security of the world as she knew it ~ to be His light and to be His love to the world at large.

Opposition to Sister Teresa's desire to leave the convent came quickly. She would have no money, no roof over her head, no companions ~ and the idea of a lone European nun living in Calcutta's slums at a time of political and communal strife filled the archbishop with angst and dismay.

The bishop believed I was too fragile to live among the poor, to dedicate my life to the hungry, the homeless, the sick and dying. He denied my request.

Sister Teresa appealed the archbishop's decision, not once, but three times! A year passed, almost two. Then, as magnificent as the universe is, something happened that plunged India into a state of panic and civil turmoil.

Struck down by an assassin's bullet, Mahatma Gandhi, the man who proved to the world that a government can be challenged and overthrown by and through nonviolence ~ India's voice of compassion ~ was suddenly silenced.

Into Calcutta streamed hundreds of thousands of desperate refugees. They had no food and no shelter and little idea of what would come tomorrow. The poor of Calcutta were in dire need of help ~ and hope.

Hope was on its way. The obedient and stubborn Sister Teresa waded through yet another year of applications and prayers and appeals and advice through the divine grapevine of the Catholic Church. She did not let up until she was, at last, given permission to go to Rome and appeal to the Vatican directly.

Upon her return, there were rumors. But that's all. Officially it was never announced. The whispering rumble was that Sister Teresa had received blessing from Pope Pius XII and was to leave the convent. Her students planned to bid farewell to her, making sure she knew she could return to their loving arms should it not work out. Suddenly, the whispers said it would be tomorrow. Her students awoke early and dressed quickly that day, eager to catch a final glimpse of their beloved Sister, but it was too late.

In the larger picture, a spiritual exchange had occurred. The great leader of India had passed his spiritual torch to Mother Teresa. She was about to embody the essence of Gandhi's teachings: *"Love is the subtlest force in the world."*

This transference was living proof of the universal balance that always comes to us, in our families and in our world. God never extinguishes one light without enkindling another. Whether it is the birth of a new life, a fire igniting the soul, a mission begun by a loved one, or an idea made real by a stranger, it is comforting to know that ultimately, there is no loss, there is no death, there is only rebirth, renewal, regeneration.

Mother Teresa was 38 years young and alone. Whereas Gandhi had made his impact on the Indian nation from the top down, she was making hers from the bottom up. Her earthly possessions comprised five rupees, three saris, and an endless reservoir of conviction. With her mission guiding her steps she walked the streets, day and night. She didn't rest; she didn't falter. Even though this kindly European woman was a strange sight, she ignored ridicule as she picked up the sick and dying, washed the maggots from their wounds, and gave the abandoned the love and care they so needed.

There was this man on the street who had much disease, he smelled so bad, no one wanted to be near him. I bathed and held him. 'Why do you do this?' he asked me. 'Because I love you,' I told him.

This vision of the street did not pass by unnoticed. A family of modest means offered her the basement of their home for her shelter and her work. In short course Mother Teresa's call within a call was echoing in many of her students' ears and in the hearts of others who simply knew this was their calling, too.

The family moved out and gave Mother the rest of their house for her missionary. And from this one home she began her works of love: homes for the sick and dying, centers for lepers, hospices for AIDS patients, clinics for mental patients, orphanages for children, soup kitchens for the hungry, dispensaries for the sick, centers from which to reach out to the poor and lonely in the cities and neighborhoods ~ from Calcutta to the world.

While I had been reading intently, there had been much movement in my cabin. Then it was quiet. Suddenly a friendly hand touched my shoulder, prodding me to look up.

What an unforgettable sight! All four men had changed into their pajamas and were standing almost at attention, politely waiting for my acknowledgment.

Chivalry was alive and well in stateroom 108A of the Rajdhani Express, bound for Calcutta and beyond. My cabin mates pulled down the shades and the top two bunks and agreed who would sleep where. They took their positions, and turned to me and bowed. The younger one motioned to me that the lower bunk I had been sitting on was all mine.

I smiled gratefully and nodded good night, and one by one they crawled under their covers.

They say a journey of a thousand miles begins by putting one foot in front of the other. For Mother Teresa, picking up more than forty-two thousand began with one. One by one, her tiny frail body picked up the sick, the hungry, the naked, the homeless and the dying.

One by one by one, more and more of her pupils from the convent showed up on her doorstep. The seeds of love and compassion she had planted inside them began flourishing. In no time, fields of "little flowers" began popping up across the surface of the globe.

Mother Teresa taught the devotion she had learned as a little girl. "I tell my Sisters, we must more and more fall in love with Christ. Let it not be said that one single woman in the world loves her husband more than we love Christ."

She instilled the tenderness and discipline Nana Loke had taught so well by example. And when she prayed for something, it was always intended for God and the good of the people, and in divine right order, those prayers were answered.

It took courage and conviction and a character of steel to hold on to a belief so strong and an idea so daring to be a light that shone so brightly that others would follow. It was the work of the volunteers, the unsung heroes of the planet, they embraced. Many left the comfort of the convent and the predictably secure life it offered. Others left their homes, their families, their childhood dreams of marriage and children, colorful clothes and family celebrations and indeed even the common comforts of a warm bath, soft bed, and three meals a day.

My dear cabin mates were all in bed now. One, two, three, their bunk lights went out. My young friend was last to get himself comfortable. He gazed at me as he lay gripping uneasily to the outside of the opposite lower bunk, head to toe with his neighbor. He looked over to me. "Calcutta?" he whispered.

"Yes." I nodded.

I kept my clothes on and pulled the blanket over me and turned my light out.

Not yet ready for sleep, I lay in the dark considering all I had seen and heard.

Mother Teresa was not eloquent. She expressed herself and her philosophies often in parables and a kind of lyric street poetry. If she had put a beat to it, she could have been the original queen of hip-hop. When she spoke with her Sisters her words were direct and firm, with no cushioning of the news.

From her Sisters she demanded complete commitment and unfailing loyalty to her ideas and her choices ~ abstinence, denial, restraint, sacrifice, and all the discomforts that leveled the playing field between those who have and those who have no other choice. With love, all apparent oppressive offerings were simply appearances that were in fact and in deed, for the passionate, the committed, the humble, a joy to give.

Thank goodness my cabin mates were not snoring loudly enough to drown out our attendant's fervent tap on the door. It was 4:30 A.M.

Quietly, I slid off my bunk, pulled a fresh though rumpled dress from my overnight bag, and slipped out of the cabin to prepare for my arrival into Calcutta.

At five, it was still pitch-black outside. The train was slowing; the four still snoring. I scooped up my five little orchids, lay them preciously atop my luggage, and tried to be as silent as I could extricating my bags and the box of film from the compartment. Oops! I was not quiet enough. My young friend stirred. "Sorry," I whispered. He sat up, eyes still closed.

The train languished and jerked to a stop. I peered out to see if we had reached the platform. In the darkness one bare lightbulb illuminated a sign in the distance. Waiting Room. A question flashed across my mind: *Have I arrived in the waiting room, and if so, what will I be waiting for?* It was a prophetic sign that I would only appreciate in the weeks to follow.

The train jerked again and inched its way along the platform. I surmised there was no one in the waiting room since the platform itself was paved with sleeping bodies.

I set about dragging and pushing my bags toward the stairwell. When we came to a final stop, how grateful I was when my Indian prince emerged from our compartment to lend a hand. In his bare feet and rumpled, blue-striped PJs he deposited my load onto the platform and waved down a porter.

It had been a wonderful train ride. Quite a joke on me, actually ~ yes, yes, I should have learned this one already ~ very little turns out as we plan. Isn't that the truth?

God's larger plan tends to overwrite our small details.

Mother Teresa's life had one simple direction, and she had stayed the course, whereas most of us from my side of the planet cannot live our lives that simply, completely committed to one focused goal. Invariably for us, all hell breaks loose when the need for more, more, more steps in.

As I stepped over and between sleeping bodies it became obvious I was in a foreign clime. I had entered a land where life is a continuous journey of the soul, experiencing and evolving each time, until we attain the state of nirvana and choose to return no more.

Was I on a path to discover every assumption I had ever made about the universe was wrong? Could it be that the ancient fragrances wafting through the air and warming my nostrils were indeed authenticating and confirming that we do indeed come into this life with a purpose and plan already written upon the timeless record of our soul's journey?

The whistle blew, steam puffed. I turned for a final glimpse of the Rajdhani as it jerked and strained to continue its crossing. My young pal, hair ruffled yet black curl still falling on his forehead and eyes still tight with sleep stood on the doorway steps, looking ever so sweet in his beddie-byes, waving bye-bye.

Waving back my priceless orchids until he and the sooty locomotive were out of sight, I felt a new kind of aloneness. The kind Gilly referred to when she said good-bye, concerned about me traveling without my entourage. They were back in America, and Nayeem was in Bombay. Comforted on the journey by my cabin friends, I was completely on my own now, standing on a foreign platform, surrounded by strangers in the dark.

"I did so enjoy spending the night with you," I called into the pitch black, sorry I hadn't even asked his name.

CHAPTER SEVEN

BE LIKE A PENCIL

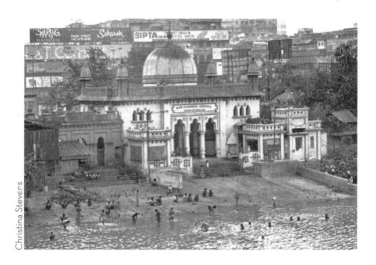

Christina Stevens

*"The moment you fully realize it is God's hand
holding the pencil that will write your life story,
you will begin your masterpiece."*

Saturday, April 3, 1993
Calcutta, India

From where I stood there were only four air-conditioned taxis in the entire city ~ luckily, one of them was waiting for me. As we drove through this infamous crumbling third world metropolis, my driver apologized for the people living in what looked like cardboard shacks. I didn't require apologies. With eyes freshly wide-open, I saw beauty where he saw shame. He gave my wonder a studied, curious look in the rearview mirror. "Where exactly have you come from?" he asked.

I couldn't answer him. I had only ever heard Calcutta referred to with the words "black hole" preceding it. And what I was seeing looked nothing like that.

We were weaving through rich, colorful, exotic thoroughfares, the sight of which I had never seen before. Not even in my history books. Squalor and poverty, I was prepared for that. Beggars' sad eyes and children's grubby hands, reaching out to touch and to take. I was even prepared for the sight and smell of the crippled and the maimed and, yes, the lepers. I was primed and ready to be sickened, to shun ~ withdraw in disgust from the streets of Calcutta ~ but that was not what happened. Something in me had shifted, and I no longer viewed my surroundings from my old perspective, rife with judgments of "good" and "bad."

What I saw was beautiful in a way that was difficult to explain. Love loomed out at me from every face I came upon, and the feeling surprised me. Smooth, deep chocolate skin glowing radiantly inside vibrantly colored silk and cotton saris. Grubby nails, dirt-encrusted toes, all beautiful to my eyes. Families living life on the street, life as they knew it and not as I might suppose it should be.

Enthralled as I was by the visual essence pulsing all around me, I wasn't quite as ready for the ceaseless, smoky, grinding roar of the city. Sounds and smells assaulted my senses from every direction. The constant honking of ear-piercing "hornmanship" as competing drivers announced their proud passage through the streets, the acrid fumes in the nostrils, the exhausting heat that bored its way beneath the skin, deeper than pores go. The taste of diesel combined with the grit of the dusty air stuck in my throat. This was Calcutta ~ terrible and wonderful all at once ~ and my heart pounded with anticipation.

Abruptly the driver turned, leaving the hectic urban rubble and inched onto a mosaic-tiled driveway that curved around and up, and up farther, out of the torrid squalor and into the palatial serenity of Calcutta's newest five-star hotel.

As the taxi drew to a stop, an opulently dressed doorman stepped majestically forward, bowing his navy-blue-and-gold-turban-wrapped head as if to a queen and, in the same fluid movement, opened the car door.

His brilliant white smile guided me through the golden revolving doors and into sudden cool relief. The instant I was inside the air-conditioned luxury of the Taj Bengal, I discovered Nayeem had prepared my way beautifully. I felt as if I had plunged into a deep pool where everything rippled with excitement and reacted to my arrival.

Before I could even think about where registration might be amid the waterfalls and the sweeping stairways and lush foliage, an exquisite Indian goddess stepped into my path.

"Welcome, Miss Christina Stevens. Welcome to our humble hotel. We have been eagerly anticipating your arrival." With one elegant gesture Monica, a former Miss India and an absolutely striking beauty, ushered me past reception, through the vast foyer, and into a waiting elevator.

"You may check in when you are comfortable. If you will forgive the liberty, we have upgraded you to a VIP suite. It is on our top floor and very quiet, understanding you are here on important business."

As she opened the door to my suite, I caught my breath. Struck by the dichotomy of India with its remembrances of formal and polite British pomp imprinted with the contrasting barefoot earthiness in plain sight, I exhaled, unaware that contradictions were to confront me at every turn of this awakening journey.

"Does it please you?" Monica asked, opening door upon door, gliding elegantly through room upon room as she went. The living room centerpiece was a meditation bay window, looking out over the park, the racecourse, and St. Peter's dome. The bedroom suite came complete with what must have been a fake fireplace, the mantel scattered with antiques of exceptional value, and the bathroom offered an endless waterfall. The knowledge that just one room of my suite was larger than the cardboard shacks I had passed on my way rankled the guilt in me. Nevertheless, after I had given Monica my passport, set up my office, and put everything away in one of my three closets, I sank into my lush bed and gratefully embraced it.

Heaven has different meanings for all of us.

> *"You are not a channel. You are an instrument.*
> *Channels give nothing of themselves,*
> *they merely let water run through them.*
> *In your action, you are an instrument in God's hand.*
> *And he writes beautifully."*

At 5:30 A.M. I left the Taj and headed for the home of Calcutta's most famous resident. The sun had not risen, yet it was already 85 degrees and the tiny fan in the front of the taxi spun, simply circulating warm air.

Accelerating and braking our way along the buzzing urban thoroughfares, down squalid alleys and across the center of town toward the Motherhouse, I gazed out the window of the cab at the people still sleeping in the gutter, or were they perhaps dead? I hoped not, but I couldn't tell.

We passed, sometimes within a few feet, mothers cooking breakfast for their children, other mothers breast-feeding infants, and men lined up for their morning shave. It was as if we were driving through people's bedrooms and bathrooms and kitchens. Nothing was hidden; nothing was private. I craned my neck to get an even closer view of children huddled in a pile of garbage.

Air, blind with grit and dust, and the taste of diesel, thick, I rolled up the window and thought of Mother Teresa, the sometimes naughty teenager who had laughed and danced and might have done any of the things most of us dream about doing, but she denied it all and chose instead to eat simple food and never take a bath in warm water again.

She was someone very much accustomed to saying no, and I had come all this way to extract a yes from her.

Her selection of the center of Calcutta as the location of the Motherhouse, the heart from which she would activate her mission and network her charity to the rest of the universe, was a visual metaphor unto itself, an allegoric source from which to indoctrinate and empower all who entered. Standing back, I gazed up at 54A Bose Road, a simple three-story cement building.

The sign on the passageway leading inside was flipped so that it read Out. It hung low over the three steps that led to the aged wooden door, so that five-feet-two Mother Teresa herself could reach up and flip it depending on whether she was going in or out.

I surmised that she was either out of town or had left very early, to begin her work for the day. I fervently hoped the latter was true.

The heavy wooden door swung open. Three Sisters mingled by the doorway, welcoming volunteers and guests for the 6 A.M. Mass. One look emerged from their faces, which indiscriminately reached out and filled the air between us. I wouldn't hazard to describe that one look ~ I could only tell you how it made me feel. Welcomed. Important. Special. Beautiful. Happy. Joyous. Graceful. Trusted. Courageous. Privileged. Full. Overflowing. Unconditionally loved.

I followed the small group up the stairs and into the chapel. I was a bit dismayed to see signs all over the Motherhouse that said clearly in bold, don't-even-question-this block letters: NO CAMERAS, NO PHOTOGRAPHING.

I was beginning to think it would take a miracle to accomplish what I had come here for, but I had forgotten there was a reported living saint involved and where there are saints, miracles are not far behind.

Letting the throng carry me up the cement stairway, I found myself in the chapel, a simple prayer room on the second level. Exquisite early light washed over the polished cement floor, rimming a glow around everyone praying. It took my breath away. I know lighting. And I know how long it can take a top Hollywood gaffer to re-create even a simple slash of natural light. It was God's glow that touched this room from sunrise to sunset, as if the fingers of God's very hands were here, caressing every person who knelt to pray.

Even in a foreign environment, I find it hard to squelch my need to take charge of my surroundings and be as helpful as needed. The fact that I am not Catholic became painfully and immediately obvious when I handed out evening prayer rosaries for morning Mass. I had no idea what I was doing. Fortunately, a young Hindu man kindly explained my error and retrieved the rosaries for me.

I then thought it best to be as unobtrusive as possible. Finding a small niche near the doorway right at the back of the chapel, I surmised it was the perfect place to stay out of everybody's way, to observe everything that unfolded, and since I was an interloper to follow (or not) along with the rituals.

I discovered singing was ever present here in the Motherhouse. I enjoy singing, and my theatrical training has given me a natural voice that projects, but as I had already made a spectacle of myself, and hesitant to hit that horrific note that spoils the rest, I simply let the chant of the Sisters' voices sweep me away.

Suddenly all around me melted. The singing became more present, and I found myself engulfed by tactile images of long ago.

"All things bright and beautiful, all creatures great and small, all things wise and wonderful, the Lord God made them all." I sang that a lot at Sunday school.

I sang that in my room, to my Bear and his friend, the dark-haired Beauty. She had beads on her dress and beads on her crown, framing her perfect face, the face that was my mother's, the face that was duplicated on the Baby Peggy dolls and in the portrait by Norman Lindsay that hung in the Art Gallery of New South Wales in Sydney. The face that was yet to be ravaged by her supposed savior, the bottle.

Beauty and the Bear hugged each other on my little stool under the windowsill where the sun didn't shine. They sat, watching me frantically dress. My good white socks, my polished black shoes. As I tied the black straps on, I lost my balance and fell. Just then, a deep and frightening voice bellowed.

"Who's that?"

"It's just me," I answered shakily.

From behind my closed door Mummy translated, "It's just Christina, Bill."

"What on earth is she doing up at this hour?"

"She's going to church," Mummy explained.

"At this hour!" he exclaimed.

I shook. They were talking as if last night never happened. I could see them both lying in bed, listening to me, and I knew they would not get out of bed to see me on my way. I hoped not, because my father frightened me. He frightened me even with his voice. Last night he'd yelled at her, and I woke when I heard a bottle smash in their bedroom. She had hiding places for her savior in every cupboard in the house.

"See this!" he shrieked. "See this! I'm going to shut you up for good, you bitch! You drunken sloth!"

Mummy was screaming, "Keep away from me," and then I heard a violent movement and her voice changed perilously. "Put that bottle opener down. Stay away." She screamed again. "Bill! Stop! Don't!" And then her voice choked into silence.

I sat up in bed, shaking. What to do? Suddenly I heard a door open. My brother, Geoffrey, brave Geoffrey, burst out of his bedroom and ran down the hallway.

"Get your hands off her! Don't you touch her!" Geoff yelled. I heard something crash to the floor.

"Who are you to speak to me?" Dad's voice boomed at him. "This is none of your business."

"This is my business. She's my mother," Geoff asserted with not a waver in his voice.

"Mother?" Dad laughed with a cruel crack in his voice. "Look at her. She's not fit to be a mother!"

I pulled the covers up to my neck and began to whimper like a frightened puppy.

All I knew was I was put here on earth to take care of my mother. To feed her coffee when she drank too much, to help Geoffrey carry her into bed, to undress her and to clean up after her, to hide all signs of her drunkenness before Daddy got home. In exchange, she would look into my eyes with boundless adoration and the world could stop right then and there. And I would know that I had been a good daughter. If that's what a mother was, then she was a wonderful mother.

Suddenly, I heard a loud tussle, slapping and falling and kicking and punching. I clenched my jaw and my courage rose. I threw the covers down, jumped out of bed, and was at my door in a flash.

As I reached for the doorknob, I heard Mummy become hysterical, ordering Geoffrey back to his room. She was no longer frightened for herself. She was frightened for her boy.

The doorknob was larger than my hand, and I had to grab it with both hands, but as I turned it, every fiber in my body froze. That was last night.

I always dreaded nightfall at our house. In the light of morning, last night's assault clung like the odor of cigar smoke to velvet curtains.

Clutching my *Book of Prayers,* I edged the doorknob around until it clicked and with my body I leaned back and the solid wooden portal opened. It was quiet now, and I was no longer in fear. Mortal fear, that is. Where I am going I will be told fear is to be expected. Fear is good, and I should live in fear ~ of God's wrath.

In the hallway last night's air hung like a veil of spent violence. I tiptoed past my parents' bedroom. The family mostly laughed at my eccentric need to go to church. Mother was my only defender. Maybe she knew I was going for her. Maybe she knew what it was that brought me to my eight-year-old knees. I had struck a bargain with God. If he could make her stop drinking, the violence would end and everyone would love one another again. In exchange I would be forever fearful and go to church every Sunday. Of course, in my family we never acknowledged the horror we lived in. Her bruises, her broken limbs ~ she laughed it aside as her own clumsiness ~ and yes, indeed it was sometimes. He said she was drunk ~ and yes indeed, she was sometimes. But we four knew.

Geoffrey cracked his door and peered at me with a sad cast to his eyes and shook his head. He had been blessed by living his formative years when they were still in love. When Father was not around, he was all she needed. She started drinking when she became pregnant with me. I knew nothing else. My elephant memory even recalled times when I was in her womb, hearing the anger and rage I was being born into. Perhaps that's why Geoffrey was so protective, why he built me a chariot to take me away from all this.

"Like mother, like daughter." Father spat that primal phrase at me, with revulsion curling his lips yet with an articulated profundity as if it were law chiseled in stone. Yes indeed, I was cast in the same mold, prone to the same fate, and, of course, hated with the same passion. Dad ruled us with an iron fist and a stinging leather strap that belied his love.

Protesting later in life that he pummeled that phrase into me to guide me away from my mother's slothful example, the imprint had been stamped. All I knew at five, six, seven, and eight was that the "father" upstairs might not judge me as harshly as the one I called Daddy.

Without fail, and with the beckoning lure of all things bright and beautiful, I made the three-mile journey to church by myself every Sunday. I had no friends outside of school and other than my brother and my cousins, Jesus was the only person I spoke with. He never ordered me to be "seen and not heard" or to "speak only when you're spoken to." He never told me he had "no time for me." My hand always went up first when asked for a volunteer, especially when it came to reading Jesus's stories aloud to the congregation. It seemed Jesus's father was about as scary as my father, but more than that, I thought Jesus was just like me.

All Jesus ever wanted was for everyone to love one another.

"Be like a pencil in God's hand.
Let him do the thinking.
Let him do the writing.
Simply allow yourself to be used."

When our growth can no longer be measured by a pencil mark on a doorframe our endless inner growth becomes rife with speculation and mystery. The only measure we have is the shift in our life experience. Walking through an open door into a world of new experiences required that I listen within and observe without. Be empty of the past, to fill up on the present.

Morning Mass was over around 6:45 A.M. I followed the crowd downstairs and shared tea with them. I felt shy and withdrawn like a child on my first day of school. Glancing around, I noticed one Sister who balanced that special glow with the power of organization. Her name was Sister Josma. I asked her where Mother Teresa was.

"She's gone."

"Where?" I asked.

"Out of the country," she answered in a clipped Indian lilt.

"Where did she go?" I pried a little more assertively, almost afraid to hear the answer.

"I'm not sure."

"Well, when do you expect her back?"

Sister Josma shrugged, appearing somewhat bothered by my curiosity. Clearly volunteers were there to work, not to fawn at Mother Teresa's feet. But she relented finally, perhaps because I couldn't quite disguise how badly I needed to know.

"Oh, maybe in a few days. Maybe not, it's hard to tell."

I had heard Mother Teresa travels like the wind and moves across the world as easily as you would walk across a room. I would soon discover this was Mother's way. Solid as the earth itself yet ephemeral as the morning dew. Like lightning, she was instantly where she needed to be, often referring to herself as a "pencil in God's hand." Indeed, she could change a bureaucrat's rules with the invisible ink of her prayer, and her pearls of ordinary wisdom could move mountains.

With my leading lady MIA, I would have immediately reached for plan B ~ if I had one. Mark and I would have put our heads together, reviewed our options, maybe rewritten the script, reorganized the schedule, and consulted anyone on the crew this glitch would impact.

But here, I had to rely on my own counsel.

Surrounded by volunteers of various ages from all over the globe, buzzing enthusiastically in languages foreign to one another, it resonated again to me that Mother Teresa's power on earth was immense, and yet it was the simplest of all powers and something every single person in the whole wide world could tap into ~ love.

That thought put me into complete calm, unwilling to entertain for a second the notion that I was not in the right place at the right time. I didn't need a summit meeting to decide my next step. I would do exactly what Mother Teresa had suggested.

In the ensuing exchanges of where everybody would head out to volunteer for the morning, I could make out French, German, Italian, Japanese, and Russian ~ very few volunteers were speaking English. Then, as I sat sipping tea on one of the wooden benches in the dining room, I heard the raucous "strine" twang of a fellow Aussie.

Having grown up in the theater, my accent is light, more a British mix that has been peppered with Americanese. However there are certain vowels and the way I end sentences that to a good ear gives away my Aussie roots.

"I thought I recognized a fellow Aussie. I'm Adriana." With her long wavy hair draping down a lithe body, her long neck, and her lost eyes, she looked as if she had stepped from a Modigliani canvas. Even her movements were languid, except for her clumsy, thick, brown leather sandals. I gathered she was in her early 30s, but her eyes spoke of an aged sadness. She talked a lot. She had been in Calcutta for two weeks and knew her way around. Deciding she would be my guide, for certainly I needed one, she suggested I first volunteer at Shishu Bhavan, the children's orphanage. She explained that Mother's homes were not a place for the faint of heart and to begin with the babies was a good bet.

It was just a short walk from the Motherhouse.

CHAPTER EIGHT

LOVE THE CHILD

Christina Stevens

*"There are no chance meetings or happy accidents.
When a certain soul has been placed in your way ~
it has been orchestrated by a higher power.
Let your conscience guide what you then must do."*

Sometimes a small journey on foot can reveal the largesse of a new friend. After a few moments of quiet, Adriana confessed to me why she had made her pilgrimage to Calcutta.

"My son died suddenly ~ my husband couldn't deal with it, but I have to."

"What did he die of?" I asked her.

"Shoo! Shoo!" Adriana cooed as she brushed away a flock of children with cupped hands and grimy bare feet who had suddenly blocked our path.

She gathered herself for a moment and then said, "Actually ~ he committed suicide."

I didn't know how to respond to such a painful admission from someone I hardly knew. Taking my own life was something I had contemplated. More than once.

I shrugged off the rock on my chest, and a few steps later I linked my arm inside Adriana's and she squeezed it. I could feel her shaking. Holding her to steady both of us we continued to stroll slowly, in silence, and it was a powerful few yards we covered. I could never know the depth of Adriana's pain, but briefly, I contemplated walking in her shoes.

As happens to me from time to time, when I touch something belonging to someone, like their keys, for instance, I instantaneously know things about them. I see visions of their future or snapshots of their past. When I touch a person, it can happen, too ~ but more intensely.

Pictures washed across my mind-screen, like snatches of slowly moving imagery. Sandy hair, youthful fuzz of a mustache, and the lightest stubble of beard. Handsome he was, yet his pale eyes reflected such torment they removed any self-assuredness, any charisma his face could have held. And then he smiled, and he glowed. He hid his pain well. Again his countenance changed and the anguish returned. And again, he transformed, his face happy, almost euphoric. It felt to me that he had experienced many highs and lows, as if drug induced. And then, just like that, he was gone from my inner sight.

As I held Adriana's arm, I felt her heart. I sensed she had already fallen into the dark abyss its breaking had opened up, bumped around all the "what ifs" and "if onlys" and arrived at the determination that she would make it through this. The pressure on my heart felt like I was in an inverted loop, pulling five Gs.

I let my hand drop and stopped in my tracks. I knew of the absurd myth surrounding suicide ~ that one's soul is damned to hell for eternity ~ and I hoped she was not carrying around any of those thoughts.

"We are walking here upon the landscape of Eastern spirituality," I said, "and from this perspective, if your son passed over before his time, it was a detour. Whether it was an accident or by his own hand, they say the worst that can happen is that he must return to go through his lesson again. And have the strength, the inner fortitude, to go through it and not around it next time."

"Mother Teresa said I should pray for him," Adriana said quietly.

"Yes. And I will, too. When you go back home it might be good for you to join a group or get a group together yourself where you could pray for his peace. Prayer is truly powerful when more than one is gathered."

I didn't know where the words were coming from ~ maybe my Sunday school classes? As she leaned upon me, all I knew was she needed to reach out to others for support when she returned home.

Adriana touched my hand. Lightly I wrapped my fingers around hers and together we took a deep and refreshing breath of life-sustaining connective air.

A moment later, I felt a tug on my coat. Standing beside me was a little boy with his hand outstretched and pleading, "Give me money, lady. I need milk. We have nothing. I just want some milk." He clutched his tummy and moaned a little melodramatically. There is a sad and piercing beam in a starving child's eyes that reaches deep into your gut and if you have seen that, you would never forget it. He wasn't hungry like that. But he sure was skinny.

"Watch out for the kids," Adriana cautioned, pulling me along. "They have all sorts of rackets operating around here. You give him some money and you'll have fifty following us in a matter of seconds."

Adriana was certainly an Aussie. They love life, they love to share their life to the fullest, but don't mistake their generous spirit ~ they don't put up with any baloney.

"No money. No money. Milk," the boy cried, casting his eyes down in a mournful fashion. I admit it. I'm an easy touch.

"Okay," I answered. "I'm not going to give you the money, but I will buy you the milk." The grubby-faced kid nodded happily and waved me over to a sidewalk store where I gave the owner a handful of rupees in exchange for a small carton of milk. I turned to the little tyke to ask him if one carton was enough; surely he needed more. But once the boy had grabbed his milk, he disappeared. A few steps later Adriana stopped, put her hands on my shoulders, and spun me around. "Look," she said.

There was the poor, hungry boy giving the store-owner back the unopened carton of milk. "I told you." Adriana laughed. "It's a scam. Calcutta Mafia. The kids work for the store owners." As we walked on, more equally talented baby beggars danced around us, asking for rupees to boost their survival on the streets.

"I can't distinguish the needy from the actors," I murmured. "But they can all do with a little more," I added as I blithely doled out coins into wretched little hands and watched them all run off happily.

Adriana retrieved my attention and opened up further.

"My son was drinking and doing drugs. After he died, I wrote to Mother Teresa, and she said I should come here and volunteer."

"Taking care of others is a sure way to begin healing," I offered.

"That's what Mother Teresa said." Adriana's eyes sparkled for the first time. I looked over to her and out of the corner of my eye I thought for a moment I saw her son beside her, reaching out to her.

Suddenly Adriana's knees seemed to buckle beneath her as if her whole body was turning to jelly. I hooked my arm through hers and took her weight upon me. "It cost everything I had to come here, but I knew it was the right thing to do," she said, almost choking on her words.

I could feel strong emotions zigzagging through her. She had confronted the terrible grief of losing her child but was not yet on the road to embracing a future without him. She was still on the roller coaster.

"Do you blame yourself for your son's death?" I sucked air, recognizing I was becoming far too personal, but she didn't seem to mind that I asked.

"I did. I did," she mumbled sincerely. "Sometimes maybe I still do, but I've seen so much here and . . ." Her voice faded and the tears tumbled. I pulled her even closer and tried to reassure her.

"You've seen, too, that ultimately, we cannot take responsibility for another's actions. We come into this life alone, with the sovereign gift of free will. The choice you made to come here and share your love with others will change your life. You know that, don't you?"

She put her hand over mine. "Thank you. Some days are good, some days aren't, but right now I feel better."

I was beyond less than qualified to have had this discussion with Adriana, yet I felt honored she shared herself so deeply with me.

Ah, the gift of friendship.

"For a child, loving is as natural as breathing."

Shishu Bhavan

The hand-lettered sign over the entrance to the orphanage read: Something Beautiful for God. It was nothing less than the truth. Once inside, more and more signs greeted us, respectfully framed and hanging over doorways, on walls, and on pillars. They were all Mother Teresa's quotes ~ simple phrases that spoke volumes. Words that swept me out of my own mundane jumble and made me focus on where I was and what I was here to do. Mother Teresa's love was in the air. She was in every bow of a head, every gentle caress, comforting word, and kind embrace.

Adriana and I entered the nursery to find more than 50 little ones awakening from their morning naps in their green-painted cots. Immediately we became immersed in their world, completely wrapped up in their crying and teething moments, wanting to sit on their potties. I was completely out of my element, yet following Adriana's lead, I tended to their needs, calming and cajoling them with singing and simple games and doing whatever was necessary to lovingly keep the peace.

Not entirely comfortable with babies, having had none of my own, out of the corner of my eye I became a follower. At midmorning, we spent perhaps an hour or more feeding the littlest ones sweet potatoes and dahl, then took them to play in the sunroom.

There were many healthy, happy babies who the Sisters told me were to be adopted within the month, but I also saw other babies who had three limbs, two limbs, one limb, and even no limbs. These brought a lump to my throat, for these, I was sure, were way too much of a burden to ever find a home. But that was my societal roots thinking. To my amazement a Sister told me that within six months, all the babies here would be gone, adopted into good homes, mostly, she emphasized, to European families.

"Mother says that as much as we love the child we cannot give what a father and mother can give ~ it is impossible."

I sat on the floor enjoying the newness and discovery of the children, with a fresh appreciation of what a child meant to a family. I had observed the news of a child as a mindless mistake of the moment, blackmail for a continuing union, and a Band-Aid upon a failing marriage. I had seen a little person treated like a toy, a plaything, a hindrance, a gift, or a duty, with the automatic expectations of high achievements to "carry on the good family name." I had seen and been a child beaten like a naughty animal, fearful and forgotten. I had seen children so loved and respected, deep sacrifices to career and lifestyles were made to assure their well-being. Yet within the complexities that brought a being into the world, no matter how inebriated or damaged the parent, I never saw a child who couldn't be loved.

"Jesus said, 'Unless you become like little children,
you cannot enter the kingdom of God.'"

With all the gaiety and laughter, you would have thought it was Christmas morning and everyone was opening their presents. One of the Sisters excitedly picked up a baby wrapped in swaddling and placed it beside me. She giggled and looked into my face, encouraging me to pick it up.

The bundle wriggled, and I couldn't resist him. Immediately I scooped him up. I unwrapped the blanket and when I looked down at the little one my heart burst open. He had no arms or legs, no limbs to hold and no eyes to see. The Sister knelt beside me and caressed his head.

"He is very special, very much loved." She cooed ever so sweetly. "It may take a little longer, but the right parents will come. They always do."

I did not want to put him down, because I could feel his happiness at simply being held. I rocked him back and forth. His joy filled me to overflowing.

It would not be the first time I had asked God that difficult question: why? But the difference was this time I did not look for an answer, because the answer was pumping from my heart and resting in my arms.

This child would do very little in his life that you and I could see, yet the gift he came to share was great indeed. He was on earth simply to be loved. I held him closer and sang softly for I knew he could hear. His little body moved gently, wriggling with my song, and an exquisite peace flowed between us.

Just a kiss. One kiss.

Just a snuggle. One hug.

That's all he needed.

"The law of love could be best understood and learned through little children." That's what Gandhi said. And here was Mother Teresa revealing his words to be true. In that moment I was the one gifted with pure love, greater than any I had ever touched before in this life.

I looked over to Adriana. Her smile was ecstatic as she held a little boy in her arms. I sensed her thoughts drifting back to the child she had once borne. Then her playfulness emerged, and all at once she gathered as many babies as she could into her welcoming arms. They crawled over her as if she were a living jungle gym. She was in ecstasy. She was unbridled and carefree, like a child herself.

Her happiness of the present and her anguish of the past seemed to be whirling together on a tightrope far above the rest of us. I could sense the tenuous string of stability to which she was holding fast. If she fell, I hoped I would be around to help catch her.

The older children came in from their potty break and when we were all played out, we tucked them into their cots and they slipped off into napland. Adriana and I hugged good-bye, and she took off across Bose Road, back to her hotel.

I watched her dodge the frenzied stampede of cars and rickshaws. She tripped as she crossed the tramline, and for a second I thought I saw the faint outline of a sandy-haired young man reach out and catch her before she could go down. She steadied herself and finished her mad dash to the safety of the sidewalk.

Spinning around, she jumped up and elegantly swept the air with her arm to make certain I caught her wave good-bye. I watched until she was out of sight.

♡♡♡

"Strangers and friends, loved ones and enemies
~ we all look the same ~
through the eyes of love."

Are we a blind world? Ever since I landed, I sensed an other-worldly force growing within me. Seeing Adriana's son shook me up a bit. I had sensed a presence before, but never had I actually "seen" someone from the other side. Crediting it to the heat or the mystical pulse of India, I wasn't ready to return to the idyllic oasis of the Taj.

The sharing with Adriana and my time with the children, especially my little love child, made me want to absorb as much raw humanity as I could. To embrace the unexpected gifts a strange land can offer, I strolled through the streets for what seemed like hours.

To my eyes there appeared to be little difference between the people of Calcutta and the people of New York, Baghdad, Sydney, Paris, London, Iceland, Denmark, Cairo. Ensconced in their safe world they brushed by you on the street and barely gave you a glance. The only difference was in Calcutta they lived their lives under the scrutiny of neighbors and passersby, like me.

Later, when I walked into the cool relief of the Taj, Monica rushed to greet me. Even though our chats had been brief, we had already formed a special bond.

"The owner of the Taj is in town," she said breathlessly. "And he wants you to be his guest of honor. We are having a big opening of our nightclub discotheque. Some of the wealthiest people in India will be here."

I was exhausted. I thought about it for a second and dismissed the idea. "I need to be up early."

"The discotheque doesn't open until eleven o'clock, but my boss is planning a small gathering in his suite to introduce you to some of Calcutta's high society."

More shocking than the fact that I had just landed yesterday and Monica was proposing my first day last 19 hours was her disclosure of Calcutta's high society.

"You mean Calcutta has a social register?" I asked. I had not even considered there was any other way of life in this city other than street life, slums, and poverty.

"Absolutely," Monica replied. "And they all want to meet you."

Monica, batting her languid dark lashes, would not take no for an answer. She grinned mischievously and added, "I will be your date."

"Wonderful." I sighed, not entirely convinced my inner clock would still be ticking but certainly willing to chance it.

Sure enough, by 9:30 that night I was lying fully dressed across my couch, drifting off when Monica arrived at my door. Her energy lifted me, and we linked arms like two happy sisters, stepping out into the evening.

"What are you doing on a date with me, Monica?" I asked her. "Don't you have a boyfriend waiting for you?"

"I don't seem to find anyone that I can really talk to," she said candidly. There was a definite air of loneliness about her that I couldn't ignore. Odd that someone so lovely and warm would be so alone. And yet her life appeared so full and happy.

Navigating the corridor, Monica graciously stopped to speak to staff and check on a wayward guest. When the penthouse elevator doors opened and she stepped in, I felt I was observing a reflection of myself. That all bonds, all relationships, good, bad, or otherwise, are a reflection of us looking at that relative part of ourselves. That if there was something in another that I didn't like, it was that shadow in me I recognized. Logically, if it wasn't within me, I could not recognize it.

As we rose skyward in the elevator, walled with a patchwork of beveled mirrors, Monica squeezed my hand excitedly and an epiphany hit me.

The arc of life could be looked at like a prism of mirrors, attracting and reflecting facets that become our personal story, mirroring what is within us. With our power of free will, we are granted the ability to adjust and refocus our mirror. If we feel love, we become the lover, if we are fearful, we inflict fear, and if we feel terror, we become the terrorist.

In all we do, we draw into our outer life the reflection of our inner life. Such a simple admonition and yet it takes constant day-to-day watchfulness. Peace, abundance, love, happiness, and all the success we desire is our gift if we remain mindful and vigilant to keeping the inner mirror clean and gleaming at all times.

Monica's clear eyes twinkled.

My bond with her was a sweet and gentle one because it was one of a shared, silent, unspoken searching.

Searching for love.

"To be attached to riches will cause you to live in fear of losing them. When you put your wealth in service of others, you will be rich beyond belief."

Moments later, the elevator doors opened to the penthouse suite and standing, ready to receive us, was Monica's employer, Jacques.

I could not guess his heritage, except that he was pale skinned, brown haired, young, bright, and charming, and from comments he made, I guessed educated in Switzerland. He took my hand and bowed graciously as Monica moved to mingle.

Jacques and I immediately toppled into discussion on the critical issues facing India. Passionately he shared with me his philosophy of spreading wealth intelligently in a third world nation. I sensed the hotel chain ran itself and he was forging a new mission, purchasing thousands of acres of land in poverty-stricken areas with plans to educate the children and provide the indigenous families with sustainable livelihoods and cultural honoring. The old adage of *"Give a man a fish and you have fed him for a night. Teach him how to fish and he will dine for a lifetime"* formed the basis for his plan.

"We will gift them the land, and it is the land that will empower them," he said, fiercely raising his fist in the air. I thought for a moment he had seen *Gone with the Wind* too many times, until he continued. "They will build their own utilities and schools and homes. I have formed a nonprofit to help, guiding them with ideas and marketing support so that they can bring in the income they need. For example, they will make wood products from the trees, like buttons from tree bark, and learn how to intelligently regenerate the forest instead of being part of massive deforestation that will wipe out their future and put our ecological balance in jeopardy. We will market the products for them and they will keep all the profits. You see, I believe if it's good for the land, then it's good for the people," Jacques opined proudly.

Feeling as if I was taking Jacques from his guests, in perfect timing, we were joined by his friend Michael. I gathered they were old school chums by the shorthand they both fell into. Michael was a doctor whose heritage was a little easier to figure. Unlike Jacques whose complexion was ruddy and build slight, Michael was tall, tanned, and muscular, not what one would expect from a doctor. His eyes were a little scary. They were so intense, I thought for a moment that if I kept looking at them the entire room would melt away. He had a Latin chisel to his face and when he spoke, he slid effortlessly from English to French in midsentence. He worked with Doctors without Borders, and he was here to advise Jacques on setting up triage units in remote, habitually needy areas, where every disease known to man was running rampant.

Flanked by two passionate and compassionate men, I felt I belonged here. I wanted to clear the room immediately, sit down, and offer to do my part for their marvelous plan. But the time and place was inappropriate. And I had my own mission to accomplish.

Gracious host Jacques made a point of introducing me to every one of his guests. What a discovery! The poorest of the poor and the richest of the rich, right there on the toxic banks of the Ganges.

The sheer beauty of Calcutta's wealthy set stunned me. I cocked a listening ear and shook hands with the very sophisticated and the very seductive as they chatted curiously of Hollywood fame, but my heart simply wasn't in it. Polite cocktail conversation and small talk have never been a favorite of mine.

By the time Monica and I made it to the nightclub, I was smiled out and the very last thing I wanted to feel was the earth move under my feet. I sat for a short time with Monica and in between music sets, she told me of the marriage her family had arranged. When she won the Miss India title, traveling opened up her life and gave her the vision to realize her own power and the courage to withdraw from a union she would not have cherished.

When the music drowned out our conversation, we watched exquisite sari-clad women glisten around the dance floor. And men dashingly put together ~ some in Ralph Lauren tuxes and others in traditional Indian garb. There seemed to be as much gold in the room as in all of the Taj Mahal itself. Their jewelry gleamed and flashed under the spotlights, looking larger and more precious than anything I had encountered, even in Hollywood. But there was one thing that caught my attention more than all the gold that glittered. They danced without touching one another. Many sitting without looking at one another, sipping their drinks almost without speaking to one another. It brought into focus what Mother Teresa meant when she spoke of the wealthy countries having the greatest poverty of all.

I sparked upon my years in New York City ~ the city of cities. Saw myself walking down Madison Avenue and smiling, trying to catch a passerby's eye, trying to coax a smile back and for the most part being shunned, avoided, or ignored. No. It was not the hungry or the homeless or the naked or the dying who were the poorest. The poverty she saw so true was the poverty of the heart. It was the protected, the isolated, the insulated, the frightened, the separated, the intimidated who were the poorest of the poor. They were all over the world.

And they included me.

"Love is the greatest teacher in the world."

Next morning

Mass was over promptly at 6:45 A.M. and the Sisters didn't waste a moment getting to their business of the day. I let the crowd carry me downstairs, where some volunteers sipped tea and nibbled dry biscuits while others connected with friends to discuss where they would assign themselves.

Not seeing Adriana I found a quiet spot for myself in the corner. I have always been extremely comfortable on the isle of my aloneness. I looked and listened. From where I was on the ground floor with its paved courtyard surrounded by corridors and rooms I could distinguish every activity. Saris were being washed, lunch was being prepared, living quarters were being swept, letters were being typed, hymns were being rehearsed, and yet the pervading quality in the air was the knowledge being absorbed.

You could almost hear the Sisters scratching notes as more than 100 novices in the Motherhouse were intent on their classic education as well as their religious studies. Everywhere you stepped, Mother Teresa's words, simply framed, hung on every wall and corridor.

The Motherhouse felt like school it even smelled like school, which made a lot of sense, since Mother Teresa was a headmistress and many of her Sisters had once been her very own pupils.

The role of a teacher is a sacred one, don't you agree? More so for a child in need. I was a rabble-rouser, so needy that throughout my school years most teachers could not contain me. Instead of listening to a lecture I would spend my time thinking up a question the lecturer couldn't answer. Stump the teacher and then crack a joke and make everyone laugh. Of course I fooled no one. Little smarty-pants spent the greater part of her education banished to a seat outside the classroom. However there was one teacher who reached into me to demonstrate an impeccable truth.

With the sounds of the Motherhouse revolving around me, I daydreamed myself back in time to Rose Bay School, to inside the large provincial schoolroom overlooking the play field. I could almost smell the chalk and wood polish. I could almost feel the hard, wooden seat of the desk with its ornate wrought-iron bases attached in lines leading to the blackboard. And there was tall, pasty-faced, skinny Miss Strickland, standing on her podium, smelling of mothballs and lavender water.

We wore traditional navy blue uniforms, navy blazers, starched white shirts, and blue-and-gold-striped ties. In winter we had to wear gloves and wide-brimmed felt hats, straw versions in the summer. We had 1,000 rules, and should you break one you got the cane. I found no joy in school. I love to learn; I hate to be taught.

We were doing a math test, never a favorite of mine, and Miss Strickland was reading quietly. When I reached the algebra section, I gave up. For a visual person such as me, A and B could never equal C. I put down my pencil and leaned back.

Without warning, the girl behind me pulled at my braid. It's a game we play, passing it on. So I reached ahead and yanked the braid of the girl sitting in front of me, and she squealed!

Thing is, squealing is not how you play.

"Who was that?" Miss Strickland leaped to her feet immediately.

The girl in front raised her hand and broke into a whine. "Tina pulled my hair."

In a flash Strickland was at my desk, snatching me out of my seat by my shirt collar.

"I didn't pull it that hard," I protested, certain she was feigning pain.

"Yes, you did. Look at her face," Strickland demanded.

The blonde angel looked up and crinkled her face and blubbered. "She hurt me."

I could have. I had a high pain threshold, and I didn't know my own strength.

Still holding my collar, Strickland pushed me to the front of the room. "This is the third time you've disrupted my class. I've warned you. The rest of you continue . . . You are coming with me."

Strickland had a choke hold on me as she dragged me down the long hallway, past the headmistress's secretary and through the open door, and shoved me toward the crotchety old wizard. Wizard, I am afraid to say, had passed me on numerous occasions as she did her rounds and while I sat in disgrace, outside the classroom.

"I let her back into my class and what does she do?"

"Obviously her parents don't teach her any discipline!" said Wizard as she rose to her full height, picking up her cane and striding toward me. "I think a little punishment might have an effect. What do you think, Miss Strickland?"

I sent her my thoughts . . . *I'm used to the cane . . . I can take it. Okay, hit me; it only burns for a little while. Hit me three times, that's enough!* But she stopped. She leaned back to her desk and peered down her nose at me.

"Hmm. You're a pretty fast runner," she stated smugly.

"Mmm," I answered weakly. *Oh God, no, not that!*

"Yes. You did well at the school games. Some kind of record, wasn't it?"

"Mmm. The hundred yards."

"Yes." She put down the cane, pulled out a cigarette, and lit it. "You're representing this school in the state games tomorrow?"

I wanted to answer, "Oh, am I? I must have forgotten, it's not important to me, you know." But all that came out was a shaky, "Yes."

The lines on her face grew, passing a smile on their way to a scowl. "No, you're not!"

I didn't want to believe my ears. I reached for any argument that might save me. "But I've been training. Mrs. Anderson and me, every morning at seven o'clock! My mother makes me steak for breakfast."

"Your mother! Does your mother do your hair?" My mother had been so impressed by my athletic record, sobriety had suddenly entered our household.

Wizard grinned at Strickland. "Look at that part ~ it's as crooked as a dog's hind leg."

"She is the last runner on our relay team," Strickland cautioned. For a second I thought she may change Wizard's mind.

I probably should have reached for tears; instead my anger popped out, and I got cocky. "I have to run. I'm the fastest."

Wizard puffed on her cigarette, staring me down. The silence was killing me. Just as my knees were starting to give way, she spoke.

"You're very slow in my book. And you will do what you're told. You will learn this lesson." She turned to Strickland. "Find Mrs. Anderson and have her choose a replacement. And take this one back to the classroom."

Eighty curious eyes watched me reenter the classroom. Through a waterfall of tears I watched as Mrs. Anderson, standing ramrod straight on the play field, holding her trusty stopwatch, searched for my replacement. *She must hate me now.*

As well as being our PE mistress, Mrs. Anderson had been my class teacher last year. At first, she, too, had me sit outside the room for disrupting the class. That wasn't bad because her classroom was a small cabin, separated from the main school and nestled among the trees. And it had a veranda. I could look at the trees and listen to the birds and feel the wind on my face. I loved nature and out there nature loved me back. Mrs. Anderson had many names for me. She called me high-spirited, a dreamer, a birdbrain.

"What's a birdbrain, Mrs. Anderson?" I bravely asked her, fearing it described someone with a tiny brain.

"Oh, you're always off with the birds," she answered with a kindly smile. Mrs. Anderson was different from other teachers. Where they either punished me or washed their hands of me, she worked with me. She took me, the worst troublemaker, and when she had to leave the room, she would sit me in her observation chair, in charge of the lesser troublemakers. She gave me responsibility. She gave me her trust and showed me she cared. And it worked.

"Christina, there's something I want to show you," she said as she pulled out a sheet with everyone in the class's name on it and a graph of their grades over the year. "Last term, you were right down here, forty-ninth in the class. This term, you're third, way up here. You've made an incredible leap. Do you know that? Do you realize what you're capable of?"

When my fourth grade with her came to an end, my IQ score moved me into Miss Strickland's class. Somehow we both knew my performance would sink again. She seemed to know there were problems at home. She saw me as a loner ~ brave enough to perform high jinks in front of everyone, yet afraid to share myself with my schoolmates. In an effort to keep me under her wing, and being our physical education teacher, she offered to improve my running. We met every day except Tuesdays at 7 A.M.

As I tore around the school grounds, she showed me running was more than just a mad dash to the finish line. She taught me about breathing, how to hold my arms at right angles to help lift me. To find my rhythm with the ground, until I felt as if the ground wasn't there, or I wasn't here.

"Hold your head high," she hollered.

Her great gift to me was that she showed me someone in the world cared about me. Somebody had time for me. She showed me that discipline, doused with responsibility, is a true expression of love, greater than that of indulgence and far more effective than punishment.

There she was, clocking for my replacement. The girls lined up, and she shot her starting gun and the girls ran, higgledy-piggledy at her. She didn't look excited, not the way she had the last time I ran.

I was wearing my brand-new spiked track shoes, and there were competitors from all the public schools in the eastern suburbs. As I broke through the ribbon, she broke judge's decorum, running to me from the finish line, her marking pen and pad flying from her hand, her face alive. She took me by the shoulders and spun me around.

"Look! Look at the others. They're still running!" she was screaming. She leaped for joy and lifted me up with her. "Your breathing was perfect."

I knew it. I felt it. I didn't even know I was running a race. I didn't know where anyone else was, and I wasn't even thinking about them. I wasn't thinking about anything. I had no thought at all! I was one with the wind.

Wizard was sitting with the other schools' headmistresses in the front section of the stands, but she didn't even crack a smile on my victory lap. My mother was there that day, and I heard her calling out my name above everyone else. She couldn't stop talking about her little runner, and my pieces of breakfast steak got bigger and she stayed sober.

My face was a mess of wetness, and I sobbed loudly. Mrs. Anderson had narrowed it down to three. My crying got louder. I had never broken down like this before. I had always been a tough soldier in front of other people; even when I got the cane, I never cried.

Some girls turned and empathized with their long looks. Some shifted in discomfort. The class clown isn't meant to cry. Here was the carefree cutup, bawling her eyes out. I didn't care. I wanted to win that race tomorrow. I wanted Mrs. Anderson to be proud of me. I wanted my mother and my father to be proud of me. And I had ruined it all.

After that, Mother returned to her drinking as if it had never stopped. Mrs. Anderson was disappointed. She asked me what had happened, and I protested innocence, but in truth, I was a troublemaker, pushing, always pushing the envelope to find the line where love would be withheld.

In the pale of sadness that shadowed Mrs. Anderson's face, it occurred to me I never found her line. She was disappointed for me, not because of me. She saw something had happened to my spirit. It was as if I had thrown a blanket over it, to keep it warm and safe. My free spirit that could break records couldn't break out of its shroud. I closed myself off even further. I didn't want to make the class laugh anymore. I no longer felt my connection to the world outside of me. But I didn't understand that then.

I wonder, was there ever an event in your life, where your inner self turned a corner?

A soft breeze brushed my moist eyelids, sweeping me forward into April in Calcutta. I couldn't recall when I finally let my spirit live and breathe again. I touched it when I danced but I think it wasn't really until I learned to fly. Then it was me ~ and the wind, once more.

As I sat in the Motherhouse amid a sea of noisy strangers all selecting where they would volunteer for the day, the sudden realization of how brilliantly we select the colorful co-stars in our personal life dramas hit me deep in my solar plexus. Thank you, Strickland; thank you, Wizard; thank you, Mummy; thank you, whiny blondie; thank you, thank you, thank you. Thank you, everyone who has ever given me a hard time, pushed me, hurt me, rejected me, not loved me, driven me crazy, turned away from me, pretty much thank you, my wonderful cast, for caring so much that you taught me the lessons I needed to learn to move onward. You were great. That play is over and the show was a raging success. You gave Academy Award–winning performances, every one. And I turn the other cheek.

And, Mrs. Anderson, wherever you are, you divine goddess ~ thank you.

CHAPTER NINE

HEAL THE INVISIBLE

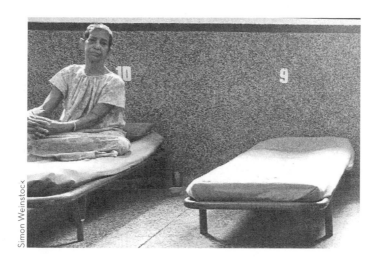

Simon Weinstock

*"When you touch the dying
you will learn lessons
you can never find in a book.
Lessons you will never forget."*

Every city has its invisible ones. Those who by the sheer ugliness of their predicament we don't see or we ignore. I had heard the vicinity of Kalighat was mostly inhabited by invisible ones. Living ghosts who, step by step, walk beside us, reminding us that *"there but for the grace of God . . ."* Their reality is as present in our lives as the expression upon our faces. If we have the courage to allow them influence, to consider their plight, to be of service to them, they may serve us well, for they can be our guides. Sometimes they may even save our lives.

Imagining I had unconditionally supportive Mrs. Anderson right beside me, I decided against the surety of the cuddly babies at the orphanage and instead sprang from my seat when word went out that the 7:30 van was leaving for Nirmal Hriday in the Kalighat area of Calcutta.

Kalighat was Mother's first home, founded to comfort and aid the destitute and dying and very close to her heart.

Sitting in the van, side by side with mostly teenage volunteers, I was impressed with their youthful inner courage, signing on for an education of the eye-opening kind. I thought I was ready for the profound lessons I would encounter. But when are we ever ready to confront death so intimately?

When we stepped out of the van in Kalighat, I could feel a looming darkness come upon us. The image beside the open entryway, welcoming us, was a raised wooden carving of the Hindu goddess Kali, with her many arms and legs, carrying various weapons and symbols, and wearing a garland of severed heads.

A young girl beside me reached over and ran her fingers across the carving, saying in French, "Kali is the greatest of all deities. Goddess of time and death." Almost immediately a disagreement ensued as her friends wanted to debate whether Kali was good or evil.

Stepping inside I saw the men's section to the left and the women's to the right. A hand-painted sign on the wall in front of me read: Let my hands heal thy broken body.

> *"When you speak with your hands*
> *and you speak with your eyes*
> *and you speak with your heart*
> *you are speaking the language of love."*

I could not have anticipated the depth of emotions that surface when a life is leaving. I could not have prepared myself for the panic, the anger, the desperation, the exhilaration, the resignation, the appreciation, the surrender, and finally the love that rises up unexpectedly from one who knows their hours of conscious life are ebbing.

Most of the volunteers went directly to the tasks they had been assigned on previous days. I stood at the foot of a large wooden staircase, waiting to be told where to go. I looked up and was caught completely off guard by a Sister standing on the landing at the top of the stairs. She was very tall, looked rather strong, and I recognized her immediately as someone I knew well. I caught her eye and waved, but she didn't respond. I would have called to her but I couldn't remember her name. We had gone to school together in Sydney ~ of that I was certain.

Just then the head Sister came to me with a wide, welcoming smile, shaking my hand as if I were an official visitor. Though her English was broken, she seemed to know exactly what I was to do.

Beckoning me to follow, she ran excitedly up two sets of stairs until we were on the roof. The sun was shining and a gentle breeze blowing. Sisters and volunteers were washing clothes, while others were hanging them on the clothesline to dry in the sun.

Sister-in-Charge handed me a stack of fresh clean towels and nightgowns and beckoned me back downstairs. I asked her about the one I knew from my schooldays in Australia, but she shook her head. "She is from Germany." And when I protested, she added, "She doesn't speak English."

Following her to the cement baths behind the ward next to the medical center, I spotted another Sister I recognized ~ from where I couldn't quite place, yet in my bones I knew her. This time I kept it to myself.

From there I could see the kitchen where lunch was being prepared, and the morgue, where two bodies were wrapped like mummies in white cotton cloth.

One of the Sisters cooking in the kitchen caught my eye. Goodness, it happened a third time ~ that nagging sense of intimate familiarity. As the Sister ran the water in the bath and described for me what I was to do, I was intent on trying to recall some past relationship with these various women, and I almost failed to appreciate that each and every one of them was speaking to a deep part of my soul, in a language beyond words. In a very real sense, they felt like family. Had we been together before? I would never know, yet I felt already we were sisters ~ sisters in the silence.

love

The instant recognition continued to deepen and weave itself in my consciousness as I made my way into the women's ward where women were all sitting or laying on green plastic mattresses.

I couldn't quite come to terms with my lapse of mistaken identities. I likened it to love at first sight. If you have ever been hit by it, you know it exists. It gets you right between the eyes. It's a chemical recognition so deep it confounds science and brings up an even larger question. Time. I had the oddest sense I was treading a path I had already walked. Or could I be walking upon multiple paths right now?

Time is an enigma to all of us who have encountered déjà vu. Is time simultaneous? Are we timeless beings? Is it our separation inside a body and our need to control that space that created the clock and the calendar in an effort to define and measure a frontier that defies explanation? Is time and our journey in it less linear and more dimensional than we can yet comprehend? Are we actually living in a holographic universe?

As sure as earth remained beneath my feet and air continued to sustain my life, this question was about to explode my universe as I fell deeper and deeper into the unseen mystical realm surrounding Mother Teresa.

I snapped my attention back to where I was ~ here and now. The Sister was explaining slowly, in her best English, that I was to lift the women out of their beds and carry them into the bathing area. There I was to undress them, wash their bodies, dry them off, dress them in a clean nightgown, and return them to their beds. If there was time, I could massage cream into their dry skin, or I could enlist other volunteers to help.

As I looked around, I noticed the others, cleaning bedpans, washing plastic bedcovers, and scrubbing floors. I felt as if I had been given an honored task and I accepted it willingly.

I knew picking up these women by myself would be a herculean feat for me, yet I would handle it. My lower back pain, ever present for lack of three lower vertebrae, would need to be put aside for the more than 20 women, all looking expectantly at me.

"Never look at the masses as your responsibility.
Look at the individual and love one person at a time.
And pretty soon, that love will spread to the masses."

Gently, as I lifted up the first dying woman, my pain no longer existed. Hers was in my face, squealing in agony.

Startled, I almost dropped her. I couldn't imagine what I was doing that was hurting her so. Swiftly I carried her limp shell of a body into the bathing area and tenderly placed her on the raised cement slab.

As I tried to remove her nightgown, she desperately pawed at me, pushing me away, cursing me in Hindi and fighting to stop me. I put my hands on her shoulders and spoke in a language she did not understand, yet in a firm, loving tone I hoped would reach beyond her fear.

"Grace," I said. "May I call you Grace?" She did not need to understand my words for them to have an effect. I gazed deep into her eyes and felt a rush of looking at my "other" grandmother who had died when I was just a teen. Churn, as my father called her, was full of Irish grace and German fortitude. Quiet, gentle, and rarely without her Bible in her lap, she was the antithesis of Madam, my mother's mother.

When I was five, Churn took me on a shopping spree for my birthday. As we crossed a busy city street, I ran ahead and was narrowly missed by a taxi wildly turning to the curb. Immediately, shopping was canceled for the day and we headed for the nearest church. Churn tossed a hanky on my head and coaxed me to my knees to thank God for his divine protection. Every time anything good happened, Churn would proclaim it God's work and call anyone in hearing distance to her lap, to thank God for his grace and compassion. What she did when something bad happened I don't recall. I think she just ignored it. The hanky on the head was a bit embarrassing but I honored her God. Even her three children, who adored her so, lovingly allowed her religious leaning, but when she was not present, they had no such kindness. Churn had the same moon-shaped face, the same deeply set eyes, same inner peace as the woman whom I christened Grace.

love

"I want you to just relax because you will feel so much better after a bath." Gradually Grace calmed enough to allow me to slip off her nightgown. I quickly draped a towel around her shoulders, attempting to give her as much privacy as possible, but she scowled and spat out more Hindi phrases I knew were unkind. She appeared angry, frustrated, and frightened. I took a deep breath, kept smiling, and continued with my task, knowing I had countless more women to wash.

The only water available was icy cold, and it would be a shock to her if I placed her immediately into the bath, so I hummed softly as I rubbed my hands together quickly to provide some heat and dipped the sponge into the water and caressed her, hand, sponge, hand, sponge. As I did this I spoke. Wishing to enhance her health and immunity, I dipped my hand into the water and did my best to be mindful of the words I spoke while working with the water.

I'll tell you why.

Returning to the Bible and Genesis. *"In the beginning God created the heavens and the earth. Now the earth was a formless void, there was darkness over the deep, and God's spirit hovered over the water. God said, 'Let there be light,' and there was light."*

God's spirit was hovering over the water. I had an inkling here that scientific tests have now proven: water holds vibration. Words spoken can change its composition. God's word was vibration, which activated the water to bring us light. Light is energy. Our body's content of water is higher than that of any other substance. It is our depletion of water that ages us. Without water, we die. Without water, our planet dies. We are cleansed and baptized by water. From our most ancient legends, oracles consulted the waters to reveal the future; the sword of King Arthur arose from the lake ~ you get my gist? I had always taken water so much for granted, and yet ~ wow! I now personally consider all water as holy. Indeed, our future may promise even the putrid water of the Ganges to be more precious than platinum.

So I half spoke, half sang to Grace as I mindfully dipped my hands into the liquid gold with the intention of activating it with words of love and healing. This calmed her immeasurably and more than once she took my hand and rubbed my palm across her cheek and by the rush of love that came from her to me, I knew it was having an effect upon her.

Tears pricked at my eyes as she held my hand against her face. I lifted her up and swung her legs out of the bath, patting dry her gray, sallow skin stretched taught over her frail bones. I looked at the pain in her eyes and understood her thoughts as easily as if she had spoken them aloud ~ "I am on my way to heaven" ~ the very words on the sign that hung in the morgue at Nirmal Hriday.

I slipped on her sun-fresh nightgown and took her face in my hands. "There, doesn't that feel good?" She smiled ever so faintly, yet it lit up the room.

Grace melted into my arms when I carried her back into the ward and she pulled at my sleeve, not wanting me to leave her. But I had many more women to bathe.

It was an honor to be given the duty of touching these women so intimately. As I bathed them, I activated the water and while I did so, I remembered many years ago, a friend had told me she believed I had a healing touch, saying she had seen green lights shooting from the palms of my hands. To her I laughed it off, but in fact, I would experiment with it from time to time and was quietly astonished by the results.

"When you give love to a stranger,
you are allowing God
to love through you.
The way you touch someone,
the way you give of yourself to someone ~
as Mother Teresa would say ~ it is
His love in action, through us."

One such time I was on a business trip in Scottsdale, Arizona. It was when I was a creative director of Ogilvy & Mather. It happened at the beginning of each year, one of my clients, Mattel Toys, held a ten-day sell-in toy fair. They took over an entire resort. During the evenings they wined and dined buyers from stores all over world, while during

love

the day they presented their product lines for the following year. This event was crucial for their business, both for their corporate success and an individual's advancement in the company.

Many millions were spent on presentations ~ careers were made or destroyed by the assuredness of a product director's performance. Since I headed up their advertising, I was invited to join them, to see the responses to our creative work, and to occasionally conduct creative brainstorming sessions with upper management for designing the following year's products.

One management associate slumped beside me at the opening dinner, almost paralyzed with severe back pain. I knew how that felt. She was panicking, certain her brand, which happened to be Barbie, the flagship line of the entire company, would suffer and she could lose her job if she didn't perform. Her stress and her pain were entwined. So I offered to massage her back in an effort to help the pain go away.

Later in my suite, we chatted and I realized we were dealing with "back" pain. I had read Louise Hay's book *Heal Your Body* on the various mental and emotional causes that aligned with different parts of the body. Certainly no expert, I understood the metaphysical aspect of a physical ailment and put it to work.

Back problems represent the past, that which is behind us. In present time, it is that which supports us. Encouraging her to stand tall and feel secure about her future, to know she was supported by her team ~ to not look back, nor entertain the remembrance of a past failure. Intuitively I hovered my hand over the painful areas around her spine. I could easily feel the heat emanating from the inflamed area and instinctively sent cooling energy from my heart through my palms. I had her affirm that "life supports me" and I breathed air and space around the cartilage and visualized the color green melting away the hot red I saw and felt in her muscles. I inhaled her pain and transported it from her back into my hands. In very few minutes I was in a weary state, slouched over and breathless while she stood energized, straight as a new woman, and awestruck.

"I don't believe it," she said. "My pain is completely gone."

She fairly danced around the room to prove it. After her lively presentation the following day, she circulated the story that their corporate "advertising heavy" was a spiritual healer. For the remainder of the trip, business associates and Mattel's CEO, no less, were hinting of one complaint after another. It embarrassed me greatly. I laughed it off as if it had been an amusing party trick, but it wasn't, because almost simultaneously with my touching, her symptoms had manifested for a brief time in my own body. A soak in a bath of Epsom salts, followed by a long swim in the pool, was the only way I could expel her pain from me.

I always knew I had not dealt properly with what was perhaps a mysterious talent or divine gift of mine. Since I had stumbled backward into this type of healing, I vowed that without the proper training I would not again touch another with the intention of taking their discomfort away.

And then one day one of my Andalusian horses, Lucena, went down with colic ~ a serious and life-threatening blockage in the intestine. After two visits for fluid flushes from the vet, she was in grave discomfort and the prognosis wasn't good. Horses can't throw up, so if the blockage wasn't removed and she didn't have a bowel movement, she had from 12 to 48 hours left to live. The vet transported her to his hospital where he would prepare her for surgery. The hitch was, she was not a young filly anymore, and surviving surgery was uncertain.

At the time I didn't know I could talk to animals, or to be more accurate, hear them; indeed, it would have embarrassed me greatly to admit this ~ suffice it to say, Lucy and I had an extraordinary connection. She had come to me in a dream to announce the birth of her filly, Harmony. And when there were life-changing decisions to make I would look in her eye and she would tell me what she wanted. In this case, she was adamant, no surgery. The vet, more than a little perturbed by this, advised me rather sternly to put her down. I asked her again, what did she want me to do? Do nothing, was her response. The vet threw up his hands and said, "Then say your prayers." And went home.

I stayed with her, massaging her intestine and visualizing the blockage breaking up and moving out, but I could feel it wasn't working. And then I did something unexpected. I held my hands four or so inches away, feeling for the heat of her intestine. I cupped it in my palm and then became like an orchestra leader, waving my hands along her torso, conducting the flow of energy and sweeping it out. Horses have thick skins and they don't feel, let alone respond to, a gentle pat. However, I wasn't even touching her yet I saw her stretch her neck and undulate her body as my hands passed all the way to her flank. During the night other owners whose horses were in for one ailment or another stopped by to watch, amazed at her physical response to my energy work. But there was no bowel movement. Seven hours later, I was limp. I asked her if it was time for me to go home and she said yes.

Early the next morning the vet woke me. "You must have some pretty serious angels hearing your prayers," he said gruffly through the phone. "I came in and she had left a big deposit in her stall."

Lucy never got colic again.

As the years moved on I discovered that not only can I communicate with my animals, others could, too. It's simply a matter of focus and intention. And then trust. Likewise, I feel we are all able to heal. And here in the Home for the Dying, in a place where it was difficult even to look upon the agony of the patients without flinching, how could I not give everything I had, heart and soul?

As I staggered into the baths carrying each woman at different stages between living and dying, I turned each task over to the power greater than myself.

My recollections were prodding me to protect myself. To visualize a force field of white light surrounding me from head to toe, forming a barrier to deflect anything outside me to enter my energy field. But I didn't. And in years to come, I would pay dearly for this omission.

When I had bathed the last lady, I was soaked from head to toe. I had been compelled to climb into the bath myself, to calm more than one woman. Another became so hysterical we settled for a simple sponge down. By noon there was just enough time left for me to massage lotion into Grace's skin and help with giving her lunch before the van showed up to take the morning volunteers back to the Motherhouse.

Somehow Grace and I had singled each other out for a silent sharing of hearts. She was my first new friend here in this Home for the Dying, and though I didn't want to entertain the thought, I could be her last.

As the van traversed the crowded alleys of Kalighat, the French students launched back into their discussion on whether the goddess Kali was good or evil while I sat in wonder of my first visit to Mother's Home for the Dying, with two dead bodies wrapped in white cotton lying at my feet.

I realized my normal preoccupation with my little self had taken a backseat to the far greater need of those around me. And it felt good. I realized, too, that one day it would be my body laid out somewhere, on its way to disposal. And that, I hadn't yet come to grips with.

On the lighter side, remembering I was here as a filmmaker on a job and with my own funds in the balance, it occurred to me this was a far cry from the requisite preproduction drinks and dinner at the Four Seasons.

"Being of service gives more,
tenfold more,
than it takes."

Tuesday, April 6, 1993

Enthusiastically, I returned the next day to Kalighat. Grace was sitting up, craning her head toward the doorway, which I was certain was an ordeal for her, yet she beamed when she saw me.

Immediately I went to her, caressed her arm, and told her I would give her the last bath of the day so we could spend a little more time together. But I realized I had overestimated my ability to communicate when I saw her watch longingly, like a disappointed child, while I carried off and bathed all the other women ahead of her.

When we had a tea break at 10:30 A.M., I questioned one of the Sisters about Grace. It seemed she had been in and out of Kalighat for some years. They had "always kept a bed" for her, though this time they weren't expecting she would leave. She disclosed to me Grace had tuberculosis and every day she was decidedly weaker. For a moment I froze at her disclosure. TB can be highly contagious, and we had been given no warning of the dangers we as volunteers faced working with dying patients. I knew I had to be vigilant with my thoughts and my cleanliness and cast out any fear of catching this disease from Grace. And I also had to have faith that while performing God's work I was divinely protected.

When it was at last Grace's turn for bathing, she was childlike in her upset with me and sulkily pushed me away. But after I carried her into the bath and sang to her, she relaxed and appreciation simply oozed from her emaciated body.

Suddenly one of the Sisters came running into the bathing room. Loud screams were bouncing off the cement walls, exploding the calm I had created.

Thrusting a wad of bandages into my hands, the Sister pulled me into the ward. Lying prone on a makeshift stretcher, with tears heavy in her eyes and flowing wet over her cheeks, a young girl screamed with her mouth, but no sound came, which made her scream even more searing.

"What happened to her?" I asked. The Sister did her best to tell me in broken English, pointing to the street outside. A car had run over the girl, and it had opened up an old wound on the girl's leg. I could see that inside a wide scar was a fresh cut, so deep it almost exposed bone, and it was bleeding profusely. I knelt down beside her in an effort to calm her but she was deaf, dumb, and blind with pain.

"She needs a doctor. Now," I said quietly to the Sister, who looked directly at me and nodded in the affirmative.

"You. You can do this," she stated confidently.

"But I am not a doctor," I said calmly while everyone gathered and my mind raced ~ *She could be in shock. Someone get a blanket and keep her warm. We need to clean and clear the area. Get antiseptic stat!*

What about an X-ray? Her breathing is labored. This isn't good. Give her some air. Oh my God.

"Yes, yes," the Sister countered knowingly. "You are doctor."

Is she understanding me? I wondered.

"Oh, dear," I muttered, looking down at the streams of blood now gushing from the young girl's leg. Blood was everywhere.

Eyes squeezing water, she opened her mouth, choking again on a scream. And then all hell broke loose. The blood pouring and pooling onto the floor and the fierceness of the girl's cry for help prompted a silent scream inside me, piercing the lock of time.

A thought flashed through my mind: *We've got to clean this up.*

As inconvenient as it might be, suddenly I was no longer present.

"Immersed in another's crisis,
you can easily forget yourself.
And just as suddenly, you may find
a part of you that you had forgotten."

I found myself swept up in a tidal wave of recall.

It was my brother's ninth birthday. I was little more than three and certainly too young to remember what occurred on this day, except for two reasons. One ~ our father had a 78 rpm record and a film made of the event, so the memory could be with us forever. The other reason was every time I looked at my brother's otherwise perfect face, the evidence of what happened that day was horrifically embedded there.

The entire Stevens clan, Geoffrey's friends from school, and their parents had come for his birthday party. Children sat cross-legged on the lawn, watching the *Punch and Judy* show. Punch clobbered Judy with a bat and the kids cracked up. They loved it. I was clinging to my father's legs, begging for attention, but he was caught up with the pretty lady who was turning to honey beside him.

Wandering the lawn were clowns performing and a magician doing tricks. Over the loudspeaker came the voice of the master of ceremonies. It was time for the birthday boy to find his special gift.

The treasure hunt began, and the MC guided Geoffrey with clues and hot and cold hints on where to find his present. There it was, a beautiful leather-bound record player, hidden behind a rosebush. Exactly what he wanted!

When the party was over, Daddy drove an old aunt and that pretty lady home and by the time he returned, Mother had cleaned up. She had cleaned up all right. She had polished off the remains of every bottle and the dregs of every cocktail left behind by guests and had passed out in the living room.

Geoffrey was in his room, playing Wagner's "The Ride of the Valkyries" from *Die Walküre* on his new record player while I was performing my interpretive dance around the house.

Headlights shone, accompanied by the sound of Father's car pulling into the driveway.

"Mummy, Mummy," I called out. She was snoring. I pulled at her but couldn't rouse her. I heard the car door slam.

When she was in this state Geoffrey and I usually hid her drunken bouts from Father. We would undress her and tuck her into bed. Then put everything away and clean up whatever mess she had made, turn off all the lights, and vanish into bed ourselves. But there was no time for that. Geoff and I had both become too occupied.

I danced back to my room. Meanwhile, Geoffrey, it seemed, had become bored with "The Ride of the Valkyries" and for some reason was now running the needle by hand, over the 78 grooves, stopping and starting the turntable so that the impassioned Valkyrie charge sounded more like the monotonous high-pitched whirr of a tired siren. It was truly annoying, and clearly he was destroying both needle and record, but he obviously loved it.

Suddenly the scratchy siren stopped. A door slammed. That's when I heard it. A scream. A terrible scream. Coming from a place that had scant to do with this world.

As fast as my little feet would carry me, I ran down the hallway. The bathroom door was shut, but I could hear everything that was going on inside.

I couldn't turn the doorknob or think of anything else to do but stand outside and pound on the door and scream: "Geoffrey. Geoffrey. Geoffrey! Come here! I need you."

Violently, the bathroom door burst open and there was Geoffrey slumped on the floor, looking out from a pool of blood. Blood all over his face, dripping from his nose, pools of bright red blood on the white tile floor, the walls of the white tub, and the sink.

I looked up at my father, his black leather shaving strap dangling from his hand. I bit my lower lip to stop it from quivering. Father made a threatening lunge as he pushed me aside, leaving Geoffrey in a puddle of red.

All I could think was that we had to clean this mess up.

Geoffrey had been blessed with our mother's elegant, perfectly straight nose, but not anymore. I wanted to cry for him, but all I could do was make a choking sound. I couldn't even breathe until I heard the front door slam shut and Dad's car pull out of the driveway.

Looking at all the blood, I thought, *We've got to clean this up before Daddy gets back.*

"The more you know who you are,
the more available for love you will be."

My knees were jelly and only the intensity of the young Hindu girl's agonizing scream could shake me to attention.

I felt helpless. I wanted to collapse into tears, but her watery brown eyes were pleading for my presence and strength. I kneeled down to her and gently touched the skin around her wound. It was on fire.

Be here now, I told myself, pushing aside the panicked mind. Why do our personal histories distract at dire moments? Is it a coping mechanism? Or is it healing? Did I just encounter that which I set out to do ~ to confront the unhappy ghosts of my soul and remove them forever from my DNA?

Looking into my young patient's beautiful face, I could see her sweet expectant soul as easily as I could see her gaunt body, the bones protruding through a thin veil of dusty brown skin. She was barely 20, but what kind of life lay ahead of her? I wondered.

Suddenly, a torrent of tears fell streaming down her face and lit up her dark eyes as they peered at me from a faraway place. I felt her silent cry, *"Why me? Why are you so healthy and rich? Why am I so sick and poor?"* Goodness, I had no short answer to that question. I could tell the young girl was depending on me, and I wanted her to feel she was in good hands.

A wave of upset swept over me. I had read a lot of criticism of Mother Teresa's homes, and here I was seeing firsthand the odd absence of knowledgeable medical help. I had been told a local doctor came on Tuesday and Thursday afternoons. My concern relaxed a little when I realized that thankfully, today was Tuesday.

Truth was, the alternative for this young girl of the slums was nothing. A girl without a family was a useless commodity. For her there would be no hospital, no shelter, no food, no bandages, no care. If the Missionaries of Charity did not exist, she would have been left on the side of the road to bleed to death, and Grace would be sitting in a gutter somewhere, if alive at all.

It occurred to me, though she is not a doctor, and though the level of medical assistance is not good, how many thousands upon thousands of people all over the world owe their lives to Mother Teresa. She did so much more than take care of their spiritual salvation. She did whatever was necessary. And I would, too.

I stroked the young woman's damp cheek and made the decision to stop judging and give with an open heart, whatever I could. I took a deep breath, acknowledged my limitations, and, as if this were my daily practice, instinctively went to work.

Quickly I brushed my hands down the young woman's legs and across her swollen belly, trying to calm all the scared energy erupting from her body.

I envisioned healing energy coming from the heavens through the top of my head, streaming through my body and into my heart. I then felt more energy coming from the depths of the earth, through the soles of my feet, soaring up my legs and into my heart. I took another breath and visualized the flow of love that I had gathered in my heart, pumping through my veins, flowing out of my fingertips, and in through the pores of her skin. Then, with my palms open, my hands hovered over the fiery flames rising from her wound. Through my palms I sent a wave of cool air, together with my own liquid energy to douse her inflamed cells, hoping to soothe the uncompromising pain she was feeling. She seemed to relax a little, the bleeding slowed and began to coagulate, and her fear subsided.

A while later she looked up at me with that agonizing question in her eyes, and what I heard this time was her wound crying out for medicine and dressing.

I had done all I could.

I turned to the volunteers who had gathered around me, since it seemed we were the only ones here.

"Is there anyone here with medical experience?" I asked calmly. To my immense relief, an Englishwoman knelt down beside me. "I'm a registered nurse; I can dress this."

"Thank God," I muttered, moving up to the young woman's head to continue calming her, while the Englishwoman efficiently took charge.

When the young girl's wound was dressed and she lay quiet, exhausted from her ordeal, the crowd dispersed. I pulled the English nurse aside. "I don't understand," I said quietly. "Why didn't the Sister give you the bandages?"

"They believe you are a doctor." The nurse shrugged matter-of-factly.

"What?" I said.

"Aren't you?" she countered.

Befuddled, I went back to find Grace, who undoubtedly was feeling extremely shortchanged by now. After a few words and a hug, she was at ease. She put her head on my lap and kissed my hands.

Gratitude is the lingering kiss good-bye.

"You and I, we have so much love to give.
But we are sometimes too shy, and we keep it bottled up inside.
When you learn to love, even if it hurts,
you will then know
how to accept love."

love

Wednesday, April 7, 1993

I awoke unusually anxious. I could hear the metronome ticking away time. "You must come soon. You must come soon," Mother Teresa had said. Okay, I was here. My crew was to arrive in a matter of days.

Only God knew where Mother Teresa was ~ and he wasn't sharing.

When I walked into the Home for the Dying the next day, I was sure I would be relegated to bedpans and floor scrubbing since word was out that I wasn't a doctor after all.

The Sister in charge greeted me perhaps even more appreciatively than yesterday and indicated I was still on bathing detail. However, one thing was different that day. Grace's condition had worsened.

She wasn't looking for me when I stepped into the room with the beds all lined up under their respective numbers. It saddened me to see she didn't quite recognize me. She fell in and out of consciousness when I bathed her, and it seemed death had begun to draw its veil over her earthly awareness. She didn't want lunch, and my instincts told me her time here was ebbing.

The best I could do was sit and hold her. I rocked her from side to side, the way I used to rock when I was a child.

I recall as a baby, and was told by a highly amused family, that while everyone slept, I didn't. I would rock and hum and gurgle and giggle with an unseen force. As soon as I could talk my supposed dreamtime then filled with chatty conversation and song. When everyone thought I would grow out of it, I arrived at full-on negotiations with my creator, making deals and trading favors, offering up years of my life and even my limbs ~ why, one time I recall seriously tendering my eyesight so that we could all love one another again. Yet as intent as I was on healing my little world, nothing was taken from me and very soon I discovered my deals hollow and one-sided. God was not listening.

I went to church every Sunday morning, diligently, walking by myself, three miles there and three miles back. "Go easy on the God stuff" was a Stevens family mantra. My reverence for a Holy Father was humorously poked at when the family gathered. Mumbling to some invisible being while eyes wafted to the heavens seeking "the almighty" brought shuddering cringes and raucous laughter from everyone on my father's side of the family. To them my lifeline was a joke. When I was no longer a child to be laughed at, I resorted to some hair-raising, life-on-the-edge antics.

Around that time, my maternal grandmother Madam, who as a woman writer/producer/director and a 20th-century trailblazer, smelled opportunity in the air. Her plan? Put Peggy back on the stage! And since that naughty Christina was old enough and had the requisite training, the theater would keep her out of trouble, too. I became the fifth generation in my family to become lured by the limelight. In truth, I was there to hold my mother together.

Peggy's return to the theatrical world was the beginning of her end. She rewrote her lines and forgot most of her cues. The only way she could descend stairs was to fall down them, and makeup no longer enhanced her beauty. Every performance became a new nail in her coffin since every curtain call had to be celebrated. If the audience didn't come, she would celebrate twice as hard to drown her disappointment.

Convinced she would one day kill herself, I waited for the sober moments to help her voluntarily check herself into private hospitals ~ but she never stayed long. Eventually they refused to admit her. Our clever "Baby Peggy" either talked her way or simply walked her way out. By the time I had exhausted all the homes in Sydney, I was the enemy. I joined Al-Anon and found the sharing and support helpful; however, Peggy was superbly crafty when it came to her survival.

The last straw came while waiting in admissions/reception as my dear darling actress mother privately met with the attending doctor. Somehow she had convinced him that I was the one in need of rehabilitation. With a wan smile he beckoned me into his office. She stood and moved beside him, smiling sympathetically at me and nodding agreement to his assertion that it was I who was in fierce denial of my problem. She was so slick the registrar nurse insisted on calling her doctor to confirm my story!

love

On the way home she suspected I was taking her to yet another rehab facility and attempted to leap from my car while traveling at 40 miles per hour.

I was shaken to my core. It was the final straw for her doctor as well. He called me to his office for a private meeting. "The way this is going, Christina, there is little chance you will ever have your own life," he said as he closed the door behind me. There was a lump in my throat the size of Texas. I had never heard her doctor speak to me so candidly. But he had seen how tenaciously we both clung to the umbilical shadow, very much the way she and her mother related, leaving little room for someone else.

The doctor sat me down on the couch as if I were his patient.

"You have only two options, Christina. You can take her to court and have her committed to a state institution. At that point she is in their hands. Apart from them being rather unsavory places, I seriously doubt you could live with yourself after doing that. Your second option, and this is the one I recommend you take: get yourself as far away from her as you can. You've done enough. Let her go."

And that's how I ended up on the other side of the camera and on the other side of the world.

It took time and a boatload of therapy for me to realize that putting oceans between myself and my roots had nothing to do with my awakening into the real world. I may have thought it was solely my parents who were playing in the field of their own private hell and I was an innocent bystander, but in truth, they were my masterpieces and the dramas were as much for my growth and illumination as theirs. Somewhere in the ether I had done what we all do in our familiar selections. I had signed on for this lesson, and it didn't matter where I was, in time or space, by hook or by crook, I was destined to learn it.

If I thought running to the other side of the world would keep the madness at bay, I was wrong. It's futile to run from what is inside you. There is no escape from the soul-chosen lessons of a lifetime.

The picture hadn't changed. Outside it looked like I had it all. Success. Freedom. Happiness. But at the end of the day my heart was empty and my cells imprisoned in their own solitary confinement. You could say I was the perfect candidate for religious rescue, but I had already tried that.

Here, without intention or forethought, I was tending to dying ladies in Calcutta, and something about it felt unusually satisfying and right.

I quietly hummed a song and Grace and I both drifted off into slumber.

Something startled me. I thought I heard a voice calling.

I looked at my watch. 2 A.M.

For a minute I didn't know where I was, and then I realized I was in my father's guest room in Sydney, Australia, and I had wet the bed. I was mystified because I had never even done that as a child. I sprang up, removed the mattress cover, and changed the sheets.

I had been told, "You must come now. She may not last the night." I was on the next flight from Los Angeles to Sydney, and 18 hours later I was following the blue line along the hospital corridor. My mother could have had a private room, but she requested a bed by the window in a ward of six. At last, the actress had her adoring audience again. And she was playing out her final act with great courage and panoply.

"Seeing you is worth a lifetime!" she announced as I turned into her ward. I could feel the others in their beds snap to attention.

Ah, enter the daughter! The scene was about to begin.

"What time did you land?" she asked, gesturing with her arms as much as her voice. "It was early this morning, wasn't it?" she stated for one and all, before I could even make it across to her bed. "Wasn't it?" she asked again.

"Yes. My flight landed at six A.M., Mummy."

"I knew it!" she stated, giving her captive audience their confirmation. "The angels told me."

"The angels?"

"Yes. They were right there," she said, pointing up. "On the ceiling." I sensed her ward mates leaning into her every utterance and nodding agreement.

"They wanted me to go with them, but I told them no!" she added fiercely, pounding the bed with her fist. "I told them! I must see Christina again!"

Over the next three weeks I found her dealing with death as if she were happily preparing to go away on holiday. I was her messenger, taking gifts of her prized possessions to friends and distant family. I encouraged them to visit her, but hospitals are hardly inviting and people are not always comfortable confronting the dying. Sad it was that I was one of the few who saw her in her final days. She was beautiful, giving out the most magnificent golden vibrations. The angels must have been whispering sweet nothings to her, for she was clearly in a magical place. The kindest gift she had to share was in showing me that death is not to be feared.

In a freshly made bed, still a little askance as to why I had wet the bed and embarrassed at how I would explain it to my father the next morning, I nestled into a warm fetal position. I wrapped my arms around my legs and slipped back to sleep, mystified as to why my body had released some kind of control.

"It's the hospital, darling." Dad woke me at 7 A.M. with a cup of tea. The head nurse was on the phone. She had a very personal attachment to my mother. Some of the patients and nurses remembered Mother from her Baby Peggy days. And the head nurse had been an avid fan, and it was a good thing. "Your mum fell into a coma," she said quietly. "So we've moved her to a private room. I wanted to let you know before you arrived. I didn't want to alarm you."

"That's kind of you. What time did she . . . ?" I asked

"I wasn't here then, but let me look at her chart." She put the phone down and went away for a moment. "Says it was two A.M."

Ah, so that's why.

The sun was setting as I sat beside her bed surrounded by her dearest mementos, silver-framed photographs of her life ~ on and off the stage. Two photographs were front and center ~ Geoffrey at the beach, playing in the water with his three children, and me wearing my flight suit leaning against the wing of my army aircraft.

Scent of gardenia, fresh and sweet, floated across me with the breeze. They were our favorite. Mummy's breathing was peaceful, except for an occasional deep sigh. As I watched the gold cross rise and fall on her chest, I remembered her words the day before.

"Your brother, Geoffrey, baptized me this morning, with water and everything." She sighed. "And he gave me this cross to wear. It seemed very important to him." In the last few months, Geoffrey had found God. For all his intellect and brilliance, there was an unquenchable innocence about him. He seized every new calling with great passion and enthusiasm.

I returned to the book I had been reading aloud to her. The nurses told me that hearing was the last thing to go.

It suddenly dawned on me that I needed to mention something to her. She had refused to speak to her own mother, Madam, the day before.

"I saw *What Ever Happened to Baby Jane?* on television last night, and it made me very angry," she told me.

This was a new turn of events. She and her mother were so close it unnerved me. They finished each other's sentences, spoke with each other on the phone, on the hour, every hour of every day. But something had risen to the surface in her final days that she would no longer brush under the rug.

"Do you know what my mother did to me?" she said, pulling me close. "I was three years old, and we were traveling around the country, performing twice a day every day, three matinees on Saturday. I was just a baby, but I was the star and everyone depended on me. In between matinees I slept." She was alive with the memory of so long ago it was astounding. Also astounding was the fact that she had never spoken to me of this time in her life before.

"You know the red fire bucket backstage?"

I nodded. To this day I still think every theater has a red fire bucket hanging nearby the curtains. "Do you know what she did? She would fill that bucket with ice and water, turn me upside down, and dunk my head in it. That's how she woke me, so that I could go on and perform." I tried to wrap my head around this kind of shock treatment for a little child, twice every day and three times on Saturdays.

In making her peace with the world, she unearthed this tiny piece of information that may have been blocked because of what it must have done to her consciousness. Suddenly my father's suspicions of schizophrenia and multiple personalities, which I myself had witnessed and had marked off to her drinking, had a plausible cause. Silently I scolded myself for not taking that extra step to look further into why she drank.

Perhaps we are all made up of multiple personalities, but some of us can simply temper and balance them more efficiently than others. Poor Baby Peggy had to wait until her final hours to return to the source.

"I'm afraid I upset your grandmother," she said sadly. "I told her once and for all, I never want to speak to her again."

I had my own little jewels of forgiveness that I had to offer up to her and so we talked about all the unconscious things we do, "in the name of love." She agreed the only conclusion now was to forgive, both her mother and herself. I squeezed her comatose hand, coaxing it to squeeze me back, but it didn't.

"Mother, don't worry about Madam; I will tell her you intended to call her. I will share with her everything we said about forgiving," I stated clearly, hoping the nurses were correct and she was indeed still listening.

The head nurse came in and lovingly leaned into my mother's face. "I'm going off now," she said quietly. "I just wanted to have another look at her. Your mother was beautiful, you know," she said without adjusting her gaze. "My sister and I, we would get so excited when we heard Baby Peggy was coming to town. We saw every performance we could. I had a Baby Peggy doll. And I wanted to sing and dance just like her. She was such a little cutup."

"She was funny?" I asked, not ever having seen that side of her.

"Oh yeah! She was a star. A real beauty." The nurse peered adoringly over at my mother again and gently touched her face. "Huh, she hasn't changed."

When she said that, I looked at my mother with new eyes. For a long time I had seen her as a sad, overweight drunk: her alabaster complexion, a mass of broken blood vessels; her soft black curls, wiry and gray. Yet in her final months Geoffrey had introduced Mother to a detox diet of vegetable juices and colonics, and the visual ravages of alcohol had all but fallen away. Her skin seemed porcelain again, her curls thick and shiny, and her eyes were clearer than I had ever known them. Her doctors were equally in awe of the fact that most people in her advanced stage of cancer are on constant morphine drips, and yet she needed no pain medication at all.

"When are you going back to America?" the nurse inquired.

"I didn't tell Mom; I booked a flight for Wednesday, but now ~ I can't leave her like this."

The nurse touched my hand. "She could be in a coma for weeks, months even. My father died just three weeks ago. I didn't leave his side for six days. And then I had to take care of some things. I went out for just a few hours and when I got back, he had gone. You know, your energy can keep her hanging on."

"I didn't know. But I can't leave her," I proclaimed. Selfishly I didn't want to let her go.

"Would you like some dinner brought in?"

"No, thanks. I can't eat."

"Well, why don't you just take a break and get some fresh air? You've been here since early this morning. I'll get you some coffee; take it out onto the balcony. Don't worry, I'll have one of the nurses stay with her."

I was standing on the balcony, drinking coffee and talking with one of the nurses about what she wanted to do with her life when a shiver ran down my spine.

"I must go back," I said abruptly, turning on my toes and leaving her in midsentence. As I entered I noticed an Asian nurse I hadn't met before was extracting a needle from my mother's arm.

"Your daughter is here, Peggy; Christina is here now," she called loudly to the sleeping goddess. The nurse offered my mother's hand to me and left. I took her hand in mine and squeezed.

"I'm here, Mummy. It's all right. Don't be afraid. If you want to leave now, it's all right. We'll be okay. If you see the light, go toward it, Mummy. You can let go now."

As if she heard me, she gave a great slow sigh, and then all breathing ceased.

The awesomeness of the moment a soul passes from this place to the next is holy indeed. Almost as if you can feel the door open and their energy slip through it. But that is not all; if you stay still long enough you can feel their upliftment as their energy expands to join with all energy. I have heard that moment called "the time of the gathering."

"Go toward the light, Mummy; it's time now," I whispered into her still ear.

With absolute perfect timing, I turned and Geoff was there, standing at the foot of the bed.

I kissed her still cheek. "I love you, Mummy."

He murmured, "Is she . . . ?" I ran the three steps to him and clung to him. He held himself erect, stoic, staring at her now-vacant body. The world would not see his pain. But I knew it was there in him, somewhere. Somewhere deep and out of reach.

The nurse returned and for a second I wanted to question her about the injection she had given my mother minutes earlier. But there was a kindness, a caring in her voice that told me to let it pass.

She spoke to our mother as if she were still listening. "Now, Peggy, I'm just going to take off your jewelry here, because your body is going to swell. Now I'm going to roll you over."

I stood with my arms wrapped around my dear brother. *Oh, Geoffrey,* my heart cried, *why do you stand here, with your business-like, blank blink? You were closer to her than I was. You took care of her when I was no longer around. You insisted she take no more blood transfusions, hoping a coma would take her before the tumor in her throat caused her to choke to death. "Awful," you said, "that's an awful way to die." And then you shuddered as if you yourself recognized that feeling all too well.*

A year later, almost to the day, Geoffrey expired in exactly the way he feared Mummy would go. Gasping for air. I wondered then, had death already whispered in his ear?

Is death the friend who comes with love to take us home, rather than the enemy who steals us in the night or on the battlefield, whom we have been taught to fear?

*"The poor are often happier than the rich.
When the rich reach out to save the poor,
the poor will save the rich."*

I looked down at Grace, who was sleeping in my lap.

Certainly, in this place Mother Teresa had created for the indigent dying, death was greeted with a loving smile.

When the van arrived to transport us back to the Motherhouse, everyone wrapped up their tasks and went to the closet to retrieve their belongings.

I cupped Grace's face in my hands. *Could the life that flows through me be a river of life for her? Could my touch revive her?*

"Or is it your time to leave?" I asked her. Her kind eyes sank deeply into mine. I quickly massaged the remainder of the lotion into her skin, around her shoulders, and down to her fingertips. I put my hand on her heart and looked into her eyes. "Perhaps you will go to heaven before I do," I said. "And if you do, would you save a place for me?" As if she understood, she closed her eyes and a rim of moisture glistened from them; I think it meant "yes."

On my way back in the van, I said a prayer for Grace. I had quickly become attached to her because she was so like a little child in the way she became upset with me, and forgave me, and loved me, all in a matter of a few overlapping moments.

I came from a part of the world where every goal issues from the concept of separation. Competing and winning ~ being the first, the biggest, the best, always measuring our success against one another. Something was shifting inside me. I realized each stranger I had met so far on my journey, I felt connected with ~ inexplicably linked to. As if my success lay in their hands and vice versa. I knew in my heart they were all a part of me and I was a part of them. What was good for me was good for them and good for all.

Gilly was right. Already a change had taken place. I would never look at another human being and consider it any other way. Our paths had crossed, our lives had intersected, and we were connected by the silver strings of a cord, woven together by the finest part of humanity. Unique. Different. Diverse.

We were one.

♡♡♡

"Your weakness is your strength."

Thursday, April 8, 1993

I woke up this morning. Grace didn't. Her bed was empty. The Sister who welcomed me gave me a sideways nod. With a heavy heart I glanced through the doorway at the sign: I Am on My Way to Heaven. Emotions choked my throat. Doing my best to push sadness away, I found it went deeper and further than the here and now.

I crept in and sat on the cement slab beside her wrapped body.

Death. Unexpected. Accompanied by the most searing of all pain had come with the sudden news of my brother's death.

It was noon, Saturday, the day Geoffrey and I were to have met in New York. Instead I was in my home office at my ranch in California, seated at my rolltop desk with its many drawers, staring numbly at the phone. I had made all my plans. I had booked my flight to London, intent on digging in to my investigation of his death. I would then accompany his body on the flight to Australia. There was one last call to make.

"Dr. Whitehouse, this is Christina."

I could picture the good doctor in his Venice apartment. Sitting by the wobbly wood phone table facing his Radionics machine. It looked like something out of a Buck Rogers movie, with its silver dials and knobs and copper-coned tubes reaching up to the ceiling. It was three times the size of Dr. Charles Whitehouse, almost taking over his tiny apartment. "The copper cones are energized by crystals inside," he explained.

The first time I saw that strange apparatus, I had the urge to spin on my toes and run the other way, fast. It wasn't long before I realized Dr. Charles is a sincere and dedicated man who works almost 24 hours a day to help heal the sick.

Proudly he handed me his scrapbook, bulging with photographs and hospital charts and letters of appreciation ~ his many documented successes. I leafed through before-and-after pictures of young children, for whom traditional medicine had no more answers yet whose diseases he had been able to eradicate or at least move onto a positive healing path. I stopped at the photograph of an older man whom Dr. Charles had been credited with having brought out of a coma. He explained to me how he worked with the patient and their family.

"It is important," he said, "that the unity of the family be an active part of the healing."

He explained how the loving fabric of a family draws a net of love around a disease and aids in removing it. He told me how a person's name and picture carry information of their illness and of their healing. He showed me the copper spiral in which he would place the photograph to focus and bolster a patient's immunity. His work was energetic in nature and miraculous in effect. After seeing him interviewed on a morning TV show, impressed with how humble he appeared, I wanted to meet him. I had learned to remain open-minded enough to look past superficial oddities. We had made another date for me to explore his work further.

"Christina, it's good to hear from you," he said warmly.

"Charles, I'm . . . I have to cancel our appointment. My brother was . . . he . . . um . . . died in London. I'm going there Monday. It was very sudden. He wasn't sick. He just left the boardroom, collapsed, and died. I don't know why I feel this, but I feel like I have to go to him. Something is not right. Something is calling me."

I had stepped out of my cautious zone. Perhaps it was because I knew I was talking to another equally eccentric human being, I felt able to say everything on my mind. I continued.

"Charles, I'm curious about how he died, but more than that, and I don't know where I'm getting this from, I just have the sense that when someone dies suddenly, they are in trauma and their spirit might be wandering around, not knowing what happened. I thought if I went to London, I could find him and accompany his body home to Sydney. He normally stays at Browns, so I would see if I could get the same room—"

"Why don't you fly straight to Sydney?" Charles immediately suggested, cutting through my nervous rambling.

"Because I have to be sure he's not lost and confused."

"But you don't need to go there, Christina," he reassured me. "We can take care of that from here." Charles's professional tone was utterly confident.

"We can?"

"It isn't difficult, dear. Hold on. Let me locate him. Geoffrey Stevens. Right." I could hear his chair rolling across the wood floor. Then the clicking of dials on his machine caused me to laugh nervously.

"You mean you can do that with your . . . machine?"

"I just need to locate him. London, you say?"

"Yes."

"Then I'll bring him into the crystals."

A minute or so went by before he said, "All right, I've got him. Now I want you to see him."

Dr. Whitehouse required my mental picture of Geoffrey to work with him, and without any effort on my part, a vivid image of Geoffrey entered my field of vision.

He was in the sunny conservatory of his home in Sydney, standing in the doorway that led to his cherished wine cellar. He was smiling, his three little kids running around obliviously playing. Suddenly I noticed baby Jessica look at him and waddle over toward him. The others apparently couldn't see him, but she could. He bent down to her, but just as I fully focused on the scene, he looked toward me and the picture blurred again.

"Do you have him?" Charles asked softly.

"No . . . I mean I did, but I lost him."

"That's all right. See him where you know him well ~ where he's comfortable."

My mind's eye reached out again to Sydney, but that wasn't what I saw.

It was raining.

I was in one of those wonderful old roomy Checker cabs driving down Park Avenue. We turned east onto 60th.

Back in Venice, I could hear Charles turning dials as he talked.

"No one tells us what to do when we die, Christina. We know how to be born, and we're told how to live, but no one teaches us how to die."

He was right. Death to us in the West is the fearful end of the story. Finding a repository for our disintegrating bones, paying our taxes, and bequeathing our earthly possessions are our last and final responsibilities. We make no allowances for our residual leftover energy, the invisible stuff we create, like the feelings and emotions we bring into a relationship ~ into a room even ~ that remain long after we have left. Metaphysical frequencies so powerful they can change the course of our life and the lives of those around us. Where do they go?

"All right, do you have him now?" Charles called through the phone.

"Yes! I see him."

I was stunned. In the numbing horrorlike haze of the last few days, I had completely forgotten that Geoffrey and I had planned to meet in New York this day. There he was, as arranged, standing under the navy-blue-monogrammed awning outside his haven in New York, the Metropolitan Club. He remembered! As the taxi pulled in toward him I caught my breath again; he looked unusually vulnerable.

My yellow taxi maneuvered close to the curb, and I leaned out of the backseat window and waved. He smiled uncertainly and stepped off the wet sidewalk. I swung open the door of the spacious Checker. Geoffrey folded his umbrella and climbed in.

Gone was the passionate yet contained, jovial yet forceful negotiator I had known for so long. His face was pale, almost ashen, his expression one of loss and helplessness.

"Where are we going?" he asked apprehensively, as if I were the one who had organized this particular journey. This, too, was unlike my big brother, the man who was always in charge.

"Somewhere special." I smiled, taking his hand. He looked at me gratefully, then out the window. I followed his gaze and at that moment, our cab left the ground.

We were no longer on Fifth Avenue. We were over the park at treetop level. Up, up, up we soared, the beads of rain on the windows evaporating as we sailed up beyond the New York skyline, beyond the clouds, beyond the blue, and into the light . . . bright and beautiful.

Geoffrey turned to me, and his face was suddenly alive again, glowing with a warmth and joy I'd never seen. He squeezed my hand. He was no longer lost.

As if he were right there in the cab with us, Charles's voice broke in. "He's there, Christina! Geoff's in the light now."

I couldn't answer, but Charles's timing was perfect. He was so right-on. Geoffrey was beaming. His entire body, bathed in glorious luminescence. Like a little boy, happy to be home and safe at last, he leaned over and kissed my cheek. "Thank you, darling."

For you this is perhaps a curious story. For me, it was a mind-expanding, life-changing moment. I daresay if Charles, from 70 miles away, hadn't chimed in at precisely the instant he did, I would have surmised this to be my own wish-fulfilling fantasy. On any other day the skeptic in me would have snickered at Charles and his supernatural machine, but not today. No way.

I reconsidered then my desire to go to London to cross-examine Geoffrey's last living moments. I found myself, like him, in the glow of peace. Suspicion and revenge can eat away at your insides. I came to the realization that it would be wiser to let it rest and let his children grow up trusting whatever was written on the "cause of death" line. Healthier to go through life with the "innocent until proven guilty" attitude.

Before I left for Australia, I did one more thing. Partly on a whim and partly because I wanted to test this newfound sense of divine right order, I thought to check the weather for New York City that Saturday morning.

Sure enough, it was a warm June morning. Yet it had been raining, just as I had seen it. Thank goodness for whims. Legitimate confirmation for me that spirit survives death. There is no end. There is simply the visible and the invisible. And we live in both worlds. And sometimes, if we can take off our blinders long enough, we can pull back the veil and catch a glimpse of the vast beyond in all its divine glory. My dear brother had bestowed upon me the supreme knowledge . . .

Death is simply returning to the loving.

"Love has exquisite timing."

My heart felt full though I had no idea this day would become one of the more remarkable days in my life. I bathed the women that morning with a renewed sense of continuum in all things and the emotion that had gripped me upon my arrival transformed into contentment.

Grace had made it home.

Traversing the slums at ten miles an hour, on the way from Kalighat back to Bose Road, it was Grace's body, wrapped in white cotton, that lay at my feet. After dropping us off at the Motherhouse, the van would continue on to deliver Grace to the burning ghats on the banks of the Ganges.

I stepped out of the van and quietly thanked Grace for bringing back to me the knowledge that our bodies are merely the chariots that house and carry around our true everlasting spirits. And that we do indeed live on.

As my van pulled away, another identical white van slid into its place. With the cluck and slide of the van door, there was an instant rush of activity and everyone around me who had been chaotically going in different directions suddenly surged as one. Curious to see what was happening, I stepped into the fray. A beggar woman dropped to her knees in front of me and, before I knew it, I was looking into the face of the most beautiful woman in the world, and she was smiling down at me.

Even though I am five foot five and she was hunching to just over four feet tall she seemed to reach down from heaven as she touched my forehead and murmured, "God bless you."

Perplexed as to why she picked me out of the crowd, I stood stock-still as the tornado of energy swept her through the alley and into the convent.

She flipped the sign to In and the wooden door closed behind her.

I could hear the excited chant of 100 happy voices calling to one another, "Mother is home. Mother is home." What a joy-filled welcome!

Their overwhelming excitement poured out of the Motherhouse windows, escaping through every crack and crevice in the cement walls. I stood with the crowd and listened.

My heart surged as the Sisters, unable to contain their joy at the return of their Mother, instantaneously broke out in song. Their happiness spread. Sound waves of love washed over us outside. It was an exquisite ripple in time. No telling how long it lasted.

Of course! Tomorrow would be Good Friday. I should have realized Mother Teresa would come home to be with her Sisters at such a holy time.

I let the crowds pass by me, not wanting to be shaken from this euphoria. Her touch pulsed warmth through my body just as it had in my meditation. And there was something about that look in Mother Teresa's eyes . . . it was a look I knew well.

It was a millisecond and yet already, from that one glance she was familiar in 1,000 ways, spanning eons I could not describe.

CHAPTER TEN

IT'S ALL IN THE FEELING

Christina Stevens

*"Hold the feeling of joy in your heart
for as long as you can.
Mark it. Remember it.
And return to it often.
It will carry you over an abyss."*

Elated, feeling as if I were cloaked in a brand-new coat, as if I had just hooked up with an old friend who I hadn't seen in a millennium, I floated, grinning down Bose Road. Mother was home! I wanted to share my happiness.

Adriana hadn't been at morning Mass for the last two days, so I danced, on air, I might add, down to the orphanage. But the Sister told me Adriana had not shown up at the children's home that day. That didn't sound like her, so I crossed over to her hotel to find out why.

Adriana's hotel was a favorite of the volunteers. The location was perfect and the price was right ~ $15 a day. But there was no air-conditioning, and the rooms were the size of my suitcase.

When I knocked on Adriana's door, I knew something was wrong. No response. I knocked again. "Adriana?"

I could hear her feet drag across the dusty floor. She opened the door a crack. When she saw me, she opened it wider, turned away, and waved me in. It was as dark as midnight in there, and the air was thick with sorrow.

"Are you all right?" I asked.

"I'm fine," she said with a shrug, but I could tell it was a lie. I've told the same one myself 100 times.

"I don't think so," I admonished her gently.

"No, really. I'm good. Just tired. I needed a little rest today. That's all."

Avoiding my gaze Adriana sat down on her tousled bed. There was only one chair in the room and it was covered in clothes, so I knelt down and touched her knee. I watched her shoulders sink into her chest as she clutched her stomach.

"I'm not feeling too well. Maybe I've been doing too much. I started working full days. The Sisters told me I shouldn't. They don't like volunteers to work in the morning and in the afternoon. They say it's too much for us. But after meeting you I was feeling so much better and I thought . . ." Adriana broke into sobs.

I had already discovered volunteer work was emotionally draining. Physically, the heat alone is exhaustive and even the locals themselves have to be alert to the contamination in their water. While working side by side with the Sisters, I noticed so many of them were young and quite fragile in appearance yet I was in awe of the sheer physical strength they received from their spiritual foundation. Mother Teresa's work had no boundaries and, I would soon discover, neither did she.

Adriana was a different matter. Her son's death had left her vulnerable. She was receiving a great spiritual gift from her service, but the strain of volunteer work was taking its toll.

"You're healing," I said immediately. "You know how, when your skin gets cut, you don't feel it at first; you're sort of numb. And then it throbs and shoots pain out to your body, sending out a message that healing is needed. And it really hurts when all the soldiers in your skin and in your bloodstream come together to begin the knitting process?" Adriana grunted agreement. "And then as time goes on, your skin grows a scar and the hurt gets less? I suspect that's what's happening with you. Give it time, and it will hurt less and less."

"I don't ever want to stop feeling him," she said abruptly.

That stopped me for a moment. How stupid of me to compare her pain to a cut. I had severed myself from my emotions so much when I was a little girl that I never quite understood those who could stop life to wallow in their pain. I was clumsy and inept when it came to understanding feelings.

In fact, we were each at opposite ends of the same predicament. Stuck. *Got to move on,* I said to myself. For Adriana it had been a few months. For me? Decades. Centuries maybe.

Deciding she needed a change from her depressing surroundings, I scooped her off the edge of her bed.

"You're coming to my hotel for a nice long lunch," I announced.

"No, no, I can't," she protested, but my will was stronger than hers at that moment. She needed someone to take charge for a little bit. I found a bright floral dress in her closet. I knew it would uplift her.

"Oh look, I think I see a butterfly!" I squealed, pointing to an open flower with the buttonhole in its center. Adriana gave it a sideways glance.

"What is that saying?" I said chattily. "Just when the caterpillar thought its world had come to an end, it turned into a butterfly."

Adriana remained silent, forcing a polite smirk. Reluctantly she slipped on the dress, and we took a taxi to my hotel.

By the expression on Adriana's face it was obvious she was not anticipating the car door to be opened by our beautiful, turbaned doorman and was speechless as he regally spirited her toward the gilded revolving doors.

Hypnotically she floated into the air-conditioned lobby, sighed deeply, and gazed up at the three-story-high ceilings and back down to the plush gold carpeting.

"This is like another world." She gasped.

"They have six different restaurants, and you can take your pick," I encouraged as I escorted her through the lobby, past the gift shops, and up the marble staircase.

"On the third floor, French cuisine, but I think it's only open for dinner. Second floor, you have your choice of German or Italian fare. I can't vouch for any of them as I have been sticking to room service. Now, first floor ~ we can offer you an English pub, a Chinese Sampan, or the pièce de résistance, Indian! Actually the names may change, but I suspect they all taste Indian."

"Chinese," Adriana groaned enthusiastically.

She ordered one dish from every category on the menu. I was happy I could share my bounty with her and give her a reprieve from the boiled eggs and white toast they served in her hot little hovel on Bose Road.

I watched her voraciously devour each dish as it arrived, like it was her last supper.

"I love spicy food," Adriana said between mouthfuls.

"I do, too. The hotter, the better. My mother once told me my insides must have been made of iron," I added, coughing on that comment. It triggered a memory in me, and though I knew I should think before I spoke, seeing Adriana in her room had shaken me, and I felt moved to say something.

"Adriana, I am not who I appear to be."

Adriana swallowed and laughed. "Who is?"

"I have tried to commit suicide." For a moment I thought Adriana was going to choke, so I rushed immediately to explain myself.

"I was young and foolish and had no concept of the consequences. I was just a little girl the first time."

Adriana dropped her chopsticks, leaned forward, mouthing "the first time" and searched my face for understanding. I had never spoken of this to anybody, and if I were able to talk about it now, it was only in the hope that it may comfort her.

"My father had a black leather shaving strap with a metal weight inside one end that would leave red welts on your bottom and your legs . . . my brother and I . . . we never knew whose turn it would be."

"What about your mother? Where was she?"

"She was out of it. I don't even know if she knew what was happening to us. She was a binge drinker, and when she wasn't drinking she was loving and tender. But just like him, we never knew what to expect."

"Your parents were horrible."

"No. They did their best. They made me strong. They made my brother strong. It's never what's done to us. It's how we deal with it. As a little person, I thought their behavior was my fault, because as a child we think the world revolves around us. Strange, isn't it, how we can blame ourselves for another's actions?"

While Adriana was chewing on that thought, Chatty Cathy me, babbled on.

"When you were a little girl, did you ever have a place where you would go where nobody could find you? I did. I was three, maybe four years old and my favorite spot was an old woodpile between our garage and the neighbor's fence. Wood . . . splinters . . . spiders . . . rusty nails . . . I really loved sitting up there. It was the safest place in the world to me, certainly the last place anyone would look for me. Sitting up there, I could hear my mother, clanging pots around, cooking in the kitchen. There was one day when I thought I heard someone call my name. I swung my legs over to our neighbor's side of the fence and shimmied my way down into their garden. I could see their laundry door was open."

At first I was narrating a story to Adriana; it was outside me, like watching a movie. But then talking about it was making it real, again.

"I knew where I was going. Boy, I knew exactly where I was going. I dove down under their laundry sink and pulled at the cupboard door and it opened."

I sucked in air quickly because if I stopped now, I might not get through it. Flash forward.

"There I was, on the cement floor pulling out boxes and bottles as if I knew exactly what I was searching for ~ and I found it! A brown glass bottle with a darker syrupy substance inside. It killed things like rodents and bugs. I had heard our neighbor Mrs. Singleton and Mummy talk about it."

Adriana's eyes widened.

"I got it all over my face; I was having a whale of a time trying to drink the stuff. It didn't taste good, but I knew full well what I was doing. I don't know how long it was until Mrs. Singleton, Mavis Singleton I think her name was ~ well, she found me. She scooped me up, grabbed the bottle, and carried me over to our place."

The scene faded slightly and I stopped. Adriana gently prodded me on. "What happened then?"

"I was there in my bedroom. It was the sunniest room in our house. I could feel the sun streaming in the window ~ it was so warm. But I felt cold. I just wanted to get closer to the sun. I could hear Mummy talking loudly and crying. And then I heard a siren. I turned toward the sunlight. It was warm and very bright, and like slow motion I was falling, and then I was floating. I was leaving my body. I saw myself rising up out of that little body. The light was getting even brighter."

Adriana squeezed my arm and snapped me back to our lunch.

I dropped my chopsticks.

Adriana was peering at me with an incredulous look on her face. "Go on . . ." she said, diving back into her meal.

"You know, I remember my mother telling me it was a miracle I lived." I laughed a little, but Adriana remained silent, her face a grim mask of seriousness.

"Some years later I was so unhappy I tried it again. I wanted so badly to be a ballerina. It was all I thought about. I ate, drank, and breathed ballet. I practiced for hours every day. I was on my toes before anyone in my class. But I couldn't do the splits. I would push and bend myself until my legs bled. I just couldn't do them. I didn't know what it was, I thought it was me. I was convinced I just wasn't good enough to take my body there, or I didn't work hard enough at it. I couldn't understand it. I was told that without that flexibility, I could never be a ballerina. I was so miserable I thought my life should end. I was no good to anybody. I cleaned my room and dressed in my Sunday best, and I asked God to look after Mummy. I went downstairs, under our house to where my father had his laboratory.

Very deliberately I ate an entire meal of rat poison. But all that preparation was for naught. All it did was make me throw up."

Enjoying every moo shu morsel, Adriana swallowed, stifling a grin, somewhat embarrassed my hardship was so entertaining.

"It was only a few years ago when I had my back X-rayed that I found out why I was never destined to be a dancer. I've always had a scar on my lower back that I thought was a birthmark. But actually it was a burn mark. By mistake or maybe she was drunk, my mother dropped a cigarette in my nappy, and when it burned through, she dropped me. Vertebra could never form. It's like my back was locked."

Suddenly Adriana stopped chewing, put her chopsticks down, and wiped sauce from the side of her mouth.

"Ronnie always knew what he was doing. I'm sure of it. His eyes were so alert, the second he opened them. He could look right through you, but then something altered in him and he stopped looking at me and he started looking somewhere else . . . he was somewhere I couldn't reach. My husband said I spoiled Ronnie. And I did. I gave him everything he wanted." Adriana peered at me through a tangle of curls.

At this point she pulled over a bowl of rice and almost in a meditative state started in on that, picking up one grain of rice at a time with her chopsticks. "Maybe I gave him too much?" she mused, peering over to encourage me to talk.

*"Love is like the ocean,
surrounding us, encompassing us,
holding us up.
Learn how to swim in it.
Or just float."*

I wanted to tell her how I felt when I did aerobatics in the sky and how I felt the air that held me up was love, but I wasn't sure she would understand.

"I don't think it's a question of 'giving' love or receiving love. It's more knowing love is always there."

I leaned in closer for I wanted her to really get the story I was about to share. "My friend Reverend Michael uses this example. There are these two fish ~ a mummy fish and a baby fish. And they live in the ocean, a vast field of water bigger than both of them. In this field of water, they are moving and living, dodging sharks and other predators, feeding and fending for themselves, and just being who they are. One fish is not responsible for the other's water, they are simply in it together, sharing the field." Not taking her eyes off me, Adriana put down her chopsticks.

"The way I see it, we are here to understand that. And to learn how to swim together in this ocean. In this ocean called love."

Adriana's attention was almost trancelike as she poured water into her glass, turning the bottle on its end. Suddenly there was water all over the table. Thankfully our waiter stepped in, grabbed the bottle from her, and mopped up the puddle.

I chuckled and continued. "There can never be too much love or too little love, because love is infinite. You can never lose love. It is always there. It is up to each of us to see that, to see ourselves totally connected to the flow of love, without inhibition."

Adriana sighed deeply. Just then a new wave of exotic dishes arrived and she picked up her chopsticks again and dove in.

"I envy you," I said. Adriana winced at my disclosure. "In my life, I have never loved anyone the way you loved your son."

Adriana stopped chewing and cocked her head.

"Oh, I have had a lot of boyfriends, and I have loved them passionately. But there's a kind of love I haven't felt. And you have."

Adriana put down her chopsticks, dabbed the corners of her mouth with her napkin, and pushed her plate aside. Her eyes welled up. Her lips pressed hard together as if she were stifling a scream.

Shut up, Christina. You talk too much. You think you know everything, and lo and behold, you put your foot in it.

The longest blink brought a lone tear to Adriana's cheek.

I reached over. "He never meant to hurt you. He just wanted his hurt to stop. He wouldn't want you to cry. He wants to see you smile again."

Her clenched mouth relaxed into a half smile. "I know."

She sat, not moving a hair. Some time passed. I was talked out. She then reached across the table and, touching my fingertips, whispered, "I'm ready for dessert now."

"In dying,
Christ showed us
that
love is, the greatest gift."

Good Friday, April 9, 1993

As every morning, I left my five-star comfort in the dark and took a taxi through Calcutta's early urban yawn to the Motherhouse. There were more visitors than I had seen before, and yet surprisingly, my inconspicuous spot, just right of the inside back door of the chapel, seemed to have an invisible Reserved for Christina sign on it.

I peered over heads, noticing the prayer room had a different glow this day. A simple wooden table between the organ and the crucifix was laid out with a white runner. Father Joseph, who was to conduct today's special service, swept in, smoothing the long purple-and-gold scarf draped around his neck. While more arrived, he busied himself by removing a gold chalice and plates from a nearby cupboard and setting them on the table beside his Bible. He looked to be a kindly man with eyes that sloped down to his cheeks, giving him a rather sad countenance. Perfect for today's sermon.

I strained to see where Mother Teresa might be, assuming it would be in an honored and prominent position in the front. But she was nowhere in sight.

love

The moment the Sister's hand touched the keys of the freestanding organ, Mother Teresa slipped quietly in through the back door and knelt down to the left, just across the aisle from me. How amazing I had selected my spot, side by side with her.

We glanced at each other for an instant. She didn't acknowledge me with a nod or anything; however, our eyes connected and then she refocused her eyes upon the air around me.

To my embarrassment, I was going through the same gyrations I had every morning. My back didn't like the kneeling position and my bony knees were in agony. Squirming, doing my best to breathe through the pain, I could not comprehend how on earth the Sisters could kneel on this cement floor and pray for hours at a time.

With Mother Teresa beside me, outwardly giving the impression of an elderly frail woman, I could at least manage a hair of discomfort.

"Surrender," Father Joseph said.

Me? Surrender? my inner voice said. *I don't think so. Surrender means give up. Do with me what you will. Let go of control. Turn it over. No. I don't think so.*

"Jesus surrendered!" Father Joseph said again, baffling my inner discourse. *Jesus could have taken off into the hills, but he gave himself up. He could have spoken up for himself, fought for his life, but instead, he was silent.*

"In doing that, Jesus, the man, became Jesus, the Christ," he added.

At times throughout the service I noticed Mother would reach down and rub her bare feet. Out of the corner of my eye I watched the way her shoulder dipped and her hand massaged her toes. Her toes twisted around one another as if when she was a little girl and her feet were growing, they had been bound or squeezed into shoes that were too small. I could almost feel the suffering those bent, misshapen feet caused her, but when I looked at her face, expecting to see that pain reflected, it simply wasn't there. Peace shone from her eyes.

My knees hurt so much, tears were squeezing through the roots of my lashes, but I sucked it in and labored through, ashamed I was being such a crybaby over my inconsequential discomfort. Blinking away the fog of wetness, the simple wooden crucifix that hung alone on the white wall of the chapel came sharply into focus.

Father Joseph was preparing Communion. Pouring wine into the golden chalice, I could barely make out his murmuring. ". . . the blood of Jesus, which is given up to you for the forgiveness of your sins." And then ". . . the body of Jesus . . . ," placing paper thin wafers on the gold plate. One by one, Mother Teresa, followed by her Sisters, the co-workers, and when they were done, the volunteers, rose to take their turn to sip Jesus's blood and hold his body on their tongue until it melted away.

Movement was all around me, and I could perhaps have relaxed my prayer stance and rolled off my knees as others did, but that seemed disrespectful. Instead, I kept my focus on the solitary crucifix. Jesus loomed out at me, almost as if he were alive and breathing. Colors swirled around him and for a moment I thought I would faint. But I held myself erect, pushing my knees into the rock-hard floor, asking the man on the cross to lift me above this torture.

In an instant, my knees were no longer connected to the ground, and I thought for a moment I saw blood streaking down his face, dripping from his palms and his feet and down the wall. Red.

"Father, forgive them, for they know not what they do."

Jesus asked that as he hung bleeding, suffering at the hands of man. Suffering such abject pain, the intensity of which you and I could never know. I knew it didn't matter to Him if I was a Jew, a Christian, a Muslim, or a Hindu, a leper, a prostitute, a Capricorn, an alcoholic, a thief, a wife beater, or a terrorist even, none of that mattered to Jesus. He just wanted us to love one another as He had loved us. And He took the hit for all of us.

On that sobering notion I inhaled big and brought myself back into my body.

My focus settled again to the words spelled out on the wall, beside the crucifix, reading simply: I Thirst.

I was puzzled. Being the only two words on the wall in Mother's chapel, it had been selected to say everything that needed to be said in this, her holy place of prayer. Its isolation was significant. But I didn't get it. Surely there was more to it than the fact that Jesus's throat was parched.

Unworthy as I felt in that moment, my throat was parched. I wanted to share in the union everyone else in the room was enjoying. I wanted to be touched by the solemn bliss they were partaking in. God, I could use a drink.

Finally, I could take it no longer. It was time for the last of the volunteers to take Communion. I rolled off my knees, hopped to my feet, and found a place at the end of the line. Silently I asked Jesus to forgive my pretense ~ sure he would not mind, just this once.

"Father, into your hands, I commend my spirit."

After Communion, we all sang and the feeling lifted us out of the room.

The visitors trickled out and the volunteers went down to the lower courtyard until it was time for the vans to depart for Mother's homes.

The Sisters immediately set about their daily chores. Even though it was Good Friday, there were no holidays at the Missionaries of Charity. I overheard a murmur throughout the volunteers, and I approached Sister Josma to confirm if what they were saying was true. Quietly she acknowledged, "Yes, Mother will go into the silence today. She speaks to no one until Sunday."

I had a crew and equipment and their nonrefundable air tickets, booked and paid for and scheduled to arrive in 96 hours. The good news was my star was in the house. Bad news: she wasn't talking.

"Choose a day, or an hour,
or whatever you can manage,
to go into silence. And be silent.
Silence has a way
of giving us a fresh new perspective
on everything."

At Kalighat, in honor of Good Friday, decorations had been hung. The walls at the head of each bed in the men's and women's wards were adorned with framed pictures telling the story of Jesus's journey from Bethany to the crucifixion. A special ceremony had been planned and our duties that day were trimmed down to basics. As all the volunteers, men and women, stood around each of the patients' beds, the Sisters told the story in stages, in English and in Hindi, and every now and then, we sang.

When we reached Grace's empty bed during the ceremony, I felt a rush of happiness. I knew it would have another grateful occupant before the day was done. When we moved into the men's section, one of the volunteers told me, "Even though the men appear stronger than the women, they tend to die faster." Looking around, I could not sense any of the men holding on with the conscious tenacity Grace displayed. They were either getting better or they were on their way.

Mother Teresa's presence infused me with the need to take action. I needed to act as if I already had her approval. One thing I know: if we aren't emotionally and intellectually aligned and ready for the opportunity, it cannot happen. Scouts' motto: be prepared.

At noon, I chose not to take the van back to the Motherhouse. Unaccustomed as I was to scouting locations alone, I had come with tools. My trusty compass, maps, Polaroid camera, blank storyboards, sketchpad, and my most valuable tool, my smile.

I set out to explore the city, ingratiating my way into strangers' houses, onto their roofs, gauging the arc of the sun and making copious notes on what time of day to schedule shots. I needed to sketch the film I saw in my mind's vision, but it was hardly up to snuff. I needed help.

As the afternoon light slowly left the dilapidated structures of this once-glorious commonwealth jewel, I put my camera away and began the trek home. Invariably, this is where I get into trouble ~ it's my sense of direction.

Lost, I came upon an ancient and deserted graveyard whose ornate wrought-iron gates didn't appear to have been opened in a century. I peered through the rusting bars. It looked as though anyone who knew someone buried here had themselves left this earth long ago. It brought back memories of a childhood I had long left behind and an aloneness I still carried with me.

Suddenly I had the uneasy sensation of falling through a tunnel, landing lightly on the ground, which felt so much closer. I looked down. And there were my toes, little, flat, unpolished toenails, poking through my favorite white leather sandals.

No one knew about the special place I went to on Saturdays. Nobody would have understood. It was a long walk from our place, yet my five-year-old legs retraced the route well.

"Sixpence worth of licorice sticks and threepence of chocolate freckles and a bottle of lemonade, please." That was pretty much my standing order at the lolly shop. Hugging the brown paper bag holding everything my pocket money could buy, I skipped along Old South Head Road, up the hill beside the Pacific Ocean cliffs, across the honeysuckled path, and through the imposing carved wrought-iron gate.

There was rarely anybody here on Saturday afternoons except the gatekeeper, and he simply gave me a wave and went back to his business of sweeping, sweeping, sweeping ~ those interminable invisible leaves from the cobblestone path.

As I passed the glorious marble headstones and soulful angels protruding from mausoleum walls, with their vases filled with flowers, lovingly strewn with wreaths and tidied with care, I stopped to add to my clutches a flower from this and a blossom from that. By the time I reached the farthermost graves, I had all I needed.

When I looked down to the graves, tucked away at the rocky end of the graveyard, tears welled inside me. *Nobody cares.* You could hardly recognize those cold, lifeless forms as graves even ~ overgrown with weeds. There was not a sign they had been visited in years.

I knelt down to one that looked most in need of attention. I rubbed off the caked dirt on the flat headstone . . . 1797–18--, the rest had broken away. I stood and bowed graciously from the waist.

"I'm so very pleased to meet you. My name is Christina, and I've come to take care of you."

Diligently, I rubbed the debris-encrusted headstones. As I scraped away their years of obscurity, stories grew from the ground. Mother and son, died during birth; father, who lived another 50 years, came at last, to rest beside them. I thought of his loneliness, and in my heart I felt it. I was only five years old, yet 50 years of solitude was something I could commiserate with.

Inch by inch, I tended the graves as best I could. With my hands I pulled the weeds, scooped the leaves from between each plot, and etched their boundaries with small rocks.

When the sun was a smidgen from meeting the ocean I knew it was time to go. I must be home by dark otherwise there would be questions. In the midst of my accomplishment I twirled around, dancing to the heavenly music that filled my head. Round and round, bowing and curtsying, dispersing my stolen booty until every grave had a flower.

"It's time we had our party," I announced to the wind.

From the brown paper bag I pulled out the bottle of lemonade and a small white bag filled with chocolate freckles and licorice sticks. My favorite!

I laid the sweets out in a circle and drank a little of the lemonade. I offered it to the cooling air as I swept my hand across the party favors.

"Would you care for one?" I asked, bowing at the waist.

"Oh, let me eat it for you," I answered, knowing my resident guests don't partake of mortal food.

One of them made a joke about the joy of giving and receiving all at once and we all laughed. I couldn't see my visitors, yet I felt their presence. They were happy now. I could feel their laughter inside me. How they love someone to visit and pay their respects. How grand it was to be with those who have been around so much longer than I, who know so much more than I do.

The reward of aloneness is wisdom, I thought.

Goodness! Was this the belief that had grown within me?

The sky was fast turning purple. Our party must end, and I must run home, never to tell a living soul of my cemetery visits since most Saturday afternoons I could be found playing in the old dairy or defending it by throwing stones at the kids who lived on the other side of the river. Most Saturday afternoons, that is.

I suddenly realized my fingers were gripping the rusty iron bars of the cemetery gate as if my life depended on it. I wasn't a little girl anymore. I was a grown woman with a somewhat odd default life. I wondered about my eccentric pastime of taking care of old graves and of my forgotten awareness of beings in a graveyard. What struck me more, though, was my strange conviction that there was a reward for aloneness, a decision little Christina had made that older Christina was living ~ that separation from my fellow man was a wise thing.

I brushed the caked rust from my hands and turned away from that lonely little girl, walking faster and faster, wishing I could simply run from those old thoughts, step out of them, the way a snake casts off an old skin that is no longer useful. But all that mental meandering had turned me upside down. I was still lost. I waved down a taxi.

As I did each day, upon my return to the hotel I glanced over to Monica's desk, but she wasn't there. Her smile would have truly added oomph to my heart. Then I made a beeline for the message center, but as had been the custom, no messages.

Wasn't anybody needing me? Missing me? Thinking of me? Surely today, of all days, Gilly would have called.

Quite frankly, I had no room in my head to deal with anything in the Western hemisphere, but I was hoping for maybe a sign of support, a word of encouragement or perhaps just wishes from home, but that was not to be.

When I reached the mirrored elevator, exhaustion reigned. The day had been long and my head was dearly longing for its pillow. The elevator doors opened and there was Dr. Michael, with a big friendly smile and a pretty girl beside him.

"Ah, Christina. *Te voir comble ma journée,*" he said warmly as they stepped out of the elevator. Translation: Seeing you completes my day.

Michael bowed and motioned to his date.

"Meet my colleague, Deane DeValle." We shook hands.

"Christina *est ici pour filmer Mère Teresa,*" he told Deane, who raised her eyebrows and nodded sweetly as she moved back a little.

"You must join us for a cocktail!" he said, moving in.

"No. Thank you. It's been a long day." I was feeling grimy, in my Kalighat slacks and T-shirt. Even though I covered it all in a silk coat, I must have been rather stinky, having traversed the streets of Calcutta for hours. I stepped back a little in case, but he stepped closer. I forgot, European men like to smell their women.

"*Ça va?*" he asked, touching my arm and leaning down to peer inquiringly into my eyes. His look was so intense I thought I would burst into tears.

"*Oui. Ça va bien.*"

I could feel Deane anxious to move along, so I backed into the elevator and waved good-bye. *Please don't ask me to say another word.*

"*Si douce est la tristesse de nos adieux.*" I think he was quoting Shakespeare, saying, "Parting is such sweet sorrow." They waved good-bye and Michael kept his eyes on me until the elevator doors closed. I felt drawn to them in a warm magnetic way and that day of all days I would have loved a cocktail.

Though I shared the fact with no one here, when I opened the door to my suite there on the coffee table in front of the meditation bed was an exquisite arrangement of fragrant lilies and a wooden jewelry box with gold inlay, lined in purple velvet. Inside ~ a card.

How did she know? Ah, my passport.

"Dear Miss Stevens, Wishing you all the very best. Happy birthday. Happy Faster. Lots of love, Monica."

CHAPTER ELEVEN

WHEN YOU WAKE THE TIGER INSIDE

Christina Stevens

*"You and I can sometimes forget
how much we need each other."*

Saturday, April 10, 1993
Calcutta

I woke late. My room was alive with sunshine. Upon realizing I had missed morning prayers, I sank back into my pillow, giving into a special kind of exhaustion. I knew full well Mother Teresa and the Sisters couldn't pull up the sheets and snuggle down for a little extra shut-eye. They could never say, "Oh, I don't think I will go to work today." Never took a holiday. Never went on vacation. Didn't take time off or even a time-out. And God forbid one had a sick day!

I readjusted my pillows and let the quiet serenade me, sending me back to dreamland. I would have gone if it had not been for the clock on the mantel.

Tick tock, tick tock. It set my mind to work. With my leading lady present, I dearly needed time to refocus on my mission here, but I knew my edge was not sharp, I was not in my element, and I had become sidetracked by my curiously weeping heart.

Mother Teresa's caution echoed, "You must come soon." Although I didn't want to consider that she would fall ill, it gave me a renewed sense of urgency that somewhere in the spiral of time and dimension and beyond my present knowledge I had been called to be here, now.

I had run out of bottled water, so I brushed my teeth with Coca-Cola and crawled into the shower, washing my hair with my eyes and mouth clenched shut. I was feeling vulnerable, in pieces almost. I didn't trust myself to transform the toxins in the water. My usual bravado had been eclipsed by some deep-down, below-the-surface bewilderment.

I dressed quickly and set out once more in search of locations.

Have I told you my sense of direction is dreadful? It is a fuzz ball I forever have to cope with. While completing cross-country training for my pilot's license, I discovered one of my own personal dichotomies. In the air, I am able to navigate without a compass. I could find a remote and unchartered airfield in the desert, in the midst of a sandstorm, but down here on planet Earth my inner compass is almost nonexistent. My close friends know even with a map and detailed directions, I can still become hopelessly lost. And though you will often catch me arguing with her, I thank God for the lady who lives inside my GPS.

As the morning progressed I found I had been spinning in circles and taken few photographs because I had lost my film somewhere, stopped into a bookstore to pick up a picture book on Calcutta and left my map on the cashier's counter, and then my compass went missing. Midafternoon, I flagged down a taxi to take me back to my hotel.

I wasn't prepared to return to my glitzy golden comfort so soon. There was so much to glean from the smells and the sounds, from the authentic breath that infused life into Calcutta.

Across the road from the Taj Bengal is the Calcutta Zoo.

On an impulse, I paid my driver, bought a soda for myself and peanuts for the elephant from a roving vendor, and followed the throng inside. As I was sipping my soda, my mind journeyed to the two words in the Motherhouse that hung beside Jesus on the cross that had seized my curiosity yesterday: I Thirst.

My musing was interrupted.

"Excuse me. What is your name?"

Deep and satiny, I was startled by a stranger's voice, which suddenly distinguished itself from the high-pitched foreign chatter surrounding me.

I turned and looked straight into the handsome, dark-brown countenance of a young Indian man. Immediately I stepped back a pace. He was much too close, definitely within that imaginary boundary of personal space we all maintain. Instead of simply answering him with some polite brush-off, I found myself unable to form even a syllable.

I did the only thing I could. I turned away. Walking quickly in the opposite direction, I searched for an opening to infiltrate the crowd. A wave of hot air rushed over me and brought with it a raw animal smell that aggressively invaded my nostrils.

"Would you like some ice cream?" His voice was so close, I could almost feel his warm breath on my neck.

"No. Thank you," I said sharply, without turning around. I picked up my pace even more, hastening to melt into the environment. But the sudden screeching of wild animals bouncing off wire cages and the deep guttural growls coming from an undisclosed source resounded in my belly.

With static between my ears, I found in my haste I had lost my way. *Where was the front gate?* Every time I slowed long enough to ask for directions, I seemed to encounter no one who spoke English.

"Can I buy you a cup of coffee?" He was still there. Following me.

I picked up my pace. I could hear footsteps echoing on the pavement. I left the walkway and waded into the bushes.

There was nothing sinister about him or his voice, but I was frightened beyond reason. And I had no idea why.

"Hullo?" he called, from where, I knew not.

I plunged through yet another crowd of strangers and slid down a gravel pathway. The lions' roars were getting louder. I dove into a clump of trees like a stalked deer. I felt like the endangered heroine in a low-budget horror film, chased by a sinister voice through a jungle of wildly tangled growth, appealing to throngs of beings who refused to help me. I turned sharply aside and concealed myself behind the House of Pythons, certain I had eluded him.

"Why are you here?" he asked, from no more than two feet away. I glanced into his confrontational, dark brown eyes. They held no threat and yet I was trembling with panic, terror gripping at my throat.

Why am I here?

His question throbbed in my head. *Good question,* I thought as I moved on. Suddenly, I found myself boxed in. I had backed into a cul-de-sac, surrounded by tigers. Bengal tigers.

I heard a nearby roar, yet when I looked through the steel bars and into the eyes of the tiger, he languished silently, eyeing me with passive, unconcerned amusement.

I stopped for a moment. Our eyes locked.

As if his fluffy paw reached through the bars and clawed for my chest, wanting to scratch a message into my heart.

You are hunting me for my skin and my meat and my body parts and you are cutting down the forests and taking away my shelter, my food, my home. Soon, I will no longer walk this planet. Do you realize what you are doing?

The tiger knew I heard him clearly. He shifted his gaze and with it, a rush of love like a silky gloved hand slipped deep inside me and caressed my stomach with the words *Help me.*

Who is asking for help? I wondered.

"Why are you here?" the stranger repeated, from right behind me.

I froze, not wanting to answer. "I'm working . . . I'm making a film," I said in a voice that sounded decidedly unlike my own. I kept my eyes fixed on the tiger, refusing to make eye contact with the man I was speaking with. "My crew is on their way."

The tiger released his stare, and I moved away, sliding by the dark foreigner, hoping our conversation would end there, but it didn't.

"I can help you," he persisted, following close on my heels. "I know a lot of locations, good locations. I have worked with a filmmaker before, and I can bring a tape to your hotel. I can help you. Where are you staying?"

The one person I needed more than anyone right now was a location scout, but the fearful chatter in my mind was overriding even that. Aside from my professional needs, I should have been guided by a quote from the Bible that I have always liked, Hebrews 13:2. "Be not forgetful to entertain strangers, for thereby some have entertained angels, unawares." But my insides churned. *No, no. Keep your distance. Stay away.*

My wish had been granted as the Bombay sage had predicted, yet lo and behold, I was waving the gift away.

Not wanting to encourage him, I lifted my head slightly and stole a glance in his direction. His expression was one of disappointment and something else I couldn't quite put words to. It was hardly evil that lurked in his eyes. The fearless Lone Ranger I imagined myself to be was still trembling in her shoes. Why was I in such terror? Why did I feel so vulnerable?

The trumpeting of an elephant call nearby spun me around, searching for the source. I felt the earth move. There was a stirring ~ an awakening in my soul and it came with the knowledge that as soon as I understood it, I would transcend it.

The earth shook again and with it, bells tinkled and the elephant broke through the trees and lumbered toward me. She wasn't stopping. Quickly I fell into step beside her, hoping she would eventually guide me to the front gate. I turned to see if the brown-eyed Indian was following, but he had vanished, as if he had never been there in the first place.

Ahh. Now I felt safe, paced with the slow and massive ancient. The elephant slackened and came to a halt for her master to tighten her ornate pink harness. I stopped with her and she looked down. Playfully she waved her trunk at me. I gave her the peanuts. And then she blinked. Her eye was deep and moist, which made her look supremely sad. Through the majesty of her charisma, her eye transmitted an awesome and wise thought to me.

You humans are the dumbest creatures in the universe. You stumble around thinking, thinking, thinking. Your brain keeps you from what is real. You think our survival depends on you. You've got it all wrong. Your survival depends on us.

Is it we humans who are the endangered species? I wondered.

She blinked and all the stories scientists have told me about the 100th monkey spreading consciousness, dolphins communicating in complete holograms, and parrots speaking and understanding complex language, felt truer than true. My throat closed up. Could it be the more we learn about our animal kingdom, the more we will understand ourselves?

Considered sacred in this land, elephants are said to never forget. I think it is that timeless memory locked in the deepest recesses of their senses rather than their immense size that instills such respect.

Is there something I am meant to remember?

Like the tiger, her eye had wrapped itself around my heart. *If only my heart could speak in terms my mind could comprehend. Is this what it's like to simply "feel"?* It was all I could do to hold myself erect and not fall down on the lawn in a sobbing mess.

A wave of warm air rushed by, and the elephant blinked again and picked up her foot, leaving a footprint so immense any creature on earth could put theirs inside it. She wiggled her foot and jingled her bells and what looked like a cute circus trick was actually one of much-needed levity for me. She placed her foot down and clomped on. I was awash again in the safety of her enormousness and grateful for resuming movement.

As she picked up speed, my steps became more sure-footed and in no time, we were at the zoo entrance and I was just that much nearer the sanctity of the Taj Bengal.

Before I could cross the road, something pulled at me. I turned around. I thought it could be the elephant's trunk, yet hoped it was the presence of the young man I had slighted that stroked my shoulder. I had brushed him off when all he wanted to do was help. I was calm enough now to entertain his conversation. But no. He was gone for good. However, something else was directly in my line of sight.

There, standing near the stone entrance, was a baby cradled in the bliss of his mother's arms, contentedly sucking on an empty bottle.

My heart swelled. I was mesmerized by the tot's big brown pools staring into space, sucking away ~ even though there was no liquid left in his bottle. He wasn't sucking for milk. My heart rose high. His round eyes caught mine, and then he gazed adoringly up at his mother. Yes! So simple. The sign in the chapel of the Motherhouse that was placed prominently beside Jesus on the cross and had been haunting me ever since I had first seen it: I Thirst.

It was Jesus's call of the heart. Thirsting for love. One love? Simple. Unconditional. The love a mother has for her child. Love for all, as one, whatever the color of our skin, whether we wore a cross, an ankh, or a star around our neck; prayed in a cathedral, a mosque, or a tree trunk; spoke in Hindi or French, Chinese, German, Portuguese, Afrikaans, or Japanese. That's why "I thirst" was so important to Mother Teresa. And why there was an absence of Catholic scripture in Mother Teresa's homes. She had reached beyond her religion, beyond all religion, into the universal realm of love.

While dodging traffic as I dashed across the road to the Taj, another revelation hit me like a hammer to the head. Contrary to everything I had been taught, I knew in that moment something Mother Teresa knew but perhaps had not openly acknowledged. "I thirst." Jesus did not come here to die for our sins, as so many would interpret. He did not waste his life and death to reinforce our dark souls or to guilt us into being better citizens. If all he saw was love, all he spoke of was love, then he came to bring us good news ~ to reveal the light and to show us the power of that love.

"I thirst" was his longing.

Upon this exposé, I felt a life force slip clear out of my body. A certainty, so ingrained in my weary and ancient soul that had propped up so many other notions, had suddenly ceased to exist within me. Whatever I may have invested in that historic belief had been exorcised.

I was dizzy. Nauseated. My head pounded, and I felt distinctly as if my temperature was soaring. I felt I must run to the safety of my room, otherwise the darkness would swallow me for good. I dragged myself up the hill and, avoiding the doorman, chose instead to enter through a side door. I had to make it to my room and fast. But I had not reached it yet and the light was growing dim, my vision fuzzy.

Praying for invisibility, I shuffled past the front desk, Monica's desk, and any other warm smiley face that might step into my path to greet me since I could not have smiled back. Praying for stability, I paced myself to the elevator, but I could hardly make out which button to push, so I thrust my fist onto all of them. Perhaps I looked like I had taken in a deadly poison, but what was really happening was I was expelling a toxic substance. My skin crawled. Every muscle in my body was turning to liquid.

I was burning up.

How I got the key into the door of my suite I don't know. Once inside, my head spinning, my heart pumping wildly, my silk coat slid from my shoulders, I dropped my bag and bottle of water and made a beeline for the bed ~ but I didn't make it.

The room turned upside down, the overhead fan *whop, whop, whopped* and then a crack of lightning pierced my head. The ceiling was coming down on top of me or maybe I rose up to meet it, I didn't know, but in the next breath everything inside me collapsed.

I surrendered to the dark.

> *"Conserve everything but love.*
> *It's the greatest energy in the world.*
> *Take it with you everywhere you go*
> *and give it freely.*
> *Like sunlight, it is the most plentiful,*
> *sustainable resource we have."*

My watch indicated 10 P.M. My face was squished into the hard floor and when I tried to move, my body was a limp mess. I fought to drag myself to my knees. In the moonlight I crawled out of my clothes and begged for strength to get me onto the bed.

At that moment, the moon was my only friend. Passing overhead, windowpane by windowpane it crept closer. I lay atop the covers bathing in its luminescent light and considered my day, fraught with uncharacteristic emotions. It was crushing to admit how much fear I felt in what was a truly harmless situation. But I had been locked in fear, paralyzed to change what was happening.

As the moon's blue glow caressed my body, revealing my shadowed emotions, I considered its gift. It showed me light can grow and illuminate the dark, but darkness is incapable of expanding anything.

Darkness sucks energy. Light inflates energy. Just as fear, the opposite of love is devoid of love, fear leads us nowhere. Love opens up the universe. When we feel love, it overpowers all sense of doubt, anxiety or stress, apprehension or paranoia. Unquestionably, love has the power to transform everything in its path. It was Mother Teresa's medium.

As the moon rose higher its illumination abandoned my room and left me adrift in its shadows. The recoiling feeling of panic returned to my stomach to remind me yet again of the encounter I'd had with the young man at the zoo. I was baffled. I wanted to think it through, but I could no longer fight sleep.

The dark swept me through a portal of time and space.

The distant roar of a lion woke me.

What roused me was a sharp rustle in the brush nearby. Alert, I sat up in bed and looked out the open window.

Remarkably I was conscious that I was not in my hotel room in Calcutta.

I was deep in a jungle wilderness. Africa, I think, or perhaps Indonesia. It was a long, long time ago. I slid quickly off my cot and onto the dirt floor. Quietly I slipped on the habit of a missionary nun and looked outside to where he slept, but he was not there this night. Wanting to call to him I searched my mind for his name . . . Tarrrk oo. Taku. There was no r in his name, but I knew to pronounce it. Taku. That was it. As soon as I found the sound of his name, the hologram of our relationship and my history with him ignited in my mind-screen.

Taku was my best friend. He had saved my life many years ago when I was 18 and had just arrived in this land. My Sisters and I had been walking this island, sharing our stories of Jesus to the indigenous people.

In some villages we were not always welcomed. Perhaps it was because we looked different, for our skin was pale and our clothing strange. Perhaps it was fear of change for our stories were empowering to many; the women and children had taken easily to the new language of English and were especially excited by the parables in Jesus's journey. More than once upon returning to a parish we would find the Bible we left burned. And fear in eyes where we had seen love.

This day we were walking from one such village and were ambushed by a band of native men. Brother James was slain immediately. My Sisters were raped and killed. I was the last to be violated.

Suddenly a very tall and powerful black man was pulling the attackers from me. What happened after that, Taku and I never spoke of. The look I saw in his eyes then I would never see again, as Taku's eyes had a warmth that was comforting and true. But that night his eyes were burning as if they would ignite to a cinder whomever they looked upon.

I had awakened the morning after that horrible incident to find Taku sitting beside me, watching. I was alone now. I felt shame and anger, and I wondered why I had been spared, to now teach everything I needed to learn.

I had no choice but to continue my work.

Holding tightly to my faith, I journeyed on, fearful. I mistrusted Taku and tried to dissuade him from following me. But I could not make him go away. Wherever I went, Taku would be there, ten paces behind. When I visited a village, he would wait, always where he could keep me in his sight. Though at first I did not speak to him or look directly at him, he remained with me as I continued my work carrying the teachings of Jesus's love to the people in the wilderness. In time, we became as one, as if our souls had made an invisible agreement that our lives would be united in this way.

The mothers and children were glad for my Bible stories, but most of the men did not like my disruption into their lives. It was difficult for me to look into a man's eyes without remembering those who had ravaged and murdered my Sisters. For a long time I saw Taku as a man, and even though he had saved me, I feared him, just like the men who had so savagely attacked my body and raped my spirit. I was reminded of the teachings of Luke 8:50. "Fear not. Believe only." And I realized Taku had risen above the gender separation and was wiser than anyone I could comprehend. Each day his presence was a healing for me. God could not have sent me a better guide and guardian and rarely did Taku leave my side.

But this time a messenger had brought word that something serious had happened to one of his family members and he was needed elsewhere. He would be gone for three days. Saying good-bye was not easy for either of us. We hugged and yet in the deep brown pools of Taku's stare as he pulled away from me, I saw a look of caution.

The sound outside came again. I took my heavy gold cross from the mantel. It was the cross I traveled with, the cross the women honored and kissed for they knew the love of Jesus would teach and guide their children. I wedged it into the tie at my waist. The love of our Jesus would be my protection. The noise in the brush became louder. At first I thought it was the echo of a leopard, but as I stepped outside into the warm air, the rustling rang out again and I was sure this time it was a human noise.

I had watched Taku many times as he listened to the colors and shapes of sounds, to distinguish one animal from another. This animal was human ~ I was sure of it. Then came a whimpering, like that of a helpless, wounded child. Oh dear. I ran across the clearing toward the bushes, the cry calling me closer to the jungle and farther from my hut. When I realized I had strayed too far for safety, it was too late. Terror gripped my throat. In the next instant there was sharp pain in my back and then a tearing in my side. I fell to my knees.

"Oh God . . . ," I called out, but my cry was cut off as my body exploded in a sensation of being torn in two. I rose up from the pain and looked down. There they were ~ two native men. One reached to my waist and pulled out my precious gold cross and held it up victoriously. The moonlight caught the warm brilliance of the crucifix.

As if speaking to me, the cross echoed, "Father, forgive them, for they know not what they do." I realized my murder was not of their making. It was my fear that had drawn them to me.

Upon this realization, the light abruptly changed and from the darkness, the sun rose up. The birds sang and a great peace fell upon the bloody violence where my body lay.

First I could hear his breath and then I saw him. Taku was running across the hills. From the pace of his breathing I knew he had been running most of the night. Taku knew. He knew the message had been a sham and our separation a plot.

In his higher knowing, he always knew how it was with me. We had been in each other's company for so long, he could feel me from a great distance. He felt my feeling. We lived beyond words.

I did not want to see Taku find me, for I did not want to see again the look of rage erupt from his eyes as I had seen the day we met. And I knew he would not want me to witness his violence.

I asked the God-ness in all man and nature to take care of Taku to ease any pain his heart would feel at my passing and to calm any anger that might grow in him. I asked God's forgiveness for my murderers.

Grateful and loving them all for their participation in this life journey, I thanked them. Then I turned from this world and went to reunite with the light.

"Might it be possible one day to harness
the power of love,
the way we harness energy?"

Easter Sunday, April 11, 1993

The sun rose and rolled across my bed like a warm, affectionate lover, returning light to my world. Intuitively, I lay quite still to let the dream that had felt so lucid, so palpable, so much a thread in my DNA, play back and settle in my consciousness. I had rested my head on the pillow last night, tense and confused, and now I was very much at peace. In the invisibility of night, light had shone upon my lagging faith and its strength had been restored. The fear that was so present in me yesterday had been completely eclipsed by the love of Taku.

I recalled reading something, and forgive me if I can't credit the author, that described what occurred when the missionaries went out into the world. It said, "When the white missionaries came, they had the Bible and we had the land. They said, 'Let us pray.' We closed our eyes. When we opened them, we had the Bible and they had the land."

Without the perspective of the bigger picture, are we all innocent bystanders until time shapes our destiny and we become history?

Easter Sunday. The day a miracle made history. To live in the moment of now, every day is a miracle. Birth, a miracle. Death, a miracle! And life in between ~ the time we are given to frolic together on this canvas of mortal dimension ~ is indeed miraculous. But what if we brought the power of the invisible into the real corporeal world? What then could we do?

The magic of the unseen world languished inside me as I stared up at the ornate ceiling with its centerpiece fan whirring overhead. Its blades invisible, like an airplane propeller that you cannot see when spinning but will surely shred you to bits should you walk into it.

If memories, dreams, and emotions are covert cohorts in our life experience, what of past lives? I was here in the land Mother Teresa had chosen as home base for her life's work, tending those whose faith was not merely intrinsic to the cycle of reincarnation ~ it was a fundamental law of their holy yet daily universe.

The Hindu belief of the body being merely temporary while the spiritual self lives on and is held accountable for all its choices, returning again and again, until it returns no more, having achieved the ultimate freedom from rebirth and reached Nirvana, seems far more plausible than poof, you're dead. Nothing.

Nothing supernatural, nothing heretical or earth-shattering. Simply a valid explanation to the crazy magnetic pull of first-sight love. And here, with each passing day, it was becoming an affirmation for those feelings I'd had since arriving: those unmistakable "instant" recognitions.

My mind raced. *Why aren't we digging around in that 80 or so percentile of our unused mind power? Could past-life regression become the objectifying therapy of the future? Likening it to traditional therapy that asks us to peel off the layers of our childhood, to resolve the barriers holding us back in life, to heal those illusive, invisible scars ~ but deeper? Could digging holographically into the life of the soul allow us to interact with the wisdom of our soul's growth from childhood to maturity? Over eons from young to old soul? Could this be the path to understand our relationship with one another on a multidimensional level so that we may wake to the vaster picture of greater awareness?*

Awake I needed to be.

I crawled out of bed and wandered the room touching every stick of furniture, making contact with every visible, solid manifestation of what I had come to believe was the real and present world, knowing my dream would remain long after the furniture was firewood.

So I ask you now ~ have you ever had a feeling, a dream, a remembrance of something that in this life you could not explain?

We are immutable energy; we are timeless beings. When we reconnect with certain other life energies, memories surface and our dreamtime becomes active in sorting out the scenario. I must have found a missing piece of myself, an aspect I didn't even know was missing, for when I showered, I threw my head back and daringly exposed my pores to the water, feeling more solid and more complete than I could recall.

I toweled down lightly, wiggling myself awake and dancing around the room to be certain I was present, in my body, to be sure I would be treading on pavement today and not on clouds, for I had much to accomplish.

I had to prove, if only to myself ~ earthbound miracles do exist.

"Each morning, as the sun rises,
like fresh orange juice spilling into a blue ocean,
we are reminded of this moment of clarity,
when the Sun of God rose up ~
to show us love can never die."

He is risen. Father. Sun. Holy Spirit.

Yes, the sun had risen and I was running late. Any apprehension I might have had was eclipsed by the knowledge that today was Easter Sunday. I dressed in anticipation. Mother Teresa was about to emerge from her silence.

My heart pumped wildly as I traveled down in the elevator, with its mirrors telling me I am just human, but with my heart wishing its doors would part and *tada!* I was miraculously trans-ported to the ground floor of the Motherhouse. My heart said yes! With discipline and faith, as in all things, we could be like Jesus and project ourselves from one place to another. I could make the quantum leap from the hotel to the Motherhouse in an instant, but my mind, my limiting mind said, *Not possible! You will never understand that equation.*

The mind can contemplate construction of the great pyramids, take us to the moon, dominate the world even, but the technolog-ical mind will not grasp mechanics it perceives are beyond its realm. That's why we must empty our minds to make space for inspiration, divinity, the creation of a miracle, the concept of ascension. That's why "the mind" can never take us home, to rest in peace.

Think less, Christina, I told myself.

It was ballet. The doorman pirouetted on his toes, sweeping me through the gold revolving doorway, bowing deeply, gliding behind me and enunciating in his finest English, "A very good day to you, Miss Christina."

"It's a wonderful day, thank you," I said, gracing his palm with rupees.

My driver was not appearing from below as he usually did. Perhaps he, too, had slept in. The doorman nodded to me that he would run to fetch him, but I waved him away saying I would find him myself.

There he was, happily snoozing at the bottom of the intricately tiled driveway, so I ventured down. As I stepped carefully over the work of art, I found myself getting lost in the hundreds of tiles. Many had a beautifully aged patina and many were new and freshly cut. I marveled at how they were chosen to fit together to create one exquisite expression of shape and color. I thought of people, young and old, all different shades and shapes, life paths and choices and how we fit together to create elaborate, complicated, multilayered lives. I stepped consciously upon the tiles as I did when I walked the cobblestone streets of Paris, knowing every stone with its own shape and size carried its own unique history. And though, just like people, their fit may be uneven at first, as time blended them, with centuries and lifetimes of people walking, horses' hooves pounding over them followed by carriages and then cars ~ the stones become molded together so they fit perfectly. Molded to mesh until they are one with each other.

Certainly it could be that way with human beings. Centuries and lifetimes of being together ~ as a mother, a father, a son, a co-worker, a neighbor, a friend, a foe even ~ weaving a family of relationships, influencing one another's characters and embedding in one another's memories until you meet, for what you believe is the very first time, and yet, in an instant and with that wealth of history, you fit! Perfectly.

My heart skipped a beat when I wondered then if that is what we in the world have to look forward to ~ everyone finding their soul connections, until we all simply merge back into one.

In the midst of my musing, my trusty chauffeur had snapped awake, pulled forward, and swish, that door was open!

What a day to be late for morning Mass, I thought. Though I gave him no inkling I was in a hurry, my driver dodged oncoming traffic as if it were the 24th hour of Le Mans. Weaving through the city, zipping along back streets, turning on two wheels, beating amber lights all the way to Bose Road, I did my part by casting all fear from my mind. And there, the checkered flag!

Two steps at a time I climbed up both staircases to the chapel, landing on my spot beside the entrance with minutes to spare, beating the rush of Sisters, volunteers, and sightseers by seconds.

White flowers of all shapes and sizes adorned the table, atop a slightly different white cloth with simple gold embroidery. And there again was the Bible, a golden plate, and a golden chalice. On the floor around the dais and beneath Jesus on the cross were more vases of white flowers with gift cards. Like fireflies, celebration sparked the sunlit air as the Sisters, all glowing in their white saris with blue borders, and the Sisters-in-training, virgin visions in all white, seemed to glide across the floor, quietly dropping to their knees in perfectly neat rows. A quiet anticipation filled the air for this special Sunday Mass. Soon, it was standing room only.

Every day in the Motherhouse the air was filled with an effervescent happiness, yet today it was even bubblier. Smiles all around. I saw "my" Sisters, the ones I "knew" from who knows where or when, and I wondered if they "recognized" me. And then, my doubting little brain jumped immediately into debate. *Stop!* I had to say. *Stop!*

If we do have lifetimes preceding this one, no wonder my poor mind has so many contradictory thoughts. No wonder we are so often in our own personal battle of wits. And how easy it is for us to erode our confidence, undermine our intention, sabotage our success, even violate our integrity. The mind is clever and profoundly creative but sometimes it can be my staunchest enemy.

A young Hindu volunteer was passing out hymnbooks, and as he handed one to the girl beside me, she dropped it. He picked it up, apologizing profusely. She waved his apology off by whispering that she is all thumbs. *There it was,* I thought. Her mind decided "I am all thumbs" and her body responded by dropping things. I'm with quantum physics on this one. *From now on,* I told myself, *watch your lazy, haphazard thoughts. Especially about yourself. Catch them if you can, clean them up, clear them out, and replace them with the thoughts you choose. Be kind to yourself. Live more from the heart and less from the mind.*

The piano began, our hearts broke open, and we burst into song, the music of the angels proclaiming, "He is risen." It seemed our bodies rose with our voices, levitating us all from the earthly floor and for the next exquisite hour or so until Mass was over, we were outside of time itself, hovering motionless, infused with the ecstasy of Easter Sunday's ethereal realization.

Once everyone had taken Communion, a hush fell over the prayer room. The only one to move was Mother Teresa. She lightly picked herself up from beside me, vanished briefly, and then reappeared, holding high, for us all to see, an intricately chiseled gold cross. Sunlight glistened upon it, and its brilliant light echoed my dream of the night before.

First the Sisters and then the volunteers, who had overflowed into the corridor outside the prayer room, came forward in a groundswell and each standing in line, inching forward, touched the cross with their lips. Mother moved to different sections of the sanctuary holding the heavy golden crucifix in front of her to give everyone the opportunity. A volunteer passed me, murmuring blissfully, "I kissed Mother's cross." Each time there was an opening in the line of people,

Mother Teresa would turn pointedly to me, seemingly perplexed as to why I would not step forward. But all sorts of emotions were churning through me, and I could not bring myself to move. I am not Catholic and I was unclear as to the meaning of kissing her cross, yet I had not forgotten my dream and the gold cross that had been my ankh, my scepter, my wand.

Finally Mother moved to the doorway and stood opposite me, offering it. Her brown eyes glowed at me. I looked at the ornate cross in her hands and the light caught it and reflected in her eyes. It was calling me, and I was paralyzed. It was her eyes that stopped me. The deep brown pools I knew so well.

Lastly, she pushed her cross straight at me, beckoning me to do what everyone else had. I smiled warmly but did not move.

I held myself erect and proud in recognition of an old and faithful friend who had been at my side and had taught me a courageous lesson: to trust my fellow man.

This was the day it all began. The event that broke history into two parts ~ the Resurrection. Today ~ the anniversary of the part that became the heart of Christianity.

Jesus, a simple Jewish rabbi, was at the epicenter of what until that time had been a small movement infused with tales of miraculous visions and healings. Yet as the story goes, on this day, of all his miracles, this was the greatest.

Broken, crying in misery, Mary Magdalene found it strange and alarming when she saw the stone rolled back and the tomb where Jesus's body, wrapped in linen cloth, was laid to rest ~ empty.

"Someone stole his body." She wept.

At first Mary mistook him for the gardener, but when he spoke, she recognized the man she loved and lost, unstained of death. Standing there before her was a vision that reawakened her heart. Sinking to her knees, she reached out to him.

"Touch me not," he said. "For I am not yet ascended to my father." Her tears flowed again, but this time they were cool and fresh, like a spring rain.

"You were dreaming, Mary. You have deceived yourself," said the disciples when she told them Jesus had risen. "Look at me and see if it is not true. Could I be this happy if Jesus were really dead?"

His apostles, who had been so dedicated and yet so terrified of being crucified along with him, denied their hearts' murmur and fled. With his piteous death, their hopes were dashed and in their bereavement lamented the confusion they felt and the failure of his mission. It was not until he broke bread with them ~ the wound of the nail clearly visible on his right hand ~ that they lifted their eyes and knew he was alive. Courage and faith swept back into their hearts, and they too were inspired to go out into the world to risk their lives and indeed some gave them, to spread the word, to tell the story.

Forty days passed between the Resurrection and the Ascension of Jesus into the Kingdom of Heaven, and in that time he was seen far and wide, on the road to Emmaus, on the shore of the Sea of Tiberias, on a mountain in Galilee. People everywhere, even those who had slain him, saw or realized there existed another dimension of their reality and they, too, became transformed.

Even James, Jesus's younger brother, who told one and all that Jesus was crazy, out of his mind while alive, would become so empowered that he risked his life and was eventually stoned to death for speaking of his brother. Jesus the man, who came back from the dead to become Jesus the Redeemer. Liberating us from our limiting beliefs.

Normally, when you rid a movement of its leader, the movement collapses and fades into history. This was the reverse. This was the day when hope grew for those who feared, and a religion was born for those who disbelieved. The day a great truth was forged: love cannot be vanquished even after it has been crucified. Hallelujah!

"Loving everyone is easy
when we love the one God in them all."

Everyone around me was gazing upon Mother with an almost pop-star adoration. For myself, a calm flowed through every fiber of my being.

As bizarre as it may seem, I knew it was Mother who resembled Taku so completely. Ever since she had touched my forehead in the alleyway, my soul had been calling out for healing on many levels. Definitely, there was a reason she had come to me in my dream, a stranger from a strange land. I had felt an indescribable closeness for someone whose personal history was so foreign to mine. And yet reaching from the deep recesses of time, my amnesia gone, those same dark eyes were peering intently at me now from behind her gold cross. She had been my guide, my protector, my teacher of faith and forgiveness. I remembered. Would she?

I was so overwhelmed with hope all I could do was let my eyes drop.

Mother Teresa was using her mind to obey the Catholic Church. Her staunch obedience to judgmental, limiting beliefs had to be in direct conflict with the supernatural testament of her work. She lived overwhelmingly from the freedom of her heart.

I wondered if she ever held discourse with her sense of certitude on the chasms between the mystical and the pragmatic, the visionary who must step outside the box, even throw the box away if need be, and the submissive who must remain inside the box, be obedient to the rules of its confinement, the rules of her Church, the eternal contradiction between the power of love and the love of power.

I tried to silence the doubting Thomas inside, who blindly refused to believe Jesus had returned from the dead until he could actually place his finger on the wounds.

Soon I will know, I told myself. I would know if she recognized me from some deep part of her soul or if this journey had truly been a flight of fancy. Soon I would have proof if I was dealing with truth or fiction. I would know because I had to know.

I was about to take a great risk with my heart because I had no other choice.

CHAPTER TWELVE

THE WISH IS ALREADY GRANTED

Christina Stevens

*"There comes a time in all things,
when there is nothing more to do
than to wait ~ in full expectation."*

Monday, April 12, 1993

Half past dawn. Monday after Easter. My heart was on the line,
and I was running again, late for morning prayers. In contrast to
yesterday, my driver was uncharacteristically sluggish in his naviga-
tion of the arising Calcutta streets. I hated being late, yet it's exactly
that trepidation, that focus of fear, that will invariably put red lights
and roadblocks in the way.

Catching my thoughts, I took control of my inner panic, and it
served me well. Breathing deep and insisting on calm must have also

tranquilized my driver as he became more deliberate and put some kind of spell on the traffic around us. We sailed through town and all parted at will.

Funny how that happens. The Los Angeles grid system of multi-dimensional crisscross highways, overpassing, underpassing, where everyone drives anywhere from 30 to 90 miles an hour can be overwhelming to the uninitiated. And then there's navigating the Champs-Élysées, or the no-limit autobahn. There must be some sort of collective consciousness we tap into when we get into our automobiles or some kind of mass meditative state we enter because there are far fewer accidents than one would expect. Some days even I will turn onto my exit thinking it a miracle I hadn't encountered a deadly pileup.

Elegantly, we pulled over to the curb on Bose Road and in the nick of time. Yesterday, there was too much excitement in the air for me to even think of approaching Mother Teresa. Today, though, felt right.

After prayers Adriana hugged me at the top of the stairs. She looked refreshed. Her face held an aliveness I hadn't noticed before.

"The fish!" she said happily.

Fishers of men? I wondered, puzzled.

Suddenly the crowd swelled, untidily separating us. I was carried off in one direction and Adriana was pulled down the stairs.

"Oh?" I called as she stood on her toes on the landing.

"The fishes swimming in the love ocean," she called out, as she was about to be swallowed by the visions in white, carrying her backward.

Cool. She got the fishes. "Yes! We're swimming in it now," I called back.

"Love. It's all love," she shouted quickly before she went out of sight on the second landing.

As if floating on my own tsunami of love, momentum swept me beyond the stairway, away from the chapel, and onto a bridge. When the crowd dispersed, I found myself on a sunny open breezeway, in the middle of a gathering of around 15 people. They all looked quite intro-spective, no doubt rehearsing their requests for prayers and blessings.

Without a word between us we found our place on three wooden benches, facing one another along the breezeway that was actually a bridge leading to Mother Teresa's office. At the end was an opening with a sheer white curtain instead of a door. I selected the bench farthest from the doorway. Instinctively I knew this was the spot for me to wait, just as I had felt the inside doorway was my place to be in the prayer room. From where I sat, I could see an open window with sheers billowing but nothing beyond the edge of a rather beaten-up wooden desk inside. All I could hear up here was an old manual typewriter feverishly tapping away in some distant room and a humming whirl of activity everywhere else.

After a short time, a tall, elegant, and rather imposing Sister strode confidently through the doorway. One by one, she leaned down to quietly question the intention of each person waiting. I had the sense she might be Sister Priscilla, who had faxed me and told me not to come. I looked straight ahead and willed myself invisible. If it worked or not I will never know, but sure enough, she passed over me.

When she was done, only five plus me remained. Beside me, a young woman shared with us all her excitement about wanting to involve Mother Teresa in a book she was intending to write. The others held their own counsel. When Mother finally emerged through the white gauze, she scanned the area and swiftly decided in what order to meet with us.

She gave a family her blessing. They thanked her profusely and left. She bid farewell to a young man who had been volunteering. He left. She now came over to the bench I sat on and no sooner had the young woman stated her intention than she gave the excited author a polite but firm "No, I do not wish to do this. It would not be right for me." Disappointment rankled the young woman's body language as she reluctantly departed.

Mother Teresa looked over to me and I smiled, fully expecting her to step in my direction. For a second our eyes locked. But then she turned away and disappeared back into her office.

Does she not want to talk with me? Have I made a terrible mistake? My nagging fears were quelled by the fact that as I watched her leave, I wasn't sure, but I had the vivid impression she was floating rather than walking. Feeling somewhat perplexed, while at the same time elated I had not been kicked out, I remained there, alone on the bench.

And waited.

♡♡♡

My back ached. I don't know how long I had been there before I realized it had been a long time. I didn't care. This was the only place I needed to be. The air was still and growing warmer. Faintly, in the distance I could hear voices singing. They stopped and began again. Ah, they were rehearsing.

The din of the street outside hung in the atmosphere like an ever-present mantra, spiced at times by the rustling of crisp, sun-dried cotton saris as the Sisters hurried about their day. A symphony of sounds traveled through the open corridors and up the floors. A typewriter tapping here, water running there, dishes clattering somewhere else, the choir rehearsing elsewhere. I was trying to put my finger on what all those disparate sounds were reminding me of, because they were creating their own seamless opus.

I focused on their rehearsal. As the pianist began her introduction, I felt myself being carried off into another more familiar musical intro. I was no longer in the Motherhouse but in the AMP theatre in Sydney, Australia, seeing images as if watching a movie.

An old, lined hand opened the sheet music to *The Pajama Game.* It was the hand of my grandmother, Madam, a towering director of the theater who took the young and not so young, the talented and not so talented, and put them on the stage. She taught them how to dance, how to sing, how to act, all with passion yet varying degrees of success.

We had our own theater company, and on Thursday and Friday nights we performed musicals and melodramas. Saturday, during the day, we put on two matinees of children's pantomimes, "Birthday parties our specialty," and on Saturday nights, we put on a modern revue or attempted Shakespeare. In between, we rehearsed.

There were a few actors seated in the darkened area of the theater waiting for their moment in the spotlight. On stage workmen were hammering a backdrop into place, and props were being wheeled across backstage, while a group of actors stood directionless center stage.

The pianist was absent and so, in her impatient style, Madam was pounding out the musical introduction to "Hernando's Hideaway." She looked up at the huddle on stage.

"Christina! Christina! Now, where is that girl?" she demanded from the cast.

The actors meekly looked at one another. One courageously stepped forward, and said, "She's not here yet."

Madam rose and proclaimed to one and all, "She thinks that because she's my granddaughter, she can come to rehearsals anytime she pleases. She hasn't made one rehearsal yet! I'll take one of her numbers out." She waggled her finger threateningly into space. "She won't like that!"

The pianist was now beside her, relieved Madam's wrath was being spent on another. "She doesn't think she needs rehearsal, you see," Madam added, tacking on a sarcastic aside with the craft of one experienced at saying something intimate for an audience of hundreds to hear clearly.

Like a gust of wind, the theater door blew open and there I was, running down the center aisle, loaded with books and bags and coats. I must have been about 17 because my clothes were no longer my mother's lopsided homemade creations. I was a working girl, breathless and occupied all the time. "Sorry I'm late. I couldn't help it."

Madam growled under her breath, and everyone relaxed, knowing they were off the hook, for now. "Since Christina has blessed us with her presence, we can continue. We'll start with her first number."

I fell into an aisle seat, hoping to catch my breath, but she swung around to me.

"Well? Get up there, my girl. Now, who gives her cue?" she inquired into the air.

Those on stage looked at one another blankly and back to Madam.

"Well, you've got the scripts," she briskly stated. "Where's your script, Christina?" Without waiting for me to say I forgot it, she rose and strode over to the piano. "Where's the music?" she asked curtly.

The pianist motioned to Madam ~ the music was already open on the piano.

Madam shushed her off the stool and sat herself down.

"Where are my glasses?" she demanded of all and sundry. No one was valiant enough to remind her that as always, her glasses were perched on her head. "Oh, it doesn't matter," she scoffed.

Two chords and then she launched, once again, into "Hernando's Hideaway." I pivoted to see a stage full of bewildered faces mirroring my own.

Once more Madam stopped and swiveled to face a small audience of actors sitting in the back of the theater. "Stop that chattering!" she ordered, and spun back to face the stage. "And stop that hammering," she demanded of the carpenters, who were not afraid of this ancient powerhouse, and they didn't stop their hammering until they chose to.

As she continued pounding out her own choppy intro, my mind reeled. *Oh God, she's in prime form today, and I don't know the words. I've never looked at the music. But I've got to do something or she'll*—my mind went blank. Panic, fear, and desperation forced all thought to exit; I was screaming inside for help. I took a few short steps in time to the music, and then I opened my mouth. Nothing came out.

She repeated the intro one more time. I took three more steps, opened my mouth, and began to sing.

From some otherworldly place the lyrics took shape, and I moved across the stage as if I had been rehearsing this for weeks.

Spontaneously the cast fell into step right behind me.

My partner grabbed me and we tangoed.

There was Madam, beaming from the piano pit while we danced as if we were glued to each other. Again, I spun away from him, singing the lyrics seamlessly.

Aggressively I grabbed him and bent him over.

Having let the pianist slide onto the piano stool and take over, Madam rose to her feet, waving her arms excitedly, herself caught in our moment of unexplained magic.

I spun away and mimed to the audience, glancing at my partner with the rest of the cast mimicking me.

I turned down the line and one by one fell backward. As if they knew I would do this, someone was always there to catch me. We connected, like we had all done it 100 times before.

When the trill of the last note rang out, we all froze in dramatic poses ~ that we did not immediately relax from. There was a stunned silence. None of us could quite believe that together we had given a flowing performance. Unrehearsed and unexplainable. Not that it would have brought the house down, but we were in complete unity. We looked to one another, silent, with wide, admiring faces.

In that moment we all understood the term *inspired performance.* It would not have been credible enough to impact me if I had experienced it alone. But the others, they knew we had all tapped in to some universal energy that we could not explain. Unified movements that spoke to an entire cast, of a oneness we rarely touch upon in our hectic, day-in-day-out lives.

Madam, perhaps for the first and last time in her almost 80 years, let a tear fall. And in her inimitable fashion she let her private moment be noticed by one and all. In the next beat she turned to the pianist and commented dispassionately, "She's the fifth generation, you know."

It wasn't me, I wanted to say. *It was all of us, together. That was the magic.* Yet it was something we could hardly address. And it's something mankind shies away from ~ the impeccable connection all human beings have with one another.

That same connection was sweeping through the entire structure I was sitting in.

Jesus said, *"The Kingdom of God is within you."* What happened to the kingdom? Do we yet know the nature of the kingdom? The nature of the invisible, the all-powerful place where the creator of heaven and earth resides? The place where the God seed in each of us lives? As one? I could feel it right there, in Mother Teresa's house.

If God resides within, then it is merely the mortal body ~ skin, bones, and a hank of hair ~ that keeps us from our creator. Could you and I each possess a fragment that is aligned with the divine and miraculous principles of creation? If so, as more and more of us come together as a collective force, if we align our thoughts and our intentions, what else may we then be?

What, truly, may we then accomplish?

"There is no time like the present to be present."

In the twinkling of an eye, I was back from my daydreaming. I was present. Here, where I needed to be. Where everything in my life up to this point required me to be. The Sister at the piano played almost as poorly as Madam, yet the Sisters' voices rang out like crystal chimes, resonating in perfect unison. Abruptly their rehearsal ended, and I lifted my head to catch a glimpse of them dispersing. There was no applause, no acknowledgment of how beautifully they harmonized. In silence, save for a swish and a swirl of their saris, they scattered in all directions, in a dance that flowed with the purpose of their next task.

The Motherhouse, three floors with countless enclaves and private rooms, was alive in movement, individual, yet as one, choreographed by a higher order. I understood then how everything was orchestrated here. Mother Teresa was the earthly conductor under her God's sublime direction.

The rustle of a sari in purposeful movement nearby brought me back. "Ah, you're waiting for Mother?" she asked without stopping.

"Yes," I responded.

"I will tell her," she called lightly over her shoulder, as she broke through the sheer curtain.

"Oh, she knows . . . ," I added, but she was gone.

I pulled out my bottle of water and took a swig. The day was heating up. The morning sun crept into the courtyard below while a warm, dry wind swept across the breezeway. I glanced at my watch. Another hour had passed. Just then a Sister arrived with a beautiful little girl who had been adopted and was leaving Shishu Bhavan.

Immediately Mother Teresa broke through the curtain, hugged the tot, and raised her up into the air, cooing, "So beautiful." She pronounced each vowel with such precision it gave the word *booutiiiifoool* a color and joy that made me smile. She held the child out to me, as if to draw my attention to the happy face of the little one who was off to a new life. The Sister peered over to me, very excited.

"Do you have a camera?" Mother asked.

You could have blown me away with fairy dust. Never without a camera in my purse, all the signs forbidding photography were so absolute I had unhesitatingly obeyed their rules. I stood up and shook my head.

"No, I'm sorry."

Mother hugged the child close, as the Sister explained to me, "She leaves us today. She goes to a very good family in France. They have been waiting a long time for her."

When Mother Teresa put her down, she continued to caress the little girl's head as she and the Sister discussed a few other details. Then Mother tilted the little girl's head up to her, cupped her chin in her palm, and said her final farewell and blessing upon the child.

The Sister and the little girl departed, and Mother turned on her bare heels and went back to her office. This time I was certain ~ her feet were definitely not touching the ground.

Sinking back into the wooden bench, I hoped when Mother was ready to speak to me, she would. Over the next hour, many Sisters passed by smiling sweetly, acknowledging my presence.

"Who are you waiting for?" one asked.

"Mother Teresa."

Another Sister passed by in the other direction, and as if in midconversation, she smiled. "She will be out to speak with you soon."

For a second or so, the lesser part of me thought that perhaps I was unworthy of Mother's attention and that this delay was a gentle hint that she had no time for me and I should just get the message and steal away. But the greater part of me knew this was not true. She did not make it her task to judge people.

I had read magazine articles where famous people had traveled oceans to talk with Mother Teresa and had been sent away without an audience. I had read where Mother Teresa had been criticized for entertaining the presence of certain others, some of whom were believed to be unsavory characters in the world of politics and human rights. I felt sure these critics did not understand her perspective.

She appeared tough, and indeed shrewd, and her awareness spread across great distances and though she was not blind to a person's failures, she looked deeper. She saw God in every face she looked upon.

From our phone calls I believed she was as human as you and me. That she felt the same anxieties and disappointments, the same frustrations and impatience you and I feel. I realized the difference with her was where we would remain stuck in the disappointment, become hurt or angry or vengeful or simply confused, she processed those emotions without pause. It was what guaranteed that she remain a clean instrument for her work. I don't believe she negated negative feelings; she simply gave them no charge, no energy, moving through them to stay focused on the higher task.

Her love extinguished anything less.

It occurred to me that speedily processing negative energy blocks could be another one of those tools needed to create a miracle. Then again it would be a good tool to navigate simple daily life.

Restlessly I looked at my watch again. Catching this I stepped back and observed myself and immediately ceased all fake and nervous activity.

I inhaled a whiff of warm Calcutta air, gasoline fumes spiced with sweet aromas of curry that became their incense. From a deep cave in my mind, words echoed. "I am right where I am meant to be." Tension fell from my shoulders, my back straightened, my toes unfurled, my body relaxed, and I was at ease. Surrendering completely to a higher schedule.

It seemed an eternity passed or no time went by, I didn't know any longer, when the white curtain wafted out and she moved directly toward me, opening her arms wide.

"Ah, you wait so long," she almost sang.

I stood to meet her.

"Mother, I would wait for you forever."

Even as I said those words, I had no idea where they came from. But they felt exactly right.

Our greeting gave me the feeling that everything we were about to say we had said before.

Impulsively I reached out and took her hands. Yes, I knew I should have asked permission to touch her. Or waited for a signal or a sign from her that it was okay. Or simply displayed a little decorum and given her the same consideration I would meeting anybody for the first time. But I didn't and I couldn't. For I felt I knew her in the depth of my soul, and she was irresistible to me. I took her hands in mine and I didn't want to ever let them go.

I have always been prepared for planned first meetings, knowing if spontaneity doesn't take over, I have a script I can rely upon. But as my gaze traveled from her hands to her eyes there was an enticement I have never before encountered, and at once I fell overboard and sank into her softness. When I resurfaced, we were sitting on the bench, our knees almost touching, our faces close, in a conversation that simply flowed.

We spoke for some time, about what I will never be able to accurately relate, not because I have forgotten, but because what she said to me is so much a part of the person I have become, it could never be expressed as words on a page. Words can be so limiting. Her thoughts, and the feelings she inspired in me are what remain, not the dialogue itself.

My entire being was experiencing a renewal, as if my cells had turned over and every part of my being was reenergized from deep within. I had always believed love came from inside us. That we conjured it up in some manner. That because we felt it so deeply that was where it was born. But being in Mother Teresa's presence taught me that love was outside of us. It could be gathered, focused, and projected. She reinforced what I had felt when flying. Love was in the air, and she energized that air around her so completely that when a person stepped into her space it was like taking a bath in the truth. I was literally "in love."

Sometime during those first few minutes I understood that while I had certainly felt love in my life, romantic love, familial love, sibling love, friendly love, puppy love, unattainable love, possessive love, crazy passionate stupid messy love, I had never touched true unconditional love in this fashion.

It snapped me back to why I had come this far.

"Mother, I have come to film you, so you may speak your message of love to the world."

"Oh, no cameras. No cameras." Her tone was light and lilting but most definitely adamant. I couldn't give up so easily.

"Cameras are tools of communication, a way to spread your message."

"It is not permitted," she said firmly, cutting me off with a conviction that should I travel to the Vatican or even approach God himself, permission would not, nay, could not be granted.

"There are so many who do not know you. So many who cannot travel the distance I have, to look into your eyes, like this. To be touched by you, like this."

"I am a humble servant."

"Yes, but one day . . ."

She squeezed my hands, pleading for me to understand and give up.

"I say no to governments, I say no to royalty. I cannot say yes to you."

"Mother, you have said the hand has five fingers. Each finger is unique. Each excels in its own different task, and yet each finger is an indispensable part of the one hand." I smiled and gently turned her hand over, stroking her palm. "I am another finger of the hand that is your work."

"Yes, God bless," she responded.

"Mother, what inspired me to . . ." I wanted to tell her of my vision and her calling to "come soon," but something spoke in my ear and said, *This is not necessary. She is here beside you, she is here with you now.* She quieted my chatter by nodding and squeezing her eyes in a smile, as if she already knew it all anyway.

Her eyes penetrated to the very soul of me, and I felt tears well up. I reentered my mind and thought I was making a mess of this whole thing.

Concern crossed her face.

Then, as she watched the single tear slide down my cheek she drew in her brow. "Oh no!" She groaned. Uneasy, she reached over and touched the naked silver chain I was wearing around my neck.

"You don't have a medal."

She immediately rose and disappeared back into her office. I felt as if the tear on my cheek had flowed all the way from whence I had decided on a future of mistrust and separation. A tear that had waited too long to be shed. In a heartbeat that tear turned into a stream, threatening to become a river and then a flood.

In the next breeze she was back on the bench beside me.

"Here is your medal. It is Our Lady." She lovingly pressed the silver oval medal with the imprint of praying hands on one side and Mother Mary on the other into my palm. My weeping stopped. I wrapped my fingers around my consolation prize.

"God bless you," she said. Her head tilted and her entire face smiled, good-bye.

And she was gone.

Wistfully I moseyed back to my hotel, quietly scolding myself for being so unprofessional that I would cry. I couldn't be certain if it was in response to her denying me permission or being in the cleansing presence of her love. Emotions have never been on my list of how to persuade even the toughest nuts, and personally, I have already told you ~ I don't cry. Or didn't.

A little tear told me that was about to change.

The gold revolving door closed out the grime of Calcutta and the serene hum of the Taj put everything on hold for the next few hours.

"Ahh. Miss Christina Stevens," called the bellman, grinning proudly from ear to ear. "I have the message. All the way from America. Your telephone rang immediately upon your departure this morning."

"Yeah! The cavalry got through," I joked.

The bellman's smile didn't widen. He had no idea how dismal the phone system was in India. Yes, I know it was just two decades ago, but back in 1993, before technical support or customer service was sent offshore and became big business for India, the nation's phone system was hardly functional. He bowed deeply as he offered a golden dish with a note, folded at its center.

It was from "Jilli." It took me a moment. *Ah, Gilly.* It read: "Mark is out of control. When are you coming home? Happy birthday. We love you. We miss you. We really miss you."

Clutching my silver medal I went up to my room. I wove my medal through the chain and put it around my neck before letting my body collapse onto the bed.

I thought Mother would see what a good idea this was. I thought she might have some recognition of me, no matter how vague. I thought she would realize I had been called, too. And although she had granted me a deeply intimate meeting, that didn't seem to be the case.

I picked up the receiver and asked the operator to get me the United States. I gave her Mark's home number, figuring he would be waking around this time.

Suddenly, once again I was overtaken by a dizzy, nauseous feeling. My stomach felt bloated and my body ached all the way to my bones. This place was making me sick. How wonderful it would be right now to shower without thinking. To eat a fresh salad without examining every ingredient. Or eat anything that didn't taste like curry. Perhaps it was time to go home. Chalk this journey up to a once-in-a-lifetime, wouldn't-trade-it-for-gold experience and get back to work. Mark was spinning out of control. I knew it. Nayeem would understand. I won't get my money back, but already this journey had been priceless. Mark will be delighted.

It took ten minutes, but the operator finally rang through.

"Goodness, I hope I didn't wake you!"

"Yes. Hello." It was Nayeem. I was not ready to talk with Nayeem, but there he was.

"Oh, Nayeem. Hello. Look . . . I'm sorry to tell you this but it appears Mother Teresa will not be giving us her permission after all."

"But she must!" Nayeem cried urgently through the earpiece.

How could I explain she was a woman who stood firmly by her beliefs and convictions? Stubborn, actually, and no correspondence would be entered into.

"If you had met her, you would understand."

"But we are all boarding the plane. Tomorrow morning! You must convince her," he said sincerely.

"I am not sure any amount of convincing will have—"

"You have come all this way to us. And we are coming to you. You must speak to her again. You must convince her!" Nayeem repeated before he hung up.

I wasn't up to arguing with anybody. My stomach turned over, and my head throbbed. I had been diligent in taking precautions against intestinal illnesses; brushing my teeth with bottled water and being very careful about what I had been eating. More than that, though, I was in emotional turmoil.

What had I been imagining? I should have donated the funds to Mother's missionary rather than wasting them on this fruitless escapade. It would have been so much easier. Write a check and hand it to her.

"When your mind is filled with worry and fear,
it is a sign of intellectual pride.
You are believing in your own power alone.
There is no room for God to enter.
Nothing can change until you let that go.
It's as simple as that."

Tuesday, April 13, 1993

I hadn't slept well, and at first light I showered and dressed. When I stepped through the revolving gilded doors, into the dark morning, my turbaned friend was not yet on duty. The good Dr. Michael was.

"De nouveau, ton sourire illumine ma journée." ~ Translation: Once again, your smile makes my day.

I thought I was smiling rather weakly, actually. He spoke in such a charming and attentive way he lifted my spirits. I touched his arm for his kindness and sensed a light electrical charge in the touch.

"You are leaving too soon!" he said.

"Oh, just early . . . ," I responded. Wondering if Michael knew what I was thinking, or if it was just his English.

"Tell me; how your filming is progressing?"

Once again, he peered into me with those intense eyes. Blue, I noticed now. He probably had a way of getting almost anything with that gaze, but there was no way I would take him into my morass of failure. "Every day is a challenge," I said lightly, looking around for my taxi. "Where are you going this early?" I asked.

"I have surgery in the provinces. May I take you somewhere? *À l'autre côté de monde, peut-être?*" I must have looked like I was searching to understand, when he said, "To another world perhaps?" Michael chuckled as his long legs strode over to give his driver the box of medical supplies in his arms.

My wimpy journey to the Motherhouse, to bid adieu to Mother Teresa, seemed so defeatist in the light of his life-and-death mission.

Michael's driver opened the door. It was a tantalizing invitation. My turbaned doorman appeared, setting his gold lapel in place just as my taxi motored up the hill.

"Ah, I am well taken care of, thank you."

"Make no mistake. Good news is on its way." Michael waved as he crawled into his car. Through the window his eyes bore into mine for one more second as they pulled out of the driveway.

Good news! I thought. Suddenly a surge of energy rose up through the soles of my feet, and a feeling of joy and success embedded itself in my tummy and tingled up to my head, all the way to my fingertips and beyond the boundaries of my body. *Good news is here!*

I didn't know Dr. Michael well, but for some reason and in that moment, I believed him wholeheartedly.

Morning prayers. Mother Teresa and I sat again on either side of the chapel doorway. Before the service got under way, my smaller self came out to play.

Who was I kidding? We were from opposite ends of the earth. She was a devout Catholic. I? A devout nothing. She was a revered holy woman. Recipient of the world's most prestigious humanitarian awards, a Nobel Peace Prize winner. I was an ad woman. I had won a bunch of CLIOs, a slew of International Broadcasting Awards, and a Gold Lion from the Venice Film Festival. Oh, and a couple of Air Show awards, one for owning a beauty of a plane and the other for landing on the right spot. We were as different as chalk and charcoal. Who was I kidding?

I was grateful when it came time to sing. What a relief. Music always shifts the frame of mind. Huh. Like the joy and health she felt when her Sisters sang for her. They gave her a sense of high when she was feeling low. When she had a change of feeling, like going from down to up, from feeling sick to feeling well, she had a change of intention ~ and it created a change of destiny. Her life turned around. She knew this to be true.

I knew I had to try, one more time, to share with her the importance of her speaking to the world. Sharing her wisdom with those who would listen. Whether there were 1, 100, 1,000, or, from my lips to Buddha's ears, 1 million people in the world who could be moved by her words, I had to risk rejection.

Love must be brave.

CHAPTER THIRTEEN

BE THE ONE

Christina Stevens

"I am you.
You are me.
We are one."

Morning prayers ended and there was the far bench, vacant and waiting for me. Where it was situated, at the end of the bridge that connected the prayer room to her office, it provided me the distance to observe who was there and how their audiences unfolded.

Across from me was a young Hindu man whom I had seen before at morning Mass. It seemed he had come to deliver a letter to Mother Teresa. Beside him, a European couple with wide smiling faces and pale complexions wanted to meet the famous "living saint." On the bench next to them waited another European couple, a British male nurse, and a volunteer whom I had seen at the orphanage.

love

On the bench beside mine were two producers representing a Japanese television show hoping to tape an interview. They were chatting away, going over their pitch, conspiring as to who would say what and when and who would close the deal.

Keeping my own counsel and tuning out their talk, I focused on what I would say to Mother when we met. In the next heartbeat a loud voice called out.

"Use your stage, Christina. Use your stage. And put that script away; you don't need it!" It was Madam's voice I was hearing as if she were sitting right beside me.

I shook my head. *No journeying off to the theater today, Christina. Stay focused.*

The warm April air of Calcutta caressed my face and snapped me back.

Everybody was waiting on the benches. Sister Pricilla had not yet come to clear the decks.

A latecomer, who had not been at morning prayers, slipped in and surreptitiously dropped down beside me. She was a young Hindu woman, who immediately became attentive to me. She reached out a very dirty hand and adoringly stroked my cream silk coat.

"So beautiful," she fussed. "I am sorry for my dirty rag. I have no husband. I have a little girl, but to have a girl is no blessing." I turned to her. Her sari was vibrant, interwoven with reds and greens and although not entirely clean, the fabric swept across her bronze body with a glorious flow.

I felt quite pale and plain beside her. "If your daughter looks anything like you I am sure she is very beautiful."

"She has a clean dress," she said as she futilely brushed at stains on her sari. "One day she will have shoes," she added, casting her eyes to her own naked, dirty feet.

"Does your little girl go to school? How old is she? What's her name? What is her favorite color?" I asked her one question after another, but she seemed unschooled in conversation and began repeating herself about shoes. Finally I reached over and touched her knee.

"I think it is wonderful God has blessed you with a little girl. I know people who can't have a child of their own, and they would say you are a very lucky woman."

She gave me her best toothless smile. I could see her panning for golden grains at the roadside and collecting old papers from the street to make a fire to cook them.

I fished into my bag and filled her hand with as many rupees as I could find, hoping it was enough for a pair of tiny shoes.

A breath later, the tall, imposing Sister zeroed in on her. She bent down to the Hindu woman, murmured something quite firm, and in the next second my needy neighbor vanished. I rooted myself to my bench as if I had been superglued to it and, again, willed myself invisible.

Gratefully, the Sister then moved on to the Japanese representatives. I could feel the producers' resistance as they fell over themselves telling the Sister how far they had traveled to interview the great lady. They were working their pitch, but it wasn't flying. The Sister spoke softly but firmly and in the next minute, the producers also reluctantly left. I realized how carefully Mother Teresa's space was protected, and I felt, as well, that instruction had come from somewhere and I was being graced in this process for a reason.

When Mother swept through the white curtain, she immediately took care of everyone's needs, one by one, until they had all been fulfilled to her satisfaction. In turn, they bowed, thanked her profusely, and left. In the next moment she looked pointedly over to me. A beat later she turned on her heel and transported herself back to her office.

I tensed up. *She is ignoring me. She has rejected me. She doesn't have time for me.* Minutes of her day are more valuable than years of my life. I scolded myself for imagining she would give me a second hearing, but then I caught those naughty thoughts, took a deep breath, wrapped them in a rose, and blew them away.

I relaxed a little, comforted by the fact I was still allowed to remain on the bench. I continued to think about what I would say to her when a peculiar thought happened to squeeze its way in and shove Christina, the producer, the controller, clean off the bench.

You don't need a script, Christina. Let conversation flow. Let it unfold. Go where it may and trust in "us" ~ trust that "we" will find the words, when "we" are ready to embrace them.

♡♡♡

"Talk to me with your eyes."

Time moved on. I lost track. The bench was getting harder and harder. The heat was creeping up. I prayed for just the hint of a breeze.

Then in a gust of wind, the white gauze curtain billowed and Mother Teresa floated forth, calling, "Ah, you wait so long."

"Mother, I would wait for you forever," I responded as I stood to greet her, wondering how this unusual greeting was now becoming "ours."

In the next moment, she was beside me and we sat on the bench and lo, before I realized it, our faces were again nose to nose.

We sat looking at each other through a long silence, though it seemed to me so much was discussed. I don't know who spoke first, but once the silence broke we toppled into conversation as if we had been waiting forever to catch up.

We talked about her work and her homes. She told me stories about the children who came to visit bringing her their pocket money and such. And she regaled me with a story about a young couple who had decided their happiness would be more complete if they forfeited their wedding outfits and celebrations to instead give her the funds saved for their nuptials. She told me of all the different people who came to call on her from every nook and cranny of the world, with their many reasons; and wrapped into every little story, there was a lesson to be shared.

"You have traveled a long way?" Mother asked.

"Yes, from California."

"I have homes in California ~ Los Angeles and San Francisco. All over the United States," she said in a deep, proud tone. "One hundred and twenty-six all over the world. I have homes wherever there are people dying of loneliness."

"I was born in Australia . . ."

Mother nodded her head. "Yes, we have homes there, too. I remember one time when I was there, I visited an old man who nobody knew was even alive. There was no one to care for him. His room was dusty and untidy, and I began to clean it up. He tried to stop me. 'Leave it alone,' he said. 'I like it that way.' I did not answer him and in the end he gave in."

She took a breath. I wanted to seize the opportunity and say, "I know, there are so many like that," but I knew not to interrupt.

"In the room there was a beautiful lamp, but it was covered with dust. I cleaned it off and I asked him, 'Why don't you light it?' He answered, 'Why should I? Nobody ever comes here, so it is of no use to me.' I asked him, 'If the Sisters came, would you turn it on?' 'Yes,' he said. Sometime later he gave the Sisters this message: 'Tell my friend that the light she turned on in my life is still burning.'"

Simple stories, beautifully told.

She had so many. And they all came down to humble acts of kindness, showing a fellow human being they were not alone, and they were loved. I knew she had better things to do than reminisce, and she gave me the cue to bring up why we were both talking.

"Mother, that is why I am here. I can help take you to those dark corners of the world, to bring your light to those people who have none in their life, to those who cannot travel the distance I have, to sit here with you. Many lonely people watch television. Old people, young ones, and their children. You can speak to them and to their families. I am here to help."

Her response did not shift an inch. "Look at the film that was made. You can use that." This time it was I who did not yield.

"But it is not the same as looking into your eyes and hearing you talk, the way you are talking to me now."

Mother Teresa shook her head again.

"It is forbidden. I have said no to everyone else. I cannot say yes to you."

"Mother, please. This will live on, long after you and I are gone." I went scarlet with embarrassment. I could not believe I had said that. I wanted to take back my words, but it was too late. However, she didn't take offense. Mother looked at me long and hard, and I felt certain in that moment she "knew" things at a very deep, almost mystical level.

"I cannot; I do not allow filming."

Once again, and who knows the source, tears formed in my eyes. I blinked them away and held onto her hands even more tightly. I was communicating with a remarkably unique human being and real truth resonated in her. I had looked deep inside myself, and I was certain my intentions were pure. I had no other motive than to share her message. I had no doubt she would see right through to the truth. My throat closed and yet my heart seemed to open up.

"I do not do this for myself, Mother." With that disclosure the tears trickled down.

"Oh," she exclaimed so sweetly. Her hands slipped out of mine and she retreated to her office. Immediately she returned, and into my hands she placed a thin blue book.

"This is my prayer for you."

I smiled and thanked her. The white curtain billowed again and she was gone.

In my taxi back to the hotel I clutched the tiny paperback. As I often do with a book, I opened it randomly, confident my eyes would find the one phrase I was seeking.

I looked down and saw something alarming. A small addition that made a huge difference. She had handwritten one phrase in pen and ink under a woodcut illustration of Jesus wearing his crown of thorns. The printed words beneath it read: "I looked for one that would comfort me and I found none." And Mother had written beside it, "Be the One."

Gandhi had said, *"Be the change you wish to see."* And here was Mother Teresa, echoing his words in her own way. Be everything you wish to see. Through all the discussion and all the silences she and I had shared, her intention was now clear to me: empowerment. Be the one. Don't look for the one. Don't wait for the one. Don't follow the one. Don't even look to me. Be the one. Don't just be as big as the world. Be the world. Do what you know in your heart you must do.

Be the one. If a loved one is in need, be the one to lend a hand. If a stranger is lost, be the one to light the way. If something needs to be done, be the one to do it.

Monica materialized from behind a palm tree and threw her arms around me when I stepped into the Taj. "How are you doing with your work? I am so much wanting to hear your report. I wish we could have a dinner, but I have been assigned a later schedule."

Briefly I filled her in on my private meetings with Mother.

"You have met with her twice. That is most impressive," she responded. Though she wanted to know every little detail, I did not want to share that Mother had said no to my requests to film her. I didn't want to divulge that it seemed heaven and earth could be moved more easily than Mother Teresa. I thought if I didn't say the words, the issue was not yet concluded.

Thankfully the bellman interrupted us.

"Miss Christina. A message. Delivered personally."

It was from Nayeem. It read: "We are here!"

I took the elevator up to my room, fantasizing I was inside a supersonic vehicle that had come this time to return me to the familiar sanctity of my home, surrounded by all things known and nurturing.

For the moment my hotel room would have to give me the solace needed to soothe my rejected nerves. Immediately I called down to the operator.

"I must get through to the United States. It's very important," I told the operator, who apologized profusely but whose tone told me I should resign myself to the fact it wasn't going to happen.

I had become so caught up in my mission here that work at home had slipped out of my conscious thoughts. But with Mother Teresa's second refusal, it returned front and center.

Mark and I have a partnership on a handshake. Not on paper. It never made me anxious before, but I knew fear ran him. And because of that he was capable of throwing our toys away, kicking sand in my face, and leaving our sandbox for good. My brain was shorting out with worry at what he might resort to in my absence. I broke out in a sweat.

And then the phone rang. "Thank you! Thank you!" I said as I dragged myself over to the phone.

"Gilly!"

"It is us!"

"Oh, Nayeem."

"We are all here. The camera. The crew. Your long lens."

"That's great, Nayeem. Look. I can't join you all for dinner tonight. I'm not feeling up to it, but I will be fine tomorrow. Please take the crew out for a lovely dinner, on me. Tell them welcome and that I am very happy you are all here. We have a lot of work to do. Will you pick up the van we talked about and be ready when I call you in the morning, after breakfast?"

Immediately I hung up. *What? Was I going to tell him we had nothing to film here? Or was I going to buy time and pretend and run them all over the city shooting this and that? For what?*

I pulled myself together and sent the message to my mind to stop thinking. *It's thinking that gets you into trouble.* I ordered one boiled egg and bottled juice and fondled the simple blue book Mother had given me. It was titled: *Mother Teaches Us to Pray.*

I have never been one for traditional prayer. For me, nature is my church and being out on a beach or in the woods or even in a garden, listening to the sounds of nature is prayer enough for me.

No. What caught me more was what she had written in her own hand. "Be the One."

I had considered religion a followers' frenzy and Mother Teresa the champion of a followers' faith. But I was wrong about her. Immeasurably wrong. I had reduced her largesse to what I had thought rather than what I was now discovering.

In my time with her I realized how I'd misunderstood her. How the world misunderstood the hunched-over European lady who wore a sari. She was her own woman who had followed her calling in the way God had laid out for her. I chuckled to myself at how this little gal with her enormously independent will must have driven the big boys in the Vatican crazy ~ though I am sure they loved her deeply. Especially since her Missionaries of Charity around the world were completely self-sustaining, with reportedly millions in their coffers.

As uncompromising and grounded in reality as she was, she was in this world ~ not of it. It was apparent from our conversations that her goal was not to indoctrinate souls into the Catholic Church. Her humility made her richer than the wealthiest church in the world, her iconic image as recognizable as Coca-Cola, and her ability to heal would grant her the longevity of sainthood. Verily, a marketing genius.

All was made clear to me by the sayings that adorned the walls throughout her homes. These were her personal sayings, reflecting her inspirations of empowerment, her guidance for caring, healing, and love. Cupid's arrow aimed at the heart of the universe. She went directly to the source. And this is where she urged us to go.

Go to love however you can get there and stay there as long as you can.

I felt sure if I told her I thought God was a flower that was growing in my garden, she would have responded, "Yes, God bless." If I had said God is the man across the road who is beating his child right now, she would have responded, "Yes, God bless."

Her own celebrity embarrassed her. She didn't want followers, and should her example be followed, should her words be heeded, that would be one's choice. She wanted to empower us all to stand up and be counted. As one. One in a world of ones. The power of one in her eyes was the power of all.

Preciously, I put the book on my bedside table. *Be the one.* The responsibility she had put into my hands swirled around inside me.

My stomach had not calmed when room service arrived. I couldn't even break open my one lonely egg. The crew was here to work and we were on a schedule and on the clock. My personal funds were also ticking away. I gathered my reference books and my location notes and laid them out before me, but my eyes kept losing focus.

I needed a break. I turned on the television searching for CNN. It was then that I noticed something had been shifted. When you live alone you become accustomed to knowing the precise order of your world. As I faced the television cabinet, something had been moved.

There, above the TV, was a VCR machine. The angels had visited me yet again. Upon my arrival and lightly, almost in passing, I had mentioned my desire for one to Monica, but later realizing that acquiring equipment like this in all of India, let alone Calcutta, is so difficult, I hadn't mentioned it again. I cast all hope for it out of my mind. But there it was, set up and ready to go.

I pulled out the tape Gilly had packed for me. The documentary made more than a decade earlier. The film Mother had suggested I use.

Richard Attenborough's dulcet tones began: *"There is a light in this world, a healing spirit more powerful than any darkness we can encounter. We sometimes lose sight of this force when there is suffering ~ too much pain. And suddenly the spirit will emerge through the lives of ordinary people, who hear a call and answer in extraordinary ways."*

I choked up. Then Mother Teresa's deep, soft voice spoke and I could breathe again. Her words were tough yet gentle, hard yet soft. If I had understood Gilly correctly, this was the film that took the producers five years to convince Mother Teresa it was the thing to do, and even then she packed them off to the Vatican for final approval. What on earth was I thinking? I had three days, not five years. And two of those days were already gone.

"When you take sides, you stop loving.
When you get stuck in politics, you forget
about people and you stop loving.
When you stand by all and not by one, you are in the loving.
That's the difference."

While I watched the film, my mind searched for a clue, a way in or around her resistance. Yet if I were to give credence to my belief in the law of attraction, what I really needed was a clue to myself, a way around my own resistance and into my own faith. I needed to believe that a miracle was possible. Or more accurately, I needed to believe the miracle had already occurred. And I just had to give thanks.

The film was half over when I caught one of the Brothers narrating a story. Mother Teresa's face on the screen pulled in my full attention.

It was 1982. War was breaking out. Shells were dropping in PLO strongholds in West Beirut. As the invasion continued, it was estimated 500 civilians had been killed and another 1,000 wounded. Mother Teresa wanted to get to West Beirut and see to the needs of the people there. Even though she had not been informed, she "had knowledge" that somewhere behind enemy lines there were people in need of her special kind of rescuing.

Frail, hunched over, wearing her diminutive thin cotton sari, she was outnumbered in a room full of upstanding, uniformed military leaders and men of the cloth dwarfing her pure intent. In no uncertain terms her desires were dismissed.

"Mother, do you hear the bombing?" the British father asked, somewhat incredulously.

"Yes, I hear it," she responded firmly.

"It's absolutely impossible for you to go there. A priest was killed two weeks ago for no reason! They just wanted to kill a priest! Even if you get over there, we may not be able to get you back. Now, this is a nice idea you have. But—"

Mother Teresa straightened up to silence his patronizing tone. "It is not an idea. It is our duty."

And then she patiently explained, as she did to so many, "You see, I always feel like this. Many years back, when I picked up the very first person, if I didn't pick up that person, at that time, I would never have picked up forty-two thousand. One at a time."

Like the beloved teacher she was, she would take everyone back to square one. Keeping it simple.

As the saga continued, he relentlessly attempted to talk her out of this foolhardy mission. "It is absolutely impossible for you to cross at this present time." The word *impossible* was not in Mother Teresa's vocabulary. "We would have to have a cease-fire first," he added.

Mother Teresa was not backing down. And he had just given her an opening.

"Oh, but I have been praying to Our Lady," Mother stated confidently. "And I have asked her to let us have a cease-fire here ~ tomorrow."

The ambassador was taken aback. He stared rather incredulously at Mother Teresa and said, "Mother, I am very glad you are on my side and that you are a woman of prayer. I believe in prayer and I believe prayer is answered. And I am a man of faith. But you are asking Our Lady to deal with Prime Minister Begin. Don't you think that the time limit is little . . . er . . . you know ~ short? That you should extend it a little further?"

Mother was firm. "Oh, no. I am certain that we will have the cease-fire tomorrow."

Trying in vain to conceal his skepticism, he placated her quietly. "Mother, if we have a cease-fire, I will personally make the arrangements to see that you go to West Beirut tomorrow."

Mother Teresa's simple and finite response to that was, "We shall pray."

The film dissolved softly to a tiny room that had been transformed into a makeshift chapel and there, on screen, was the image of Mother Teresa surrounded by her Sisters, all on their knees, praying together.

Through the night they prayed.

This would add to the growing body of evidence that when people unify with focused, specific intention and feeling, even in a nondenominational mass prayer, they can produce effects that reach far beyond the sanctuary where the prayer had been given.

The sound track of the film became quiet as the camera recorded the sun rising over Beirut the next morning. Suddenly the voice of the British Red Cross captain came through. In contrast to the discussion of the night before, he spoke with an almost comic awestruck tone as he said, "I think we should take full advantage of the fact that we have a cease-fire of sorts." Very quickly, he pulled out a map and unfolded it for Mother Teresa to grasp the situation fully. "There are sixty totally deficient spastic children in a center, here. There is no staff there to look after them and it's been shelled a number of times. Many people have been killed." He leaned close to Mother Teresa and added, "I should like to take you there."

While watching the film of Mother Teresa leading an armada of Red Cross vans across enemy lines, waving her arms, directing the operation, totally in her element, I could feel the intensity of her mission. Rescuing the abandoned children who would certainly have been killed or would have died without water, food, and care ~ suddenly, I knew what I had to do.

I continued watching as Mother Teresa and her Sisters scoured the center, picking up children. I watched while the picture remained focused on one of the Sisters as she caressed a spastic child's crooked and contorted body. Her hand was cupped in a manner I recognized, as if she were spiraling air to conjure and disperse energy. She spoke with the little child, and though I didn't see her lips move, what became apparent was they were communicating ~ with each stroke of the Sister's hand, the little girl's stiff and twisted body relaxed and straightened, her taut, pained face softened, and in the next moment broke into a smile. This was a true mystic at work. And it began with prayer.

I knew my prayer could not be a request or a plea, for that would simply reinforce disbelief and create space for the possibility of failure. No. From my training in the Science of Mind and the power of affirmations, when I was asked to pray for someone, as if I had just been given direct access to the power of creation, I would snap immediately to the knowledge that "it was done." And so it was. My prayer was an echo of gratitude. I took a deep breath.

The prayer had already been answered.

Yes, God bless.

CHAPTER FOURTEEN

SEE EVERY DAY AS A MIRACLE

"In love, you can never be small.
The moment you open yourself up to love,
you become infinite."

I was dealing with someone who worked in a universe of miracles. Having the curse of an analytical mind, I wanted to know what it was the Sisters actually did that caused a cease-fire to happen. Being a visual person, I needed a picture.

What does a miracle look like? What does it feel like? What occurs right before a miracle? Is there something that brings it on? Do we momentarily elevate ourselves into a higher state, see it done, and then come back to earth to wait for the outcome? How many layers of consciousness do we as spiritual beings possess, and how many can we as physical beings access?

Before I could step into my spiritual self, I had to envision the physical disappearing. I nestled into my meditation couch, closed my eyes, and inhaled ~ breathing air and space into every pore of my body. It took a little time to separate from the discomforts of physicality, yet pretty soon there was nothing inside or outside of me. All had melded together and become one. The floor, the walls, the ceiling, up to the heavens and down to the core of the earth, all of it became a living, breathing part of me. My head opened up and expanded with light. In a swooping slow rush of air, I left the ground and was no longer in my hotel room.

I was on a beach. It was dusk, that perfect moment when the clouds turn orange and resonate with the still blue of the sky, electrifying the water. Suddenly I felt the wet sensation of the sea lick my toes.

Then I saw the fishing boats. Long, wooden boats moored at the water's edge, their nets empty. I felt the presence of people around me. So I turned and saw them, everywhere, scattered as far as the horizon. Thousands of people, standing in the dry grass and over the dunes. And farther where the cypress trees rimmed the hills, they were there, too. There was something remarkable about everything I saw. As if I had stepped into an oil painting, a lucid landscape. Where the people were a part of the sky and the sky part of the sea, and the sand and trees, all flowing into one another and all pulsing like a heartbeat, as if it were one giant living organism. To add to that, my arrival sent ripples across the liquid canvas, as if my presence was now an integral part of this living picture.

I felt called to leave the shore and make my way through the crowd, over the dunes, and up toward the cypress woods. As I moved I felt buoyant, as light as air. The people made a path for me, the way water embraces you at first and then separates as you swim through it.

I noticed how, from the colors of their skin to the clothes they wore, each person was unique and yet very much the same, and I couldn't help but feel a part of them. When I reached the crest of the hill I found a great multitude, sitting, listening to a man who stood before them. When I stopped, the movement around me ceased. It made me feel as if I were important and my actions made a difference.

The sun rested upon his face as he spoke. I did not see his lips move yet I felt his intention and I saw and heard his gentleness. He was sending out love, beyond words and comprehension. This love was flowing through the air, and everyone was inhaling it as if it were their breath of life. As if we were all part of this creation, a little boy emerged from us, offering a basket.

The speaker took the basket from the boy's willing hand and held it high for the multitude to see. At that moment a wave pulsed through us all. Almost like a camera lens we focused on the basket and what was inside. The speaker dipped in his hand and pulled out a loaf of bread and three small fish and handed them to someone close. Then he did it again. And again. As I observed, more bread and fish were being taken from the basket than could ever be in there. Then as I watched, the food that went from one hand to another multiplied as each person touched it. It seemed very natural.

A small loaf and fish were handed to me. I turned to the neighbor beside me and gave it. I noticed he did the same. The unusual thing is, he still had the bread and fish in his hands and so did I. On and on the bread and fish were shared, though our hands remained full. My eyes were not deceiving me: one small loaf and three little fish were multiplying from one to another, man to woman, woman to child, ad infinitum, with endless fluidity.

It was not the speaker who was performing this miracle. It was us. Everyone.

A small jug of water was offered, and as I looked out, I saw it ~ the jug itself was being passed from one to another, never needing to be replaced. And the fish were being enjoyed with the bread and the water and a great feast was under way.

Something profound was occurring. There was a glow surrounding all of us. A unity. An impeccable closeness I had never felt before. I looked more carefully, thinking perhaps everyone was speaking with one another, yet I saw no mouths moving. I felt sure they were communing. And then I realized what was really happening.

People were sharing without fear and whatever they shared without fear, multiplied. That was the secret. If for an instant just one had thought, "I wonder, will there be enough to go around?" or feared, "I don't think I should give it away, for it is all I have," or reached out in greed, "I should take more than my share, in case there is no more," everything would have stopped. The miracle would have vanished. Right then and there.

From horizon to horizon, this was a world without separation, without boundaries, without borders. This was a world without end. Where we were all individual and unique beings, having taken our journeys from unconscious union to conscious separation and then onward to this place of conscious union, confident and secure in our differences and able to enter into the equality of one consciousness. All one unifying tone ~ where all was taken care of.

Love connected us as if it were a golden strand running through us, drawing us together, and in that union, we were complete and perfect.

I took a deep breath, and it brought me back into the density of my body temple. For a time I couldn't move. Reentering my earth-bound vehicle, I thought about where I had just been and what I had been a part of.

Suddenly I heard myself chuckle. Dr. Whitehouse and his funny Radionics machine crossed my mind because of how his mode of healing requires the whole family to focus upon their loved one. I thought about the Sisters kneeling together in prayer. I thought of other times when people gather to pray, to chant, to meditate, to commune and how it fills them up.

What immense strength and power togetherness brings. And how vital the power of one really is.

"Love doesn't ask that you succeed in everything, but that you remain faithful. However right something may feel, it is better not to become attached to its outcome. Be prepared to give it up. Without losing your peace."

Wednesday, April 14, 1993

Like clockwork, I was on the bridge leading to her office for the third time. A small group of visitors had been attended to and as had become the custom, I was left alone, waiting on what I now considered my bench.

Again, the sounds of Sisters going about their daily tasks wafted through the courtyard below and up the stairs. I knew I could leave right at that moment and not regret a second of my journey. She had told me no, twice. Surely it was time to honor her wishes.

We can never really know why an impulse takes over. Ordinarily my work would never have brought me here, volunteering in Mother's homes and then to actually privately meet her. Perhaps that was the reason behind my vision. Inside her influence I had learned so much about myself and the world around me. In some ways I was feeling reborn. Not to a faith, but to myself. When you move through life and work at the speed of sound, driven by ambition, technology estranging us from one another, with an occasional day off to run errands and catch up on paperwork, there is hardly time to explore the substance of life, to look at where you came from and how you got to where you are. Or even explore your heart for that missing chip inside your perceived happiness.

From the moment the Rajdhani Express pulled out of the station I had been in the waiting room. In that nothing space, on the precipice of the unknown while a clock ticked somewhere, nudging me to explore all that had led me here. And here I was. Back on the bench, waiting. I had spent so much time here I wondered if someone wouldn't come by soon and ask for rent.

Tingling to my toes, an overwhelming sense of gratitude rushed through my body for this unusual, heaven-sent gift to my life. The sensation was exquisitely matched by the chimes of a celestial voice.

"Ah, you wait so long," came her greeting.

I was on my feet immediately. I had to hold myself back from running into her arms. She was gliding, *swoosh,* through the air toward me. I needed just one step until her hands were in mine.

"Mother, I would wait for you forever."

I knew in that moment I was back here because I was in love.

Her arrival was always perfect. And I wondered for a second if she observed me through the sheer curtain, waiting for the chatter in my mind to dissipate. Waiting for me to find my peace. For nothing comes to a being unready.

We sat down together, and she smiled cutely and bowed her head and we touched, forehead to forehead. I simply melted into these moments with her, wanting them never to end. Her face was luminous in the soft light ~ a face I wanted the world to see more than anything else.

Sitting on the bench beside her, I finally came around to accepting the fact that I would have to break the news to Nayeem and my crew that we would not be filming in Calcutta.

Perhaps I could give it one last run, I thought.

Deliberately, I squeezed her hands, but my mind was a blank. Many times I had rehearsed my speech, my final plea, but no words came. It was as if an unseen hand had stilled my voice. A sense of relief swept over me. I breathed a sigh. At last! Stripped of the desire for an outcome, I had accomplished the simplest and the hardest of tasks.

I had let go of letting go.

I looked into her eyes ~ the kindest I have ever seen. There was a silence now between us that we hadn't shared before. It was extraordinarily comfortable. Indeed I felt no need to fill the void, no desire to be intelligent or persuasive. Everything felt perfect. The air between us, around us, and through us became refined, as if we were 30,000 feet high and the world of form and density that separated us no longer existed. In that moment, and the next, we connected, as if we were exchanging places.

I felt her love for me as I felt my love for her. As if the breath that was giving me life was the same breath flowing through her. How long it lasted, I will never know, yet upon my return into myself, I was able to speak again.

"Mother, I cannot do what you do," I said softly, wondering where on earth those words came from.

"I know," she replied. "And I cannot do what you do."

With that, she stood, just over five feet high, yet towering and powerful.

This is it, I thought. *I'm going to be banished forever for my persistence. She'll go back to saving lives, and I'll return to making commercials.*

Then, an almost mischievous look of resolve swept over her face and she smiled.

"Together, we shall do something beautiful for God."

I smiled back. I had stopped asking. My mind flickered, *Does that mean . . . ? Is she saying . . . ?* Aloud, I finally found the courage to ask, "Are you saying I can film you?"

She gave me a twinkly grin and a hushed, "Yes."

"Tomorrow?" I breathed, chasing after her.

"In the afternoon," she answered. "I have Sisters from all over the world here right now and I am very busy."

"Mother, I must tell you. A thirty-five-millimeter camera is a very big camera." I wanted to be certain she understood it wouldn't just be me with a tiny video recorder. I wanted to be certain she knew I was bringing a camera into her home that required a crew.

"Yes, yes," she said.

"I will only take fifteen minutes of your time, Mother. I will do it as quickly as possible."

"Yes." She nodded.

"I will need light on your face."

I had done my homework, and at two o'clock in the afternoon the light in the lower courtyard was exquisite.

This was her home. Though I had seen some of the most naturally lit, perfect shots ever in the more private portals of the Motherhouse, I didn't want to be invasive of her cloistered space. If it had been anywhere else or anyone else I would have cajoled and begged and stood on my head to get those visions on film. In deference to her style, it was vital we create something very simple.

"The courtyard is beautiful in the afternoon, Mother. Perhaps there?"

"Yes, that will be good. You may set it up with Sister Priscilla."

I caught my breath.

Mother noticed and smiled. "Is there another Sister you would prefer to work with?" *Goodness,* I laughed to myself. *Is there anything she doesn't know?*

"I know Sister Josma."

"Very well, you speak to her, and I will also tell her." And then she released my hands. The white curtain billowed and she drifted away like an angel with the noon breeze.

I was beside myself with excitement and fairly danced down the stairs to the ground floor where I went searching for Sister Josma. There she was! Scribbling out a shopping list in the dining room.

"Sister Josma!" I called breathlessly. "I am coming tomorrow. Mother has agreed. I will be here at one o'clock with a film crew. Mother has agreed to be filmed."

Sister Josma stopped what she was busy about, looked carefully at me, and shook her head ~ rather pityingly I might add. "Oh, no. You are mistaken. Mother would never allow that."

"But we talked about the size of the camera and about the light in the courtyard." Sister Josma wrinkled her brow, reached out, and kindly touched my arm.

"I'm afraid you have misunderstood her."

"Speak with her, she will tell you," I insisted. "We will need to be here at one, to set up and be ready to film by two o'clock."

She rolled her eyes, convinced I was wrong, and for one shaky second she pushed my sudden elation right off its pedestal. Another second later, I knew what I knew. But then two seconds after that I worried. *Have my daydreams been just that? Have I simply conjured all this up in my mind, like a little child who sits on a bench and entertains herself with fantasy?*

"Mother will tell you," I reassured her confidently.

Sister Josma's smile remained benevolent.

And I departed with uncertainty nipping at my heels.

Back at my hotel, Nayeem and the crew all proudly stood at attention in front of a van that looked so dilapidated it would be rusting in a junkyard in any other city.

"Ah, our chariot awaits," I said appreciatively as our trusty driver slid open the back door and I crawled in. Careful to dodge the gaping, rusty hole dead center on the floor, I put my bottom on the cold metal slab that was the seat. Peering down at the wobbly tailpipe and the road beneath, I chuckled quietly to myself. It reminded me of the chariot Geoffrey had made for me out of fruit crates when we were children. Perfect!

"Let's go scout the locations I found."

After a few scratchy attempts, the engine caught, and pretty soon we were off, rattling down the mosaic driveway of the Taj, with me feeling quite the queen.

Perhaps it was the frenetic pulse of Calcutta's 15 million people that made it impossible to resist, or simply that for a filmmaker, its colorful canvas is so seductive. I knew it would be the perfect complement to Mother Teresa's words.

Nayeem cheered at the news that we were to film Mother Teresa the following day.

Jehangir, our cameraman, a tall and very handsome man, had no idea how touch and go it had been. He liked to tell jokes, and he spoke excellent English, so we were able to converse easily and enjoy the ride. I had brought lighting, mood, and composition references from my collection of Wyeth family books, and when I was interviewing cinematographers, Jehangir recognized the subtleties of their work; we were immediately in sync.

The rest of the crew spoke little or no English, and I had a hard time remembering their very foreign names. I've never been good at names ~ faces, I remember. Dialogue, from my theatrical upbringing, I recall exactly. And now feelings were becoming unforgettable for me. Like the exquisite softness of the palm of Mother's hand as it wrapped around mine, or the look deep in her eyes reflecting everything in her heart.

Jehangir, with his lanky legs, sat next to me on the metal slab and his wonderful sense of humor kept us all jovial through the bumps and grinds and fumes. His camera assistant, another member of Ismail Merchant's family, chuckled at everything he said. I laughed, too, grateful for the levity, yet I wasn't certain if I always got the joke since Jehangir spoke half Hindi and half English so as not to offend anyone.

The expensive man with the expensive lens sat opposite us, clutching the lens on his lap. He didn't speak a lick of English and didn't say a word ~ in fact he was entirely expressionless throughout the journey. He came to life briefly when the van broke down near the racecourse, and for a second he placed his precious lens on the ground and crawled under the van with the driver. Then he stoically resumed his role as the silent keeper of the long lens that would indeed prove itself invaluable.

I had found the courage to knock on doors and bribe and charm my way to the roofs of houses and buildings where I hoped we could get good shots of the expansive city and rooftop living. With the crew in tow, I revisited those locations and at last, my long lens proved itself to be a star.

"Let us begin a revolution. A revolution of love."

Thursday, April 15, 1993

At sunrise my smiling crew greeted me with their wonderfully bright, white teeth. We left the dingy, rickety van in the driveway of my hotel and crawled around the roof of the Taj Bengal to capture some beautiful footage of the haloed sun popping out of the blue mist over St. Peter's Church. Later we went to the fruit and flower markets, religious shops, and tea stalls and captured one of the most colorful cities in the world, crawling out from under its covers, opening its arms wide and yawning. We grabbed an early lunch before heading to the Motherhouse.

"Are you sure Mother Teresa has given her approval?" Jehangir asked. "I have heard stories. She is not a fan of the camera."

"Oh, yes," I reassured my nervous DP even though I myself was holding onto the bare threads of conviction that all would go as planned.

At precisely one o'clock we approached the door of the Motherhouse.

I held my breath as I knocked, envisioning Sister Josma opening it and shaking her head in an I-told-you-so fashion. My fears were unwarranted. It was like a royal welcome. Three Sisters opened the door wide, smiled broadly, and beckoned us all in, even wanting to help the men carry their equipment.

More Sisters than I had ever seen in the Motherhouse came out of their classrooms and offices and prayer rooms to greet us. The courtyard was rimmed with an overhanging balcony that swept the entire circumference. Many stopped what they were doing and leaned over the balcony to watch us set up. Tea and cream-filled biscuits were preciously laid out for us even though I had only ever seen the Sisters eat plain ones. I knew these were the kind they saved for special occasions and special visitors. The crew chuckled among themselves, commenting that they felt like celebrities. As with everything Mother Teresa touched, I found her generosity never ending.

Wall to wall, the Motherhouse was inside and out, cement and stone. Yet there was one spot nature touched. It was a grotto nestled in the far corner of the courtyard, with green plants growing at the foot of a statue of Mary. Light shone down and kissed the plants in the afternoon. We didn't bring in any lights and were relying on the natural light in the courtyard. We were set up and ready for Mother in less than 15 minutes. One of the Sisters brought a chair for Mother, but instead I thought it would be more aesthetically natural for Mother to sit on the edge of the grotto, if she approved.

It was 2 P.M. Sunlight flooded the courtyard. Film loaded and in the gate. Sound check completed. Everything in working order and the crew at the ready.

By 2:30 the light in the courtyard was glowing. The crew relaxed a little.

At 3 P.M. the light was softer yet still magnificent. Nayeem had grown fidgety. Jehangir and his assistant were sitting on the lens cases. Mike, our soundman, who was leaning against a pillar, had nodded off.

At 3:30, a dark shadow began its inevitable crawl across the stone enclosure. Nayeem was chewing his nails.

At 4, Nayeem was pacing in the shadows that had swallowed all light in the lower courtyard, and the green plants surrounding the statue of Mary were in darkness. To top it off, it was now ear-piercing, peak-hour traffic on Bose Road.

At 4:15, Mother appeared on the top-floor balcony.

"Ah, you wait so long," she called as she came down the stairway. I stood and smiled, relieved and happy to see her.

"Mother, we would wait for you forever." Everyone scrambled to resume their positions.

Mother Teresa moved like the wind, with the force of a locomotive, yet she appeared so frail. I watched her looking at the crew, not really smiling, but acknowledging each of them intensely. It was something I later saw the Dalai Lama do, and I have come to understand they often look at the space and the energy around people rather than directly at the people themselves.

As I approached Mother I detected a hint of nervousness. I was beginning to think she was superhuman, and she was, really. Yet that little bit of uncertainty prompted me to move quickly toward her and protectively escort her across the courtyard.

I linked my arm in hers and walked her over to the stone grotto.

"Will you be comfortable sitting here?" I asked. She smiled and nodded and sat down. When I leaned toward her to attach the microphone to her sari, she pulled away and looked at me questioningly.

"Do I need makeup?" she asked sweetly.

"No, Mother." I caressed her soft cheek. "You have no need of makeup."

As I leaned in to attach the lavalier microphone, I noticed how worn and frayed the fabric of her sari was, and immediately I thought to tuck the edges under so that in close-up no one would see her sari was almost in tatters.

As if she read my mind, she said gratefully, "The lepers make our saris." She caressed the black crucifix, attached with a safety pin on her left shoulder.

"It is good for us and good for them," she added, smoothing and straightening the folds of her thin white cotton sari as if it were a precious velvet gown, a jewel-encrusted robe worthy of a queen of heaven. I immediately let go of my foolish worries over superficial appearances and gave in to an overwhelming urge to hug her.

Before taking up my position out of camera range, I sat beside her briefly to explain that I would not be interviewing her on camera, but that I would be simply letting her speak directly to the camera, and to take her time. Reminding her of the many subjects we had covered during our time together, I guided her to speak just the way she had spoken to me or as if she was talking to one of her Sisters or to one of her eager volunteers.

I had promised we would take only 15 minutes of her time, and the crew knew we would shoot only one 1,000-foot roll of film. And then Nayeem rushed in with the clapperboard.

Mother sat, hunched over in a most humble and beautiful fashion. I turned to Jehangir to be certain he was moving the camera across her hands and feet before she began to speak. But he was standing back, his jaw dropped open in awe. Then Mother spoke.

"Jesus came to bring us the good news . . ."

Facing the camera, she was unusually nervous. She didn't want to look into the lens and instead focused upon me. However, as she spoke, she became more inspired and comfortable "winging it" and punctuated her sentences by blinking into the camera, which at certain moments was perfect.

Everyone was mesmerized. I was falling in love with her all over again, not for what she said, even though she was a sage of simplicity, but for the pure light of her presence and the love, the deep love, that emanated from those wise, gentle eyes that showered peace upon everyone she looked at.

At one point she stopped and waved her hand around, trying to silence the hammering and the *clackety-clack* of an old manual typewriter inside the Motherhouse. The cacophony of noise outside continued to bounce off the cement walls. Regardless, she continued . . .

"Love begins at home. And it can spread like a burning fire from house to house."

When she said this, I knew I had the core of her message. Instantly I connected her statement back to the loaves and the fishes and how easily love can spread when more and more of us participate and what truly miraculous events we can bring about.

As if she read my mind, she looked over to me, uncertain of what more there was to say about the joy of loving. I quickly went to sit beside her and reminded her of the "theme" we had discussed. When a message is short, it needs a brief wrap-up.

"Remember, the revolution?" I said to her.

"Ah, yes," she said, and looked back to the camera, like a real pro. "I call it a revolution. A revolution of love."

She gave a final smile as the last of the film clattered through the camera. Nobody moved. Mother turned her focus to me.

"Finished?" she inquired, with the bright expression of a little girl who had just completed her homework and now wishes to be released to go outside to play.

I scanned my senses as I always did before calling "Cut" for that "yes" realization.

"Yes, Mother. You were perfect." I stood and moved toward her. I had no idea if I had anything usable in the can. Logic and experience told me the light was so poor it was highly unlikely we had an image on the negative, but that was out of my control. I had used up my 15 minutes, and I knew to keep impeccably to my word.

I stepped in to unhook the microphone from her sari, and she considered me with an odd look. I would call it gracious appreciation, surprised satisfaction, but those words wouldn't quite fit the silent message in her attitude.

She didn't move, seeming as if she didn't want to leave immediately. Instead she pulled me down to sit beside her and, clutching my hands, whispered, "Works of love are works of peace." Then she pulled me closer, adding, "I will pray for peace in the world." She then became very still for a moment and, holding my hand even tighter, she began. "I pray for peace. I pray for healing and the upliftment of humanity, for the end to suffering of small children. I pray for the bombings to stop. I pray for no more little children's legs to be blown off by land mines. I pray for the lame to walk again, and for the sick to rise in the splendor and the glory and to remember who they truly are, as divine children of God. I pray for peace to find its way into the heart."

Mother touched my hand one more time and murmured, "I pray for peace," and then she seemed to float upward and was gone.

I looked over to Mike, our soundman, noting he was playing back the tape in his headphones. I saw from his expression, his concern was as deep as mine. Mother's delicate voice had been up against the invasive sounds inside the Motherhouse, the bouncing echoes of cars and carriages and trams and rickshaws that were stopping and starting on the six-lane road outside. Mixed with the cacophony of horns honking, brakes screeching, and engines clanging and the always-present people noise.

"I can't make out one word," Mike said quietly, shaking his head.

That night, I took the sound equipment and listened to the DAT in the quiet of my room. Our fears were confirmed. Calcutta had imprinted itself all over Mother Teresa's soft voice. Her message was barely audible. And if it were audible, the only solution would be to cut away to scenes of the street so the viewer understood where the muddle of noise and clatter was coming from. Perhaps if I could record Mother's voice in the quietude of an interior office and lay it over afterward ~ perhaps I could make it work. As for the light and whatever image we may have on the film, since I was carrying the unprocessed negative back with me, I wouldn't know what we had until I returned to Los Angeles.

CHAPTER FIFTEEN

TWO MAGIC WORDS

Christina Stevens

*"You don't need words
to tell someone you
appreciate them."*

Friday, April 16, 1993

It was a happy crew who could sleep in the next morning. Not so for me. As much as I hated to request any more of her valuable time, I rose at dawn and went to the Motherhouse to ask Mother Teresa if I could record her voice in a quiet place.

When I reached the breezeway to her office, I was sent back on my heels. There were what looked like 100 people milling around, all waiting to see her. The four wooden benches were not even visible. I had never seen this many people before; certainly Mother

Teresa and I could never have had our three private meetings amid this kind of scene.

I was concerned and sought out Sister Josma.

"What's going on? Has something happened? What are all these people doing here?" Sister Josma looked at me curiously. "It is like this every day."

"No." *How could she say that?* She looked at me even more incredulously, adding, "You have been here. You have seen how many people come to see Mother. Always."

This exchange threw me. I raced back upstairs to be sure my eyes were not failing me. And yes, the crowd was overwhelming. I realized something significant had shifted.

Suddenly, the tidal wave of nations parted with Mother at its epicenter. As if she knew I was there. Her eyes squeezed into a smile, and she made her way through the crowd directly to me.

As she had done with the little girl who was leaving her care and going off to be adopted by a European family, Mother grabbed my head with both her hands and affectionately pulled me to her.

"How was it? Good?" she asked me excitedly, her face wreathed in joy.

"Oh, Mother, I don't know. The sound wasn't good. I don't know if I got everything you said. If we could just record your voice again?"

She held up her hand to silence my anxiety. There was a knowing twinkle in her eye, and I felt like her little daughter whose mother knew better.

"Then we shall pray," she said, smiling with great conviction. I knew I was not to ask her again. I was to take this leap of faith, and I was not to worry. Somehow the power of her prayer would bring her face out of the shadow and into the light and her voice out of the muddle of noise and into clarity.

I reached out and touched her hand.

"Yes." I beamed.

In the next instant, she was swallowed up by her adoring fans.

"If you don't laugh,
you won't know how to love,
for laughter is the music of the soul."

That afternoon, we all began our trek north to Sikkim on the Indian border of Tibet to film the second message in the series, from His Holiness, the Dalai Lama. It was an arduous journey. Two and a half days by air and over land, through unfriendly territories, dangerous terrain, and numerous armed checkpoints for which I, especially, had to present my special letters of entry and wait while I was examined and cross-examined.

We made it to Gangtok, a most serene mountain village at the foot of the Himalayas at sunset on the third day.

I found His Holiness sweet, enchanting, very flirty with the camera and yet so mirroring Mother in energy, they were almost like the flip side of the same coin. He had a seriousness about him that was breezy. When we first saw each other I was standing beside Jehangir, who was idly resting his camera on his hip. I nudged Jehangir.

"Let's shoot this," I said, to his surprise.

He squirmed beside me and frowned, whispering, "But we haven't loaded any film. I didn't know we were going to—"

"Well," I whispered. "Pretend!"

Our flight out of Calcutta had brought into play many of those extra rupees and some of my stash of dollars to get us all on the flight. Thankfully we got our camera and lenses on board.

When it came to the cans of film, we had a problem.

We had no other choice than to put the film on the mountain bus with a PA. This was a big risk. We had a firm appointment with the Dalai Lama and no idea if the bus would make it up the mountain pass in time. I was forced to pretend I was pregnant and smuggle one can of film under my dress. This 1,000-foot roll could have been all we had. Enough for the Dalai Lama to deliver his message but not enough to shoot anything else.

You would think by this time, I would have had more faith.

It was an amazing sight. His Holiness was greeting his people ~ Tibetans who had risked life and limb to smuggle themselves under the cover of night across the border from Tibet to India simply to catch a glimpse or maybe even a touch of their holy leader. As they filed by him preciously holding out their silk white scarves for his blessings, we were directly in his line of vision, and in between salutations he would squeeze his eyes at us, lift his hand, give the camera a cute finger wave followed by a squeeze of his shoulders and a high-pitched giggle. His eyes sparkled when he did this and they magnetized you into his realm. The moment was so endearing I didn't feel guilty in pretending we had film in the camera, yet I will forever be disappointed we hadn't captured it.

From the time His Holiness stepped foot in Sikkim, 48 years earlier, having been smuggled out of Tibet, he had been living his life under a never-ending cloud of death threats. Back in his homeland, if the reports were true, his people were tortured, their places of worship destroyed, and his religious heritage and legacy reduced to rubble. Yet he carried an air of joyousness and laughter with him that defied explanation.

On our first day, we lunched together and discussed his message. He thought to speak of the Tibetan plight, but I discouraged it. I knew if he had a political axe to grind I could not get it aired. I am like Mother Teresa in this manner; I don't get mixed up in politics. I guided him to address more universal issues, such as creating our own inner peace, one quality I knew Buddhism promoted and he was a champion for.

Following that, he held a press conference where journalists from all over the world pressured him to speak out against his foes, the Chinese government. He would not. His Holiness countered every confrontation with a serious response albeit punctuated by humor and lightness. Strategically, he was right-on, completely softening the barbs and disarming his audience.

I have since heard him bless his enemies. Allowing others to speak out for the plight of his Tibetans and his flight from his mountain paradise, he has turned the spotlight onto the teachings he was born into. Today he is unofficially welcomed the world over. Spreading the Buddhist philosophy ~ inspiring and empowering many who would never have heard of him if peace had reigned and he had remained a spiritual leader ensconced high up there in his beloved Tibetan home.

The next morning the bus with our trusty PA who was carrying our film arrived. We were able to wade through the throngs of Tibetans and Buddhists from all over the globe to capture monks praying in the sunrise, children playing in the morning mist, families loving one another, and His Holiness's innate joyfulness.

Finally it was time to focus on his message. At first he surprised me because this simple man whose people could be among the materially poorest on the planet began by stating that it was a good thing to want wealth and possessions, yet it was "our power within" that was our greatest asset because it gave us the ability to transform ourselves and all those around us. He was as eloquent about achieving our inner calm as Mother Teresa was about being a warrior of love.

When I nodded that we had finished, all at once his security net swooped in to surround him, forming a protective cloak under which to whisk him away to his waiting motorcade.

Suddenly he held up his hands to halt their movement. A hush fell across the crowd. He broke through his security force and strode directly toward me. They stood at a distance and kept the hundreds who had gathered around us at arm's length.

His Holiness stopped within a foot of me. He smiled. Reaching out, he took both my hands in his and giggled in what I had come to know as his charmingly playful manner. He looked deeply into my eyes and said with great purpose, "Thank you." Then he squeezed my hands, nodded, and blinked!

It was one forceful, head-nodding blink!

He sent waves of energy through my hands, up my arms, rippling across my body, and landing directly in my stomach, the solar plexus that is our power center. As if my belly had a propeller attached to it that he had just started up, I felt as if my feet were about to lift off terra firma.

I will never forget that blink.

"Thank you," I responded.

He squeezed my hands one more time as if to punctuate the feeling that purposefully he had transmitted something to me. To this day, I am not quite sure what it was. As we watched the throng carry him away, I thought, *I shall have to ask him sometime.* Because somehow I knew I would see him again.

Five years later I would be requested to film him; this time, we would be under the Bodhi tree in Bodh Gaya, the place where Buddha gained his enlightenment. I spent many days filming His Holiness for a world peace project. I did not get the opportunity to ask him that time either. However, I know I will see him again. And if I am still curious, I shall ask him then.

As his motorcade carried him up, up, and away into the Himalayan mist, the dizzying crowd left us on the grassy hill and we all breathed a sigh of relief.

We were done.

The plan was for the crew to fly home to Bombay and me to Calcutta, for my return flight to Los Angeles. Who knows, perhaps it was His Holiness's blink, perhaps not, but the invisible finger of caution was tapping me on the shoulder telling me that I could not release the crew. Not yet.

"Nayeem, I have to take you and the boys back to Calcutta with me."

"So you have fallen in love with us, Christina," Nayeem chortled, making eyes at me to the crew's utter enjoyment. We had spent so much time together that with mere expressions and sounds, mostly a lot of hand waving and laughter, we were all communicating.

On the long journey overland, I had been editing the film in my mind.

"Truth is, guys, I don't have the final scene for Mother Teresa's message." I showed them a photograph from a small photo book of Calcutta.

"I need this shot on the banks of the Ganges!" They all looked dumbly at me. "Okay. This is how it plays out. Mother Teresa's message will begin at the water's edge with words written in the sand. Then we cut to her and the scenes we shot in Calcutta. In the end I want to bookend it, by panning up from the water's edge again, this time slowly going up to the heavens. And then I can either put my title there, or go back to the beach."

"But, Miss Christina, you have already exceeded your budget," Nayeem said, like a concerned production manager. "And no air travel is refundable in India."

The heightened pitch of Nayeem's words reminded me that we had twice returned to the American Express office for more bags of rupee cash ~ that being the most effective mode of purchasing services, airfares, and favors in India. I bit my lip.

"You understand it will mean more days for the crew, all new flight tickets and hotel rooms. It will almost double your original budget. And for one shot?" Nayeem's eyes were bugging out of his head. I could tell he thought I was nuts. I would also have to make last-minute changes to my flight home, with still more penalties attached to that.

Quietly I knew this was the price I had to pay for not having a location scout and for not having prepared the shoot in my usual manner. I remain ever grateful American Express has no spending limit.

Once again, after our journey overland, through armed check-points and the like, bribing more government officials than I could count, and with my pretense of being a pregnant damsel to explain the bulge of film cans under my dress, the crew were given seats on the only flight bound for Calcutta.

*"It's rather wonderful when you realize
there is a higher power involved, even in your daily activities.
It takes all the pressure off you and puts
a higher purpose into each day."*

Monday, April 26, 1993
Calcutta

Before sunrise we all jumped back into our old, reliable, rickety van and rattled through the streets of Calcutta, where people were bathing away their cobwebs from the night. We stopped briefly to capture men doing yoga in the park and children happily having breakfast while sitting in a pile of garbage under the bridge. The sun was just over the horizon when we turned onto the entrance to the famed Howrah Bridge, spanning the Ganges, connecting India's rural land to the city of Calcutta and built to carry the masses to work every day.

"Stop. Stop here," I called to Nayeem, waving my guidebook at him. "This is the spot." Before he could lightly tap the driver on the shoulder as he had done for me every other time I spotted a place to put the camera, the van's engine coughed and died.

"Ha," I said, assessing we were right in the middle. "This is a perfect place for us to break down."

Being one of the largest cantilever bridges in the world, the Howrah offered us an unencumbered voyeur's view of the river, its bathers, and the city skyline all in one sweeping crescendo. The perfect finale. I shot out of the van as if my feet were on fire.

"This is it," I told Jehangir. "Put the camera right here." Then I showed him how we would pan up from the water to the sky and across and higher, telling him I would then dissolve into Mother Teresa's image to speak her final words from the heavens.

As the rest of the crew crawled out of the van, a group of uniformed, armed policemen standing nearby turned and looked in our direction. *Uh-oh!*

Every time we pulled out the camera, Jehangir would remind me of the perils of shooting without a permit. He would state them in English and Hindi, so everyone was in the know.

He motioned for his assistant to leave the camera in the van.

The driver crawled out from under it, signaling to Nayeem that it was the same old problem and he could fix it in no time. Nayeem motioned to Jehangir that he should take the camera out of the van.

That's when it began.

Gently at first, but then it hit us violently. The massive single-span steel structure began to sway. As if the bridge itself were a breathing, living organism, it commenced expanding and contracting, billowing in the wind. Then it moved into shudder-and-vibrate mode. I hugged the steel girder beside me and reached out to steady Jehangir.

"I think we're having an earthquake!"

Jehangir chuckled at my California girl comment. He then grimaced and nodded to behind me. After steadying myself, I turned to see a truly awesome sight. Thousands, literally thousands of people, so colorful they put the rainbow to shame, emptying out of buses and trams and goodness knows what else to begin their morning charge across the bridge on their way into the city.

With the arrival of the masses the police force nearby suddenly became extremely attentive. More uniformed constabularies emerged from their vans brandishing weapons.

The camera assistant was loading the long lens onto the body of the camera and Jehangir suddenly fell into a fit of anxiety. When the camera assistant stepped back signaling he was ready, I breathed a sigh.

The crowd was 100 feet away and charging. And Jehangir selected that moment to take a deep breath, cross his arms and legs, and lean upon the bridge strut to pontificate.

"I do not understand it," he said deliberately. "I made a film for the Indian Tourist Board and we wanted to shoot here, right here on this bridge, but we were not allowed. Even we, who were working for our own government, were told we could not shoot here. Not here, not anywhere in Calcutta! But look, right there, the policemen have seen us and they do nothing. I cannot understand this. Either they are blind or they have already called the paddy wagon to come pick us up. I think perhaps we must leave now."

Then, he said it all over again in Hindi, so that each one of us could contemplate his dilemma. As the assistant dismantled the lens to pack it back into the van, it was all I could do not to pick up the camera and whack Jehangir over the head with it.

I was beside myself. I pulled Nayeem to me. "Nayeem, I must have this shot." He alone knew what it had cost me.

Nayeem ordered everyone to stop.

Though I couldn't quite understand what he was saying, two words popped out. *Spiritual government.* Then the assistant cameraman repeated them. Ah, he was telling them about the predictions from the ancient palm reader in Bombay. Even Jehangir straightened up and pulled in his brow at those two mystical words, considering them solemnly.

Then, without any further ado, and under the stoic gaze of the police, the long lens carrier brought the lens back out of the van, the assistant cameraman returned to remounting it, and Jehangir focused on planning the camera move in his mind.

With the crowds bearing down on us from one side of the bridge, the police slapping batons on their legs from the other side, Nayeem, as if he read my mind, stood poised to fly and said, "Do you want me to run down to the water's edge and chase the birds?"

"Yes," I responded. "Go now. We'll be ready when you get there." We didn't have walkie-talkies or any of the sophisticated equipment I was used to, so I pulled at my red scarf and motioned to Nayeem that I would wave it to cue his birds. And off he sprinted.

Some of the citizens on their way to work had reached us and stopped to stare at the camera. I was sure it would begin a dangerous pileup of people.

It was a race against time. It was a godsend that our van had broken down. It gave us an excuse to remain, when all vehicles were being cleared from the bridge. And now it helped as a buffer between us and the onslaught.

The bridge was now swaying under the weight of the thousands heading our way. *Nothing will stop them. The van will topple, and we will surely be crushed.*

Suddenly the police force banded together, shoulder to shoulder, and faced what looked like a marching army.

The film was locked in the gate. Just a little more threading . . .

I took off my red scarf. Nayeem hadn't made it to the river yet.

I wasn't quite sure what to do, except exude confidence and pretend. Pretend we had permits. Pretend we had the permission of God and government and the sacred tiger itself. And not let a fearful, wary thought cross my brow.

Go to that place of bliss. Get yourself to that place of absolute peace, I ordered my mind. I had survived some very hairy landings in crosswinds that should have taken me out. And what saved me? Some odd transportation out of this time and space to a place where fear did not exist.

But the sight in front of me spoke of instances in India where the masses surge forth and people are trampled to death. And I had never seen this many people coming at me before. *Where, oh where were my magic slippers? Click. Click. There's no place like home. There's no place like home.*

The bridge was now in full swing. The crowds were about to overtake us. I bundled up my scarf, ready to release it into the wind. I peered over to see if I could spot Nayeem in the distance. "Okay. Are we ready?" I asked.

I don't know what was scarier. The oncoming crowd or the cops who were all lined up now.

Instead of putting his eye to the lens, Jehangir, along with the rest of the crew, eyed the police, looked to the others, and nodded seriously. Almost in response, the police slapped their thighs with their batons and continued to look right through us. And the paddy wagon had yet to arrive. Consensus was we were working under the divine protection of a higher power and all was as it should be. Smiles and relief all around.

Finally. Roll film.

We were within a few feet of the mass blitz when the sun emerged and sparkled upon the rooftops. I released my red scarf into the wind and a flock of birds exploded from the steps of the River Ganges and soared up into the heavens. It was perfect.

As if the world started up again, the van sprang to life. The crowd and the police dispersed around us. We all piled in and drove across the bridge to pick up Nayeem.

Jehangir, relieved and energized, spoke rapidly to the others, and though I didn't understand what he was saying, I picked up on the phrase *spiritual government* right before he began to laugh. The rest of the crew nodded their heads intently and then they, too, broke into laughter. Nayeem interjected something and their mirth faded. Whatever the exchange, I could tell he was referring to the old sage. A quiet filled the van, and I saw again how they honor matters of the spiritual kind with such great reverence and respect. Thank God for my ancient fortune-teller.

It was time to say thank you and good-bye.

Knowing how valuable and scarce film equipment was in India, I gave my unexposed negative to the camera assistant. I had seen how preciously Jehangir had fondled my two rather expensive Pro-Mist filters, and I gifted them to him. Jehangir was wonderful in his understanding of composition and texture and light, and like all of us, whether we're creating a movie or creating a life, he simply needed the tools.

Speechless, the look in his eyes said it all. *Thank you.* Two words, two little words that mean so much.

Nayeem put the crew on a night flight to Bombay, and I wandered the hotel gift shops gathering presents for everyone at home.

"When you love,
there are no good-byes."

Tuesday, April 27, 1993
Taj Bengal, Calcutta

After big hugs and teary thank-yous to Monica, golden handshakes with the phone operator, the bellman, all the waiters, and pretty much everyone who was working in the hotel that day, and finally the doorman, I went one last time to the Motherhouse to see Mother Teresa. I thought it would be a brief good-bye, but I should have known no time with Mother could ever be referred to as "brief."

When I arrived, Sister Josma stood at the doorway as if expecting me.

"Ah, it is you!" she said with a sweet smile. "I had a dream about you last night."

"You did?"

"Yes," she answered, gazing into my face. "I dreamed about the one who was born when Mother began the Missionaries of Charity."

"Oh," I responded, recalling that I was, indeed, born in the springtime of its founding. I wanted to know what her dream had been, but I didn't want to pry. Besides, my time here was almost over and there was something about Sister Josma that was contained and private, and a search for details would have been slow.

"Would you take the mail back to the United States for us?" Sister Josma asked.

"I would be happy to."

She disappeared into an office and returned with two shopping bags filled with addressed letters from Mother and packages for the Missionaries of Charity in the United States.

"Here is a tape Mother made," she said, handing me a small cassette tape. "It was a talk she gave to the volunteers a few years ago. I thought you would like it, or, who knows, you may need to use it."

I wanted to hug Sister Josma, but I felt her space was very much her own, and so I touched her arm and she in turn touched mine in exactly the same way.

I journeyed upstairs, cautiously, unsure if I would see a crowd of 100 or the small group I had become accustomed to. My flight was departing in two hours, and Nayeem was to arrive with a car and my luggage in ten minutes, so I was anxious about how long I would need to wait to see Mother.

Morning prayers had ended, and there were less than a handful of people waiting in the breezeway. She dealt with them as she had before, briefly and lovingly, and this time miraculously, it was just a few minutes before we were alone on the bench, for the last time.

"I am leaving today," I said, fighting back tears. We took each other's hands and held on tightly. We spoke as if we both knew this would be the last time we would speak in the flesh.

We touched upon the subject of dying, and without her telling me, I sensed she looked forward to one day going home to God. I encouraged her to relax her rules a little and permit interviews and allow people to take photographs of her and her work so that she would remain alive in people's hearts and minds after she had gone.

"Yes, God bless" was her response. I am happy to say in the few years that followed she opened up herself and her work to many authors and photographers.

love

I knew time was of the essence here, but I did not want to leave her. Briefly, we sat in silence, just holding hands. And then I felt the emotions rising in me. Thank goodness she spoke.

"You are a carrier of God's love," she said softly. "Say this with me." Still holding hands, she turned our palms up and cupped my hands in hers, and as if we were two little girls playing a game, she lifted my hands up and down to the rhythm of our chanting.

"Make me a channel of your peace,
that where there is hatred I may bring love,
where there is wrong I may bring the spirit of forgiveness,
where there is doubt I may bring faith,
where there is sadness I may bring joy."

She then held my hands even tighter and pulled me close.

"Promise me," she said seriously, "that from now on you will only work for God and the good of the people."

"I promise," I replied, lowering my head to hide the evidence of my sadness over our parting. I was choking up. She leaned in, cupped her hand under my chin, and spoke in a voice as deep as the sea is blue.

"It is by forgetting self that one finds God. It is by forgiving that one is forgiven. It is by dying that one awakens to eternal life."

Her smile was wide and happy. We both knew what she was saying to me.

I could not hold my tears inside any longer. I couldn't swallow them, and I couldn't blink them away. A tidal wave of emotion burst forth from within me.

"Oh, no," she murmured. Just the way she had done those other times when she had returned with a gift. The white curtain billowed, and she was gone. I didn't quite see her leave, and it felt to me as if she had simply transported herself back into her office. She reappeared the same way and slipped down on the bench beside me. Taking my hand, she pressed into my palm a silver ring with a cross on top of it.

Have you ever had a vision that felt so real you were certain it was a memory? You knew it could not be a memory of who you are today, but it touched you so deeply that it may have been you in some other time? Something so indelibly inscribed upon your soul you know it has come to enlighten you again? Something that emerges when you least expect, prompted by the blush of a sensory recollection ~ even something as insignificant as a touch?

She pressed the ring into my hand and the cross on the end of it pressured the hollow of my palm. What flooded back into my consciousness was wholly more than a vision. It was complete knowledge in the snapshot of a hologram. So deep I could barely frame it.

As I look upon it now, it summed up every feeling I had with Mother Teresa as she progressively lifted the limiting human veil of time and space, shaking me from my conscious sleep.

If I were to describe the hologram I saw in that moment, it would have come with the heavens opening up, divinely called forth by angels singing ~ heralding hallelujah and revelation.

It was an early time in Egypt, and Jesus had not been born yet, but his arrival was anticipated in the privacy of our home. My mother would gather groups of people together and speak to them of a great teacher who was soon to be born. He was coming to remind us of that which mankind was quickly forgetting. Only the few who gathered with her knew what she was referring to. As she told it, he would display talents and powers destined to change the minds of men and alter the course of the world.

As anticipation of this revolution became stronger, my mother's health weakened. In prophecy of the new world we were about to see born, she was also predicting her own demise. And as the time of his birth grew nearer, my mother's life force grew weaker.

Then one day she did not rise from her bed. She told me she was to be beside him in his life, and she needed to leave this place to prepare. She held me close, for it was time for her to be on her way to heaven, and she knew I would feel a deep sadness and a great lonliness.

She had done her best to teach me all about "knowing," but I was just a child, and I wasn't always paying attention. Yet from my birth she had prepared me. Gifting me with knowledge and revealing to me my natural talents.

One thing she wanted to impress upon me was the importance of a box.

It was vital, she said, that I remember where it was hidden so when the guards came to take her body away, I could retrieve it. The box, she promised, assured I would not grow up in slavery. It was not physical slavery that concerned her ~ it was slavery of the mind. She did not wish for me to fall under the spell of fragmented thought, pulled into the societal whirlpool of the masses.

I was reluctant to listen to her speak of leaving me, but she was getting weaker and weaker, and nothing I did helped. I cooked and served her all the right herbs, cleaned the house, and kept to the spirit of love she had always encouraged ~ sharing what we had with anyone who called. But her life force was fading.

Huddled beside her bed, I prayed for hours, but she wasn't getting better.

For days I sat on the hard floor, holding her hand, watching her chest rise and fall, listening to the crackle in her lungs. My mother, who had always been so vibrant and alive, looked as if she were slipping off into a deep sleep. Eventually she refused all food and water, and I knew it was only a matter of time ~ and all I could do was wait.

Every minute of those last days I remained close to her.

Then one day the sky grew dark and the rains came. Perhaps this was her call to return home, because she lifted her head and tilted her eyes to me and said breathlessly, "Oh, you wait so long."

And I answered, "Mother, I would wait for you forever."

She gave a great sigh, and then she was gone.

When the guards came to take her remains, even though I knew she was no longer present in her body, I cried and cried anyway. And then I remembered the box.

For a moment I had forgotten where she had hidden it. But I saw it again, in my mind's eye. And there it was. Concealed behind a series of loose bricks, wedged in a tiny passageway, was the simple wooden box.

It creaked open. Inside were three perfectly forged silver bracelets set with deep blue lapis stones. I remember her wearing them on special occasions when we had gatherings of close friends. I moved them around in the box, and the sound they made as they touched resonated in the room. It brought back to me the joyous times when she wore them and the room "felt" different. When she lifted her hand and waved, the bracelets would ring out a frequency and a call for attention, and the chatter all around ceased and a certain peace came upon everyone.

One by one, I pulled the bracelets out of the box. When I let all three come together, their sound echoed through me, almost as if they were awakening the divinity of the soul. All at once, I heard her words again as if she were beside me, speaking in my ear. And all those many things she had taught me filled me with knowing.

She had prepared me well for this day, schooling me in the mysteries and gifting me with talents that some said with mankind's evolution would be forgotten. Distractions from outside would crucify the jewels of within. She did not leave me with the practical knowledge of how human beings function in the outer world; instead her teachings focused on our inner realm. I knew how to recall my soul journey and how to hold consciousness so that I could gather information while in dreamtime. She taught me how to navigate dimensions so that I could step through to the other side. She showed me how to read energy, how to communicate with animals, and how to heal. What many would consider supernatural, she made for me as natural as breathing.

Beneath the bracelets was a necklace woven with ankhs, the symbol of Isis: the signature of eternal life. Each ankh connected to another in an intricate web significant of the layering of life experience and the multiplication of form and the eternal transmutation of energy. The many becoming one. One. One. One. And the one becoming many.

Finally, there was a soft cloth, dyed the color of deep purple grapes. Inside its folds was a ring. It wasn't really a ring you would wear ~ it was a ring you held to pray with. It was heavy forged silver, with a deep purple stone in its center.

I looked deeper into the box. I knew there was something more in there. I ran my fingers around inside but felt nothing. It appeared empty. Faintly, I recalled my mother suggesting this was the most precious gift of all. I turned it upside down and shook it, wondering if whatever it was had left a speck or a hint. And then it came back to me.

love

She had trained me in sensory recall. How I was to close my eyes and stop the mind chatter. How I would slow my breath and my body activity down to see through the eye in between my eyes. The intuitive third eye.

I held the simple wood box up high, and there it was! Dead center, flashing through an almost imperceivable hairline crack. In that pinprick hole I saw again what she wanted me to remember. The tiny crack looked like a lightning bolt. I held it up to my eyes and was struck again by her intention ~ "It is the one thing no one sees; yet without it, we see nothing."

A pinpoint of a vivacity, glittering like a diamond in the sky. It was light! It was clarity and respect. It was compassion and understanding ~ joy and happiness. It was the moment of recognition. It was love.

The fire from that tiny hairline was the revelation I would carry with me all the days of my life. Reverently, I held the simple box close to my heart, evoking its truth to forever trust that which I could not see, yet would always feel. Recognizing it as the essence of love deep in my heart. It would fill that place of emptiness and I would no longer look without to fix or heal what was within. My tears stopped and the sadness lifted from my being.

She was gone from my sight. Yet she had not gone at all. I knew that.

In death, I knew she would be closer than she had ever been to me in life.

CHAPTER SIXTEEN

TRUST LOVE

Robert Black

*"Love arrives in an instant,
enters everywhere, and
lives on throughout eternity."*

Mother Teresa pressed the ring deep into my palm. Her soft, generous hands folded mine around it. I was dumbfounded. Our last words in that life were our first words every time we greeted each other in this life. It was like a ritual or a code, for I could never fathom where those words came from. In that moment, sunlight shone down upon us and my tears evaporated.

"When you write . . . ," she said with great intent.

Into my mind shot the thought, *How did she know I wrote? I never told her. She has only seen me as a woman with a camera and a film crew.* I gazed at her in wonder.

Mother squeezed my hand and looked deeply into my eyes to be sure I did not forget what she was about to say. Her voice was penetrating and unwavering.

"When you write, wear this ring and God will write through you."

I braved a smile, and we hugged good-bye. In a flash of light she was gone.

Certain I would never see her again in this life, tears welled in my eyes. My whole body began to shake. Quickly I gathered myself, and slipped away down the stairs and through the courtyard.

Once I stepped into the clinging heat that hung in the alleyway my wet cheeks became dry and only my hands were quivering. It was still early morning and quiet on Bose Road.

I looked for Nayeem and the car, but he had not yet arrived. So I sat down on the Motherhouse stoop and waited.

Composing myself, I wondered if this had all been a dream or a journey back into the world of my own personal akashic record. As I sat there watching a strange yet familiar world go by, fondling the silver ring in my hand with Mother's last words still resonating, I was in awe of the gift I had just received. The gift of remembering.

The knowledge that we are all uniquely gifted beings, living multidimensional, nonlinear existences. We are all mystics who can choose or not to push away the darkness to reveal what our present consciousness has hidden.

We all carry this knowledge. We all know this truth.

And it's the truth that shall set us free.

Nayeem threw open the car door, and I crawled in.

"We will make it, but just in the nick of time," he said, and we took off in a screech of tires. *Uh-oh, we've got Mario Andretti at the wheel.* Maybe I was silently saying my prayers or perhaps I was sad to say good-bye to Nayeem ~ our ride to the airport went by in silence as we wove through the streets like a colorful thread making its way in and out of a delicate sari.

Nayeem ran ahead with my precious cargo of unprocessed negative, carefully encased in aluminum-lined bags and inscribed with the fervent plea, "Please DO NOT X-RAY!" I would not be able to carry it aboard, and I would have to check it as cargo. Fragile, delicate, breakable cargo.

Having appointed himself to be my protector of sorts, Nayeem went to great pains to explain to the ticket agent that the negative film I carried contained a message from Mother Teresa. I saw the response two words, *Mother Teresa*, brought ~ gasps and smiles and bows of the head. Willing and complete compliance to his wishes.

Nayeem flatly refused to leave until he had seen both me and the negative safely aboard my flight to Thailand.

The agent took my passport and tickets and beckoned over the airline concierge who was then followed by an airline attendant. She had him put my film on a cart and motioned for me to follow them both through a door marked Entrance Prohibited.

Nayeem and I hurriedly exchanged personal gifts we had each picked up on our journey and hugged good-bye with promises to write, to call, to see each other again. I would be forever grateful to him.

The airline attendant rushed me down a very long corridor, up a small flight of stairs, and into an elevator, explaining she wanted me to witness my negative being put into a secure, pressurized, temperature-controlled part of the aircraft. "When I return to my office I will call ahead to Bangkok and make similar arrangements for your layover there and your continuing flight to Los Angeles."

A waiting male attendant unlocked a compartment in the midsection of the plane and slid my negative in between two large containers of what looked like refrigerated medical supplies. The airline concierge shot me a smile, gave the film a kindly pat and a giggle, nodding as she said, "Mother Teresa." After they locked the door, she escorted me back up in the elevator where the ticket agent handed me my processed passport and tickets and in a flurry of thank-yous, delivered me into the aircraft. The doors closed immediately behind me.

When our wheels left the ground ~ what can I say? It never fails to overwhelm me. The miracle of flight. Why do I liken flight to love?

love

Because it's impossible, implausible, irrational, and inconceivable to believe we human earth inhabitants could mesh with another, in a moment of exquisite perfection to seed another moment of perfection from the union. The miracle of love.

When the wheels locked into the wheel bay, I was grateful for the empty seat beside me and wriggled down. I took a deep breath of gratitude, and the tension left my body. Relaxation tugged between my shoulder blades, and I gazed out at the clouds that seemed to be engulfing us. At 30,000 feet, I was home.

"Time to turn your no into YES!"

Content that I had fulfilled my mission ~ which to some I had encountered at the Motherhouse was an impossible dream ~ my eyes wandered across the clouds outside. Grateful for the absence of a plan or a desire, at least for the next few hours, I stared out the portal into that spaceless zone and let my mind merge with its living shapes. Ahh, *victory!*

Perhaps it was merely fluttering, but I thought I heard my heart whispering so faintly I could not make out what it was saying, yet a second later, his smoky deep voice murmured, *"Le destin nous me à l'épreuve."* Translation: Fate is testing us!

He slid down into the seat beside me and followed the direction of my porthole gaze.

"Voilà! The *Winged Victory!*" Dr. Michael said.

"You see that, too?" I asked rather incredulously. How rare is it that someone else sees the same shape you do in a cloud? *Is this man wooing my heart or what?*

I looked at him, and those eyes got me again. My pulse raced. I was falling into his deep blues.

"When I lived in Paris I had an apartment very close to the Louvre. It was before I learned to fly. I would spend my weekends sitting under the *Winged Victory.* Sitting on the stairs, studying her, and drawing her. I knew every fold of her gown and every feather in her wings. She was my touchstone."

Uh-oh. This is another thing I do when nervous. I talk. I chatter. I fill up and block every opening of discovery.

I took a deep breath. "Do you live in Paris?" I asked.

"Non." He shook his head. "I studied medicine there. My mother is French."

"And your father?"

"He is from Colombia."

The blue eyes ~ definitely from his mother. There was a warm compassion in his eyes that my quick glances hadn't seen before. I considered that they had looked upon worlds I had not and probably would never see in this life. He was not the kind of doctor who came to know his patients. Landing from a distant star to heal the sick, rescue the dying, and manage the pain of the desperate, perhaps never to know gratitude from those he saved. My eyes rested upon his broad and not quite perfect nose and his impeccably tanned skin. These and his smooth, poetic way with words ~ they would be from his father. Busy wrapping my head around the exotic combination playing itself out exquisitely in the good doctor, the flight attendant returned to the galley for another tray setting and brought it over to Michael. He waved her away and said he would return to his seat. My heart sank.

"Will you be spending time in Bangkok?" he asked, rising out of his seat and giving me that steely, penetrating stare that unnerved me so the first time we met.

"Yes," I responded.

"Do you have friends?" he inquired, having shifted to English.

"No. I am just on a layover until my flight to Los Angeles tomorrow."

"Would you like to have dinner with me?" he asked, looking deep, probing for more of a comeback than yes or no.

My mind sorted through its file of acceptable responses: *Oh, thank you so much but what a pity. I have work to do. Kind of you to ask, but I'm on a very early flight tomorrow. I will be asleep by dinnertime.* Always I had my excuses ready, but without permission my mouth dismissed them. "That would be lovely," I said, immediately rationalizing to my inner terror: *I have earned this detour.* "I am staying at the Oriental," I offered.

"I will call you before seven," he said, and returned to his seat. Immediately the butterflies in my stomach took flight, circling in chaos and crashing into one another.

I had just about organized them into manageable formation when our wheels touched down in Bangkok. It was a little before noon, and I was immediately concerned for the film's survival in 90-plus-degree heat. Despite Mother's efforts to impart her unconditional faith to me, I hadn't yet fully grasped there was a spiritual power at work that could not be derailed by my futile worry.

When the hatch swung open, a VIP attendant boarded the plane, whisked me past the deplaning passengers, and escorted me down to the tarmac. There I watched as my priceless cargo that had traveled side by side with what I now realized were Michael's medical supplies was removed and hand-carried into an air-conditioned holding room where it would remain until the next day. Word of its importance had preceded me. The young woman at my side smiled at my obvious relief, took my passport and tickets, and assured me that all would be ready for my departure the following morning.

Already I had seen it a dozen times ~ on my boarding ticket, my customs exit form, my visa documents, customs entry forms, and I wrote it on my traveler's checks, but I didn't actually "see" it until I signed the hotel registration book. The date. April 27. It was Geoffrey's birthday. This date would forever signify my father's gift to him of a broken nose. Horrific it was, and until this trip I had cast out all memory of how he got that bump on an otherwise perfect cherub's face. Had I recalled it I would have understood why Geoffrey hated our father so much. He had not masked it or pushed it down.

Yet, in a healthy fashion, when he was ready, Geoffrey forgave our father, and six months before his death they agreed to go into business together. Forgiveness in itself is freedom. Without the perspective of the larger picture it can be an expansive human achievement. Knowing that what others say and do to you is a projection of their reality and has nothing to do with you is living from a higher realm. It brings compassion and understanding into every relationship.

I lunched on my balcony, overlooking the waterways of Bangkok's metropolis and its urban skyline dotted with ancient Buddhist temples and gleaming golden palaces. The timelessness of Thailand's capital city, rich with ancient history, thriving presence, and soaring future, mingled perfectly with the day I'd had so far. In Calcutta I had spent time with Mother Teresa, journeyed back to a time before Christ, been treated like a queen while taking an international flight, stopped in briefly to recall my life in Paris, and now I was plopped down into five-star Asian luxury. And goodness, it was only lunchtime!

I lifted the handset to schedule a massage, but there was no dial tone. Instead, his sultry bedside voice was right there.

"Can you be ready and downstairs in two hours?" Straight to English no less.

"Ready? For what?" I was quite taken aback.

"We are going to a friend's restaurant on the beach. It is the journey of an hour. Dress to be comfortable. *C'est bien?*"

"*Oui.*"

"Forgiveness brings peace.
And peace is freedom.
Freedom at last."

Having no time for a massage, I opted for a luxuriating bath. I could feel all the stories I had looked upon lately as if they were just that ~ stories. I slipped into the bath and let the rush of water rise over me as it filled the tub.

April 27. It marked also the day we last spoke ~ Geoffrey's 42nd birthday. Celebrations in my family were nonevents. Money or gifts rarely considered, a card or a letter, sometimes. Still, the birthday person could always expect "the phone call." I, engrossed in my corporate ecosphere 12,000 miles away, completely forgot what day it was. Geoff and Rosie took it upon themselves to call me from Sydney. In between their waiting silences, they laughed and giggled. Surprised by their unusual gaiety and a little aggravated by a pointless phone call at 2 A.M., I missed the joke. I missed the opportunity as well.

A hint of regret crept into my heart, and for a moment I felt myself sliding back into the past. I caught it and wondered why it was still with me. I meditated on it for a moment. What I saw was a seed sitting in my belly. It looked and felt like a peach seed, with tiny rough thorns around its edges, gnawing at my insides. I had let most things go, but the one thing I hadn't liberated was the mystery under which Geoffrey died. I never found out what the autopsy actually said. Rosie told it to me, or maybe I heard it, in a jumble of lymphoma, bronchitis, or could it be pneumonia. I saw myself again, sitting in the conservatory with her, holding baby Jessica, and watching the children play around the staircase that led down to Geoffrey's beloved wine cellar.

A wave of undoubting love washed over me for those four little innocents. Who was I to take away their sweet naïveté with my dark suspicions? They did not need my burdensome uncertainties imprinting their blossoming into the world. When I took him to the other side he made no claims upon revenge. Revenge being more an unhappy ghost visited upon the living rather than a prayer of peace for the dead.

Watching droplets of cleansing water as they trickled over my body like trails of personal history, to merge with the waterways of the more universal ocean of humanity, I watched my tiny drama transform and become one with all water. *If I don't get lost in the drama, if I don't use my "stories"' as excuses and reasons, if I can simply learn to let go of a thought should it not be one of loving, either for myself or another, then I may get to see my life path with a clear and healthy detachment. I may even achieve a life unencumbered by my own small importance.*

I sank deeper and let the water rush over my head.

Ah, the ocean of love and the fish! The fish for Adriana. When all the drama has disappeared into one, could we, humanity, find ourselves swimming effortlessly in the sea of love? That magnificent ocean where Mother Teresa is a permanent resident?

Bubbles were forming on top. I scooped them up and blew. They popped and were gone. I reflected on the last couple of months where I had reached deep inside and unearthed a whole heap of broken past in order to be clear enough to put myself in Mother Teresa's presence. Then lo and behold, as I let go of my human adventure, I came upon an even deeper past, the adventure of the soul. For who is to say when a life journey really begins? When a belief came about? When a talent was learned? When a burden was taken on? When an agreement was made? When a disease or a challenge entered our body? Who is to say indeed.

We live two lives simultaneously. One of the body and the other of the spirit. One has an expiration date stamped on it and the other? None we know of. I have heard many say we are spiritual beings having a human experience. And though I know the heart is an organ of the body, it seems to be the one most connected to the spirit. Could it be the master interpreter, the connector for the soul? It certainly is the organ most like the soul.

The heart can always be mended. The soul can never be broken.

"Real love is innocent.
It opens its arms wide,
free of expectations, boundaries,
and judgments."

Standing under a massive umbrella of red hibiscus, soaking in the sweet perfume of star jasmine, I was looking for a car or maybe even a limo to find its way out of the steaming, pulsating Bangkok traffic. Suddenly a BMW motorcycle slid like butter into the curb in front of me. I couldn't see his blue eyes through his helmet, but I sure recognized those Latin hips as he lifted up from his seat, pushed down the parking step, and swung himself off the bike.

"C'est bien." Translation for this moment and the look on his face was his appreciation of how intelligently I had dressed, almost as if I had known I would be sitting astride a motorcycle.

love

I knew where he was taking me. Or should I say, I knew where we were heading. No. I couldn't tell you the name of the restaurant, what beach it was on, or even in what direction from the city it was. But I felt it immediately when he slipped a helmet on my head and gently tucked back my long hair from my cheeks. His hands were strong and yet his touch was tender. The connection of our energy was just as you would expect from a doctor, as if his fingertips were sensing information. Momentarily his right hand slid around to the back of my neck and rested there. A tiny thrill squiggled down my spine and exploded.

"I think this is where you most like to be kissed," he murmured.

I loved that he was right ~ but it also made me uncomfortable. A scary indication he knew more. *What else?* I wondered. He could know things ~ things I don't want to share with him. But then, why wouldn't I? What is sharing of yourself, other than opening another to your truth? *Why not own who you are,* I told myself. *Why not be real, take a risk, enjoy?*

I sensed Michael's capacity for caring when he guided me to climb on behind him and intimately pulled me into him, hugging my legs to hold him tight. We knew so little about each other, and yet I suspected we knew so much more than many I had spent years beside. More than many I considered good friends ~ more than some I called family even.

Anticipation roared in my throat when he kicked open the engine and every atom in my sensual body tingled and woke as if they had been dozing out there in the ether for centuries.

Accelerating in a burst of power, we swerved and swayed our way through the grinding city traffic where I found myself close to kissing more than one smiling, toothless tuk tuk driver. It occurred to me how last minute my change-of-flight plans were and how this side trip was such a sweet coincidence. Ah, but I knew better . . . and I knew, too, this was no side trip.

Am I ready for this? I marveled. I knew the mission Michael had chosen had no room for a traditional home and family. I knew our moments together would be time stolen. A weekend here. A layover there. Always on the honeymoon. I knew also there were others in his life. I would have to stretch myself to overcome the challenges of loving that I had previously failed at so dismally ~ to love without condition, to share without jealousy, and, most difficult of all, to give without expectation. I steeled my heart and said yes. Like the tug that had irresistibly drawn me to Mother Teresa, I was being reeled in by another golden thread of destiny. There was no turning back.

All sense of time vanished. We left the grit of Bangkok behind us and veered off under an archway of lush foliage onto a dirt road. Michael geared down and pulled over to the roadside. To allow me appreciation of the warm fragrant air, he took off my helmet. The infectious laughter of children nearby caught my heart. I turned to see there, through branches of orchids, a handful of children, draped in silks and laced in smiles, playing as if conceived in a dream. Before I could turn back, Michael's lips pressed moist against the nape of my neck. And so it began.

We both knew the slow approaching night and the road before us was about to become extraordinarily long and deliriously lost in translation.

With his soft lips still there, I closed my eyes and didn't move. *I shall carry this moment with me into my future. I shall see it and feel it and have it again when other moments arise that are not as blessed. I shall replace anything less with this love. This impeccable feeling will imprint its happiness and it will see me through for the rest of my days.*

Blessed I was. Blessed we are.

CHAPTER SEVENTEEN

IT'S WHY WE ARE ALIVE

Christina Stevens

*"From love we came
and
to love we return.
There is no reason
to fear the journey in between."*

Thursday, April 29, 1993
Hollywood, California

Back on earth, I had changed clothes from girl on a tropical adventure to springtime in business for my reentry onto US soil. Nevertheless, I was still in the clouds. As I exited the plane I tripped over the coat that trailed from my arm and dropped my handbag. It fell open, papers flew out, pens rolled down the ramp, and mascara followed the pens. Clumsy! Falling in love has always made me clumsy. I lose my head. I get giddy. I was hardly able to mumble a "thank you" to the helpful strangers who stopped to retrieve my belongings.

My journey through customs was just as haphazard. No VIP airline executive to meet me. No porters to carry my chattel atop wrapped turbans. The royal treatment was over. I loaded my cart in a hurried, lopsided manner and lost it all a couple of times before I made it out into the California sunshine. Had I murmured to anyone I was struggling with film of Mother Teresa, in a plea for help, I would not have gotten a glance. I was in that "other" world, where someone was struggling with the fact that they had just spotted, in the flesh, Brad Pitt or Julia Roberts or some other more revered celebrity.

I was far from the mystical milieus of India, bereft of Mother Teresa's soft voice and strong hands holding mine, but she was hardly gone from my life ~ still, worry once again prickled at the back of my neck. I had not let anyone know I was arriving home. I wanted to reenter unencumbered by questions and the exchange of information, to keep soaking in my experience of the last three weeks. And last night. I would need to get used to being carried off on a magic carpet ride, only to land on earth the next day to deal with business as usual.

I was back in production mode, and so directly from the airport, I took my sealed rolls of negative to FotoKem.

I crossed my fingers, prayed, and sketched hearts and flowers all over the requisition form as I handed over the negative for processing. Then I went home to wait. I would know in a matter of hours.

Have you ever walked into the familiarity of your home and felt that everything had changed?

Sitting quietly on my couch, waiting for the film lab to call with their results, I had the uneasy yet peaceful sense that everything in my house had shifted. My "things," my precious possessions ~ paintings, handed down in my family for generations; the silver candlesticks I had unearthed in a Parisian flea market; my stamped and hand-signed Lalique vase that I coveted every morning for six months while it sat alone on a black marble slab in the window of an antique store on Rue de Balzac; my crystal skull, a cherished gift from an unnamed monk ~ all the treasures I had collected over the years felt different. Though nothing had been disturbed or moved. The actuality was they felt less mine and more like exquisite works of art that belonged not to me but to themselves. My attachment to "things" had loosened and I felt wonderfully free.

I pulled out the conch shell found on a beach in Thailand and held it close to my heart hoping Michael's warmth was still there. Grains of sand fell. Yes. Simple. Real. This was my freedom. I placed it on the mantel beside the silver candlesticks. Slipping back onto the couch, I imagined my lone shell being joined by others from distant shores. As if my visualization was a prediction, in time, Michael's sweet forever love and our mutual passion for the ocean would build a collection that would make any beachcomber green with envy.

Peace was interrupted when the shrill ring of the phone startled me. My anxiety shot right back to a fever pitch when I realized this was it. I would know ~ if the light in the courtyard had been enough for an image. I would know ~ if I had dragged home rolls of negative with nothing on them.

"Great footage," said the technician without preface or introduction.

"What?"

"Great footage," he repeated. "Your numbers are good. Looks like good work."

"Can you see her face?"

"Huh?"

"Can you see her face? Mother Teresa's face?"

"Hang on a second. I haven't really looked at all of it." He dropped his phone with a clatter.

Years inched by while I waited with the handset pressed hard against my ear, straining to hear his conclusion. Finally I heard a scraping noise as he scooped up the receiver. "She looks beautiful," was all he said, but it was enough.

"That's the power of prayer."

"What?"

"Never mind . . . thank you, thank you for everything."

We had an image! Amazed yet extraordinarily grateful Kodak's D97 stock could have captured anything in that low light. My heart wrapped around my wonderful crew's technical expertise and the faith of loyal associates, without whom there would be no film, and my dear sweet Mother whose prayers . . . what could I say?

I breathed a sigh of relief. I had put so much pressure upon myself for this moment. Every cell in my body gave way. I fell to the floor and wept.

♡♡♡

Next morning

Considering it wise to return to my regular schedule, I headed off to the gym. Pierce was on the bicycle when I arrived, and passing him on my way to the ladies' changing room, I called out, "I bring you greetings from India."

"Is that where you've been?"

"Yes. I was working with Merchant Ivory and the family wanted to be remembered to you."

"Oh," Pierce said quietly. I caught his expression as 1,000 emotions rippled across his deep blue eyes. *Oh, Christina,* I said to myself, *sometimes you just don't think before you speak!* I had touched a nerve. It was while filming *The Deceivers* in India with Merchant Ivory that Cassandra, Pierce's wife, had first fallen ill to the cancer that eventually took her life. What was that they say? *India forces you to come face-to-face with yourself to return home, changed forever.*

Before I could apologize to Pierce for unconsciously opening up the wound he was working hard at healing, Jackson put me on the treadmill to warm up. I had barely broken a sweat when my whole body throbbed with a pain so great my knees almost gave way. With no more exchanges, I begged off my session and returned home. To bed.

What childhood memory is about to surface now? I wondered, captive audience that I was. But nothing came. In fact, as the hours rolled on, I lay staring up at the ceiling, feeling like death warmed over but also like something very tiny that had just crawled out of her cocoon. I realized the memories had gone. Search as I might, my personal past had somehow been erased. Or maybe better still, healed. There were no scars on my heart, no negative murmurs in my mind, and no judgments upon my soul. The sadness and longing that I had known all my life had left. I was a blank sheet, a clean slate. It was dawn of a new era.

"Victory!" Gilly called through the earpiece.

"Yes," I said weakly.

"We all heard how beautiful your film is . . . Are you all right?"

"I will be." My energy was sapped, while Gilly's was bursting like popcorn.

"I want to know everything. Blow by blow. What was she like? How on earth did you get her to say yes?"

I grunted. Gilly sensed I didn't have the wherewithal to engage in conversation, so she just kept going.

"Everyone is talking about your dailies. And I guess you can imagine that Mark is, er, he's not happy. He lost it a few days ago. We went way over budget on the Chrysler shoot; we had no weather insurance. Hmm, and he says he's moving everything to Canada." She gurgled nervously through the phone.

"He's been threatening to do that for a long time," I slurred. I didn't have the strength to reassure her that she would be okay. That I would make sure of it. "I think I have to go back to sleep."

She acknowledged that I was in my three-day innocuous malady period after an intense shoot, and she let me go.

Indeed I was, but there was a distinct difference to this discomfort. My entire being felt raw and exposed. As if I had simply reenergized my spirit back to Los Angeles, but the remainder of me was somewhere else, getting that upgrade I had applied for somewhere in the ether.

On the third day, with no relief in sight, I dragged my weak body to my friend Dawnea. She is an energetic therapist whose hair changes color often, as long as it highlights the tattoo emblazoned on her lower back. She pulled me into her office, a tiny house on the cliffs of Zuma Beach, and laid me out on her massage table.

Staring up at the ceiling reproduction of the *Hand of God* detail from the Sistine Chapel, she went to work. I have done all kinds of aerobatics, put my body through wrenching g-forces, but all her prodding and pushing and shifting energy around in the atmosphere had no effect until she said, "I keep seeing the image of something that looks like an Indian goddess with all these arms protruding from her back." Dawnea had neatly described Kali, the Indian goddess of destruction, the relief statue beside the doorway of Kalighat, Mother's Home for the Dying.

It clicked. So intent on calming the ailing women and taking away as much pain as I could, I realized I had not taken the necessary precaution of surrounding myself with protective white light or moving whatever energies I took in, out. It seemed as if I had inadvertently absorbed some of it.

One year later, however, I would collapse while on location in Hawaii, and after a battery of tests the doctor confirmed I was having a relapse.

"A relapse of what?" I asked.

"Hepatitis," I was told.

"What?"

Upon further questioning by the internist, we identified that it was hepatitis that I had contracted while in India.

"But I had no idea. I wasn't sick when I was there, and I only felt strange for a week or so after I came back. I just chalked it up to exhaustion."

Some inner strength in me had pushed it aside, undetected and forbidden to interfere with my work.

Perhaps Dawnea realized we were dealing with more than simple fatigue and absorption of lethargic energies, because she canceled other appointments and insisted I return each day for longer sessions. Three days later I was feeling more complete and up to returning to the office.

"Good," she said. "Because you're going off on a new job next week." I didn't want to burst her bubble, because Dawnea rarely spoke of future events without confidence or accuracy. However, I knew that could not be the case. There was nothing scheduled. We had not even had any inquiries. Even the accelerated bidding process takes at least a week.

I waltzed into the office refreshed and relaxed. I was prepared to deal successfully with Mark and his anxieties, only to find Gilly juggling a waterfall of balls and the office buzzing with excitement. New life had suddenly been breathed into a $3 million project I had bid on months earlier. We had the green light if we could bring it in for $2 million. Needless to say, Mark was energized and the payback I was expecting for my absence would be postponed.

I jumped feetfirst into preproduction for the new project. I had fashioned the original bid with us traveling all over the United States for a month, which for this new price was impossible. Immediately I sent our location scout off to scour the country for one 60-mile radius that could provide us with the cornfields of Kansas, the rolling hills of Wyoming, the rivers of Mississippi, the lakes of Illinois, the waterfalls of New York, the sandy beaches of California, the wide-open spaces of Texas, and the red rocks and snowy mountaintops of Colorado. He returned with a file thick with all that and more, in one rather magical location: on and around Mount Shasta in Northern California.

Before we left for Mount Shasta, I asked Gilly to run through an audiotape of Mother Teresa's sound track and transcribe it.

"We've never done that before," she noted, perplexed.

"Something tells me this is the way to begin." To hand over such a mess to the editor, goodness, it would take him a month of Saturdays to sort out.

After an hour, she reappeared, her entire face crinkled in a frown. "Blimey. There are things on there that for the life of me I can't make heads or tails of. Did you film her on a freeway?"

This was exactly what I was afraid of. I took a deep breath. "Just write out everything you can hear and understand," I begged her, refusing to give in to the doubting. "Even if it's just a word here or there."

She shrugged her shoulders and toodle-oo, off she went. Hours later she returned energized as if she had been off frolicking in the park. She handed me five pages of notes. On them was exactly what I had asked for. Words that didn't flow! Half sentences! Syllables even! Confounded and in shock at the puzzle in my hands I found myself taken aback by the bizarre challenge ahead.

Out of the maze of her notes and with a recollection of what Mother had said, I wrote a script. Without referring to the video, I remembered while filming her that I knew I had the heart of her message when she said, "And it's something so beautiful that love begins at home and can spread like a burning fire from house to house." I took a big risk with an editor's patience and deft ability when I pulled one word from one sentence and one word from another and stuck them together. I then faxed it over to Bobby Volpe, the editor.

Normally, we would have begun the editing process by sitting together in the theater and screening the footage, while I called out the scenes I liked and he took notes. Then, adding in his preferences, he would assemble a rough cut. We would screen his cut and as was normal, we would then spend a week cutting it this way and that until we were both happy. The final step would be to trim it for time. That normally took a day or so until we had whittled it down to our favorite takes, creating a decent piece of communication that fulfilled all the network guidelines.

This time, for reasons I can't quite explain, I didn't approach it that way. We sent over the film with my written script attached. If Bobby questioned my method, he didn't say anything. I confess I felt guilty not being man enough to watch it with him.

Unexpectedly he called me a few hours later, suggesting I come to his office.

"What? Why?" I asked.

"Nothing. Just come on over," he said, and hung up.

I was beyond nervous, totally prepared for him to hand the whole thing back to me. We've all been there. It's one thing to sign on for a "love" job ~ it's quite something else to put your reputation on the line to wade through a heap of unintelligible footage and say you can do something with it.

He was sitting on the couch in his edit suite having a late lunch when I arrived. Immediately he tossed his pasta aside and sprang to his feet, making a beeline for the console. *Oh God,* I thought. *He is going to show me how bad it is, before he gives it back. He's going to rub my nose in it!*

Bobby is Italian. A passionate yet quiet Italian. His cool makes him a great editor. Nothing fazes him. As I followed him over to the console, he had an odd glow in his eyes and an unusual joviality in his demeanor. *Is he going to turn this whole thing into a joke?* I did not know what to expect. As he sat and poised his fingers over the start button, he turned to me, looking like he had just been kissed by a pixie.

He then prefaced what he was about to show me with nothing other than, "I did a few things with the footage of the streets of Calcutta that I think you will like."

"Yes, but what about Mother?" I pleaded, fearful of his response.

"What do you mean? She was perfect. She cut like butter," Bobby said so offhandedly I thought for a moment he was joking. He noticed I had stopped breathing. I was waiting for the other shoe to drop. He winked and his grin widened. "Don't worry. The sound track is just fine. We got everything we need."

"You mean you already have a cut?"

Bobby's face was enveloped in delight.

If I didn't know better I would have thought he, too, had been divinely touched by the powerful little lady of Calcutta. He swirled his finger around in the air and aimed it at the start button, but stopped dramatically short. "Oh, and the best part ~ watch this!" Bobby pounded his timer and it turned to a bunch of zeros.

He pushed the roll tape button and the clock began. He had followed my script to the letter. Every cut he made ~ deft; every word she spoke ~ clear. Even when I suggested he build a sentence with a word from here and a word from there ~ her phrasing emerged, seamless.

I have been in the studio with some of the world's most experienced voice-over announcers and accomplished actors, and any attempt to build sentences out of disassociated words can be nearly impossible. The inflections don't blend. Not so with Mother Teresa. I realized each of her words carried the same tonal quality so we could pull a word from one sentence and a word from another to create whole cloth out of fragmented threads. Bobby had craftily disguised those loose ends by cutting away to the street scenes and my rooftop shots of Calcutta.

And the best part? Yep. Timing was exact. A rarer-than-rare experience.

You should know this sort of complex commercial film normally takes 100 cuts of going back and forth, looking for something better, shaving off a second here and a millisecond there. Fade in, fade out. Substituting a better shot here and a sweeter take there. But no. Perfect! In record time!

"Play it again, Bobby," came a voice from the doorway. Bobby's boss, Rye, stepped in, beaming. Doing work pro-bono can be risky business. This would become close to a six-figure favor gifted from Rye's heart. Mostly it's deeply rewarding, but sometimes a film can be so challenging you regret your decision and forget why you said yes in the first place. "Fantastic!" Rye said.

We had created a concise and beautiful message, and it never changed from that very first edit.

"How can I thank you?" I said as Rye hugged me from behind.

"Hey, we've never had it so good!" Rye chuckled. I knew when I asked him for help that he had no idea what I would bring back in the can from India.

This caused me to wonder at the fine balance and steady consistency that made up the fabric of Mother Teresa's being ~ about the authority she put into my hands and the power her prayer provided.

Word spread quickly around Hollywood studios that there was a film with Mother Teresa in need of a music track. I had offers from some Academy Award–winning musicians. Gilly sent out tapes for their producers to look at before we left for Mount Shasta.

I thought we were simply off on another commercial shoot.

I did not know then that the entire crew was about to embark on an adventure of such mystical proportions even Mark may never again question the power of the invisible.

Mount Shasta, California

Dealing with our all-too-visible, four-billion-year-old carbon universe was no longer the challenge it had been.

"Do you know we have landed in one of the foremost spiritual centers of the world?" Gilly was agog with all the sacred spaces she could explore. After her initial journey into the town of Mt. Shasta, her sexy pleated skirts turned into colorful, flowing Indian robes and her tailored cropped jackets were now draped with scarves and crystals. On top of that, Gilly, who had always been glued to her desk 24/7, relaxed even her own controlling work ethic.

For myself, behind our hotel, in the town of Weed, I found a wonderful windy dirt road about four miles long that I could jog through each morning. The most surprising thing was that although the elevation was high, the altitude had zero effect on me. I didn't need to adjust my breathing and I swear there were even wings on my heels.

Effortlessly, production details fell into place. We functioned like a well-oiled machine, and when shooting began, it continued. When the first weekend hit, everyone except Mark and I had an adventure planned. Mountain hikes, cave excursions, wilderness camping, volcano exploring, bird-watching, or just heavy partying by the pool.

I had a lot of catch-up work. However, at 6 A.M. Saturday, my phone rang. "You want to come for a run with me?" Mark asked. Reluctantly, I said, "Okay. If we can run the road behind the hotel. I know the route."

"Meet you by the pool in ten," he said quickly, and hung up. Already I was unsure about breaking my vow not to run with him. I need not have worried.

We set out in silence. Less than a mile away from the hotel I was settling comfortably in my stride. It was time to pick up the pace. Out of the corner of my eye I noticed Mark was not beside me. At the first bend in the road I turned and was shocked to see him trailing by 20 yards. I ran a few circles so he could catch up. The next straight expanse of road was around three-quarters of a mile long.

My breathing smooth, I was feeling as light as the thin air, one with the ground and the trees and everything surrounding me.

"Come on then," I encouraged Mark, but I could see his legs were heavy and his breathing labored. I could do nothing else but let my happy feet fly.

My head held high, my arms at right angles, *God, it felt good. Mrs. Anderson would be proud of me.* When I reached the end of the road, the four-mile marker, I turned around and headed back. Mark was nowhere to be seen.

Once over the railroad track around the two-mile line, not a wisp of breeze and nothing to cool, I came upon a huffing, puffing Mark. His face was beet-red. He had eaten enough of my dust.

"Hey, babe. There's nothing ahead." I could have run all day that day, but I didn't. "Let's walk back; I'm exhausted," I lied, to which he enthusiastically agreed. Silently I was cheering inside.

At the end of that weekend, I gathered the crew together for a dinner. The 12 of them arrived at the New Age health food restaurant looking different somehow ~ transformed.

Sean, our client from New York whose pasty complexion attested to the fact that he was hardly the athletic type, had ventured off with Dale, our lead makeup artist, a longtime pal of mine and a practitioner at Agape, the Church of Religious Science. That afternoon they had gone on a hike into the volcanic caves at Medicine Lake.

The distinguishing thing about Sean was that he never smiled. When he entered a room his countenance literally sucked the energy out of it. In fact, he seemed to walk around with a perpetual dark cloud over his head. True to form, as we waited for our organic cocktails, he launched into a story about being attacked by killer bees.

"Now you have to understand," he began, "the greatest fear in my life has been bees. And there we were, so far under the ground my legs were buckling and suddenly out of nowhere, I mean, nowhere natural where bees could even appear, there they were ~ coming at me like Messerschmitts flying sorties over France. I thought, 'I'm gonna die.'"

The only reason I wasn't startled by his story was that he was here in front of us, unscathed. And on his face, a grin as welcoming as the Brooklyn Bridge.

"It was alarming and breathtaking at the same time," Dale added.

"Go on. What happened?" Mark said, repositioning himself on the edge of his seat, surprisingly intent on something other than business. Conversation at the table fell to a hush.

"They circled my head. I mean, they were everywhere, all around me, about four inches from my eyes, going around and around. It was terrifying. All my life I have had this . . ." He shuddered. "Bees have been my deepest terror!"

"I immediately went into prayer," Dale injected.

"She did!" Sean agreed, and without a breath he continued. "Then poof! Like, snap your fingers, they were gone! I mean, they didn't just flap their wings and fly away or anything, they were gone! Poof! Vaporized!"

"It's true," Dale added.

"Thank God you were there," Sean said, reaching over and squeezing Dale's arm. It wasn't a sexual, let's-fall-in-love touch, but it wasn't a brotherly nudge either. It was a sweet bond, right in the middle.

I shot a glance to Mark ,who had suddenly become quite pensive.

""Kindness converts
more people than
enthusiasm, eloquence, or science."

By our last weekend, we had shot more film than originally planned and were nicely ahead of schedule. Gilly organized a group to participate in an Indian sweat while Mark and I were in full-on preparation for our next job for AT&T. Upon our return we had two weeks before we were to leave for Sydney, Australia, and Papua New Guinea. Still, I thought we had earned an afternoon off.

"Let's go for a hike," I suggested to Mark. Though we had not spoken of it, privately he had not recovered from our little jog and my newfound strength. Ever so subtly, he had withdrawn from us all. I recognized this interior shifting all too well and sensed he needed a friend.

Mark and I agreed that Panther Meadow, about 7,500 feet above sea level, would be our destination, touted as home to a natural healing spring and meadows of flora and fauna rare to the area.

"It will only take us an hour, right? No more than that, right?"

"Indeed," I reassured Mark.

It took us two hours to reach the meadow. Yet by that time Mark was no longer referring to his watch. We didn't stop there.

The pathway forward unfolded like a spiral dance up a chakra color chart as if the visualization that began my meditation practice had come to full immersive life.

We hiked through lines of ruby-red boulders so large and spaced so geometrically they resembled the roots of a tree that had broken through the earth.

The path then curled gently up to a field scattered with masses of wild orange California poppies. As we strode around them they gave the impression of being tiny hands, applauding our arrival.

As we climbed higher the poppies gave way to rugs of sunny yellow buttercups. A soft breeze rushed by, and the yellow blossoms glowed and sparkled, waving us on, making my tummy feel so happy.

Next, the blossoms were gone and what was in their place was a carpet of green. Deep green grass and moss paved the entryway to a forest lush with emerald pines. My heart burst with happiness as we stepped along a neatly worn path guiding us through the wilderness. Once the last tree was behind us, the world opened up.

Surprisingly groomed, almost cartoonlike in its perfection, the landscape exploded before us like a choir of angels singing. A ceiling of intense cobalt blue sat like a wide-brimmed hat over our heads.

"Let's follow the water." I sang as I danced beside the creek, which snaked upward. Dodging occasional seats of white rocks and purple flowers that dotted the sloping earth, we traversed higher and higher until the trickle of water turned into a brook, running downhill. The light was radiant, unlike any glow I had ever seen.

When we reached the bubbling source of the brook, we both turned around and beheld what was all around us.

"Panther Meadow." Mark and I gasped in unison, realizing we'd had to get up that high to actually appreciate it. We inhaled a long, holy moment of silence.

Gilly organized a picnic lunch for us and we were famished. We found a wonderful rock formation just off the natural path, two large, smooth boulders shaped like big pillows on either side of the emergence of the spring.

It was good at last to relax with Mark. Relieved I could share with him my journey to India and my time with Mother Teresa and all the amazing things that unfolded for me.

"You know I don't believe in anything I can't see," Mark stated.

"You can't see the wind; does that mean it doesn't exist for you?"

"That's different," he countered.

I talked and talked, taking him all the way to Mother's gift of the ring. He didn't interrupt, and he didn't roll his eyes or show me any of his previous judgments of disrespect. He was intent and listening.

I knew words would not do it. And I sensed our time together as business partners was coming to a close. I wanted so much to give him a little more faith in the world and a little more insight into how integral he was in its evolution.

Ask and ye shall receive.

After lunch, the hectic workweek took its toll. The sun baked hot and the air was light. We each knelt down and sipped water from the natural spring that flowed between us. The water tasted clean and cool, going down like the breath of morning frost. We then stretched out on our own respective pillow-like boulders, soaking up rays. In a matter of moments we were both drifting off into slumber land.

*"One day it will hit you
and you will wonder why on earth
you thought otherwise ~
everything is alive!
I hope I am around when that day comes."*

There was no telling how long we dozed, but something was tickling my cheek and a soft breeze was tapping the side of my nose. Slowly I lifted my lids and whoosh! Two luminescent wings fluttered in front of my eye line. Dancing before me was the most remarkable butterfly I had ever seen. I lay there content, staring up at the sky, following the butterfly's intricate yet precise movements.

"Mark. Are you awake?" I whispered.

"Yeah. I'm watching this butterfly. I think it likes me."

I didn't move my head. "I have a butterfly, too. It's swirling around making figure eights."

"Mine, too," he added.

Neither of us shifted a hair, not wanting to disturb whatever hypnotic spell the butterflies were weaving.

"Christina?"

"Yes."

"Am I lying on a rock?"

I slid my glance across and looked over at Mark, spread out on the giant flat boulder. "Yes."

"It's moving."

"What?"

"I'm telling you, the rock is moving. It's breathing. I mean, it's alive."

"Well, of course it's alive," I said.

I turned to give Mark a discourse on our "living" planet, no matter how solid and immovable something may appear ~ yet as I turned, the butterfly left my airspace and flew toward Mark's butterfly.

I rolled onto my side and gazed at them. I swear my eyes were not deceiving me. Something that I always thought was one way was now suddenly another way. The rock under Mark was undulating. And I could see it!

"Whoa," Mark whispered. "I want to get off. But it feels too good."

I hadn't noticed actually, but the rock I was on was moving, too. I rolled over and lay across it with my legs sprawled out. I put my head down on the rock and melted into it, and that's when I felt it breathing.

"I feel like I am on a water bed and someone's jumping up and down, in slow motion," Mark said, lying back and letting it move him.

The butterflies came back into view over the spring. Twirling above, they exploded the space between us with their excitement, landing for a short time on a mossy pebble in the spring and then taking off again to engulf us like Saint Teresa among a flock of angels.

I sat up and looked around. I could hardly believe my eyes. The entire mountainside was rising and falling in a slow, rhythmic breathing gesture, almost aligned with my heartbeat and the butterfly dance. All one. Breathing with us and for us.

"This is not normal," Mark whispered. With my peripheral vision I saw Mark gripping the rock like he grips the portal of a jet plane ~ his fingertips turning white.

"Mark. This is what's real. Can you see now, how much a part of nature we are? Can you feel how connected we all are?"

"Am I going crazy?"

"No, you're not. Take a deep breath and relax."

"But it's alive."

"Of course, that's what I have been telling you. Everything on our planet Is alive. Even a rock! And it's all connected through our aliveness and to our breath. That's how important we are to each other," I said, in awe of my own discovery.

Mark had been rendered speechless. So I seized my moment.

"Just because a rock is dense and solid, seemingly without consciousness or movement, doesn't mean it's any less alive than you are. You are as much a part of it as it is of you." Amazed and in awe of the confirmation of universal unity we were both experiencing, I immediately accepted this enchanting magic, whereas Mark was still cautious and breathing heavily.

"Can you sit up?" I asked.

"Mmm." Mark gingerly raised himself onto his elbows. As he did, everything about his countenance settled. His face, the lines that were there, had smoothed, like years of worry ~ fallen away.

"Look. We're fine. How could anything this beautiful be scary? Look at the butterflies, how they follow each other. So precisely and in sync. Oh, Mark, look!"

Suddenly the butterflies soared straight up in the sky, turned, and in one sweeping brushstroke zoomed down straight toward us. They came nearer, then slowed and separated ~ one settled gently on my hand and the other greased a landing on Mark's shoulder.

They folded their wings and in a blink all movement around us subsided. The rocks stopped their undulating, and whatever had occurred ceased.

"This is surreal," Mark whispered without moving.

We didn't talk or move for the longest time.

When the meadow was in shadow and daylight had left the mountain I slid off my boulder and gathered up our picnic leftovers.

"I feel so good," Mark noted as we traversed our way through the trees and back down the mountain face. Both of us took particular pains to tread lightly. When you realize how alive a blade of grass is, you become mindful about trampling it.

When we reached the heel of the trail and the tree line, darkness was swirling quickly around us. I turned, wanting to inhale one last breath of the magical summit. It wasn't easy to pull away from van Gogh's living canvas of a *Starry Night.*

"Uh-oh, listen to this!" Mark had found a visitors' sign at the entrance. "'Shasta Mountain figures prominently in the world of creation myths and legends of the Native Americans. Many Indian people, unless under very special circumstances, will not ascend the mountain beyond this tree line.'" Mark read on silently until he could no longer contain his shock. "Do you know it's called Panther Meadow because the Native Americans who lived here would change into panthers?" he said, his voice becoming somewhat shrill. "Now we find this out?"

"You looked like Mark to me, but who knows? What else does it say?" I added lightly.

"'Those who were indigenous to the area knew this was a dangerous place, and without the proper preparation a person could get lost, seriously injured, or go crazy and perhaps never return.'"

"Well, we made it," I cheered, ever so thankful we didn't see this sign earlier.

The sky above moved into a pitch blue-black, geometrically illuminated by a netting of stars, all bouncing light, all connected, one to the other. Mark, holding onto the wood sign, followed my gaze. It felt as if we were encased under Buckminster Fuller's geodesic dome. The stuff fairy tales were made of.

With all the stories we heard from the crew, we weren't the only ones whose eyes had peered beneath the veil. The town's bookstores were filled with fables written by people just like us who had also left this place carrying a rainbow in their hearts that had not been there before.

Mark and I never again referred to that day, though it fired up something miraculous in him, reminiscent of young Moses and the Burning Bush. He had a newfound respect for the unconscious solid rock. That afternoon hike and the butterfly dance ignited a transformation in him that would unfurl and become his touchstone in the uncertain times ahead.

Wednesday, May 26, 1993
Hollywood, California

The small human phenomena had not ended.

"Gilly, I didn't mean for anyone to record finished music."

Gilly couldn't hide a sorry but guilty face. "I guess it moved them," she said, making it sound as if she had nothing whatsoever to do with the wealth of talent on the tapes in my hands. We had sent out rough cuts of Mother Teresa's message to three of Hollywood's finest composers, for their review and maybe rough suggestions, certainly not for completed, perfectly mixed music.

"But isn't it fabulous! Now you can finish it." Gilly smiled.

"No. Not one of them sounds right. They're beautiful, but the music is fighting her words rather than supporting them." Editing had been so easy, and I was perplexed why finding the right music was proving so difficult.

love

I had to say, thank you, but no thank you, which would be a hard thing to do when exquisite pieces of music had been lovingly written and recorded, for free. "It will be fine without music," I said, not really feeling that way, but I knew if these pros couldn't crack it, no one could.

Just then I picked up the phone, though I had not yet heard it ring. Nevertheless, I picked it up. And wouldn't you know, the line was alive and a voice spoke.

"Christina. It's Dawnea. How are you feeling?"

"Good. Great, in fact." Everything had moved so quickly, I had all but forgotten her sure healing and accurate prediction.

"And what about the film?"

Somewhat perplexed as to why she was inquiring about my work, I filled her in on how beautifully the footage cut together. I shared with her the music snafu and that I'd decided I would complete it without music.

"Call my client Suzanne Ciani. I think she will be able to help you."

I loved Suzanne's music; in fact I had taken one of her albums to India with me, and for some reason, one track had become my favorite. It echoed my journey.

I described it to Suzanne.

"Oh yes. I called that 'Mother's Song,'" she said, peppering her words with laughter. I hadn't even noticed. Indeed Suzanne had written the song with Mother Teresa in mind, many years earlier. Say no more!

We overnighted the film to her. Within 24 hours she called, exuberant.

"This has never happened to me before," Suzanne said. "I opened it up, took one look, and went to work immediately. I worked with it through the night and it was effortless. I could feel Mother's presence in the studio with me. She was right here, Christina. And would you believe? The track sliced like butter. I didn't have to record anything new." Suzanne's experience was effortless, just like Bobby's had been.

"Nothing?"

"No. It was all there, as if you had choreographed your film to it."

"What about the ninety-second version and the shorter ones?" Bobby had cut various versions, 60 seconds, 30 seconds, even a 20-second spot, so that stations could have their pick of time slots.

"Every one of them. It was all so perfect. I've never experienced anything like it," she said, laughing jubilantly.

"Me neither," I agreed, and we both fell into a long-distance moment of grace.

When Suzanne's tracks arrived, they were, as she said, as if we had designed every cut, every note, every movement with precision. Mother's voice wrapped around her melody in perfect pitch and perfect timing.

I sent out a long-distance high five to the invisible realm.

I felt pretty cocky returning to my office clutching the completed film and copies to send to Mother Teresa. Gilly greeted me with a red Hindu dot between her brows and in true paradox floated off to the refrigerator for a bottle of '85 Dom Perignon.

Mark came into my office carrying an exquisitely intricate antique Indian wall hanging, a white-and-gold-encrusted sari resting in a woven antique Indian food basket.

"What is this for?" I asked him. Tweaked by the fact that I had just returned from the country where these treasures originated, albeit some centuries earlier, I realized he had probably paid a king's ransom for them.

"I know you didn't buy anything like this for yourself, and I wanted you to have something special," he said.

This would be his parting gift.

I thought I had the Holy Grail in my hands. Doors I wasn't even knocking on were opening wide.

"Send us a copy of your Mother Teresa message," my pal Baird from Bonneville Communications in Utah said. "I want to show it to everyone here because I think we can handle distribution for you." Yet again, a process that would normally require effort and negotiation and a modicum of begging, in this case, required nothing.

I had produced public service announcements for the Church of Latter-day Saints and was ever moved by the fact their work focused less on nonsecular teachings and more on a heartfelt universal message. Without missing a beat they offered to carry the burden of designing and printing the color brochures and tape labels and all costs associated with network and cable distribution. This was a bighearted, many-thousands-of-dollars gift from the Mormons. A generous donation acknowledging that indeed there is a place in the heart that supersedes religious doctrines.

That was indicative of the small yet powerful revolution of love that swept up friends, business associates, and strangers who would become friends, many of whom I have never met and many who would never meet one another. You name it, Jews, Muslims, Christians, Catholics, Mormons, Buddhists, Science of Minders, all woven in there and all stepped up and acted as one, to be sure the message from Mother Teresa was sent across the airwaves. When it was all said and done, we were gifted with around $20 million worth of free airtime.

If what I experienced after returning to the United States with my cans of negative film was any indication of what would happen when her message went out into the global public arena ~ love on earth would be home free.

Truth has always been simple. Love will always be contagious.

*"Your last and final act will be to give
the gift of life back to God.
Give it willingly and with love."*

Friday, September 5, 1997
Santa Paula, California

Every time Christmas came around, I thought I would jump on a plane for Calcutta and celebrate with Mother Teresa, imagining how simple and love-filled it would be. Four years went by in a blink. And then suddenly, without warning, she was gone. But not without coming back to give me one last gift.

As you know, each time we met and whenever tears filled my eyes, she ran to her office, only to return with something special for me. For the tough, harsh, unyielding woman I knew Mother Teresa, founder of the Missionaries of Charity, to be, she could not bear to see me cry. A mother's love.

This time was no different. Although it would not be her last lifting of the veil that separated us, she came with another present for me. And this one was as real as the medal, the book, and the ring.

No matter how prepared we are for a visitation from the other side, it still has the ability to shake you to your core. And what that visit may give you, you may not in that moment be ready to accept. Or in my case, remember.

It was the middle of the night and yet what filled my room sparkled bright like the sun.

I thought God had come to take me.

Light was all around me. Alive it was, flitting here and there like lightning bugs. So alluring, so full of energy, so beautiful I wanted to give myself over to it, become part of it, certain I would be engulfed in its ecstasy. So I thought of nothing but the light and whoosh! I was in . . . in the midst of what seemed like a great gathering.

I was no longer inside a body. The energy coursing through me became me. Elevated. Magnificent. Vibrating me, lifting me from all of earth's boundaries. Soaring me higher and farther than any airship ever could. I was a galaxy of light. The most impeccable light, pulsing and pumping, aglow with the endless breath of new life.

My thought was not a thought but an action. I was hurtling through space. All around me I saw light igniting light. Endless explosions of light. Feeling my beginning, your beginning, our beginnings, as a brilliant orb that touched and merged and separated, reproducing itself, again and again. Eternal and infinite. No beginning or ending. Pow. Pow. Pow. And those flashes, right before each explosion was the moment of birth, in all its wondrous exuberance.

I am lost for how to explain what I felt next in this stratosphere of unbridled freedom, vision, and sound overtaking. Like a sonic boom, I was hurtled beyond human imagination and possibility, into a frequency of indescribable elevation. Climaxing with the stars.

I was no longer. I was the cosmos. I was everything and nothing, all at once.

No longer seeking God, I had joined creation.

I thought if I stayed there one more moment I would die. And yet, I was willing to die, because in that instance, I was all life. *I was God. I was love.*

Suddenly, I felt myself. I felt myself step back through the gateway and become again contained in an ethereal body. Faintly I felt the sensation of falling. And I was me again. With my memory and my consciousness.

I was back. In my world. In my room. In my bed. In my body. She had taken me to where only love exists and she had brought me back.

Love. It's all about love, I thought. And then she spoke the words that only now, so many years later, do I hear.

"When you write, you will remember this. When you write, you will be like a pencil in God's hand and you will write of this."

So now I have written it down for you.

Was it God who wrote these pages for you through me? Or has it simply been someone, who after years of seeking that magnificent part we each possess, gathering thoughts as they roamed the ether, sat down and wrote the hologram of a personal tale on a mirror for you?

It was not Mother Teresa's ghost that came to visit me on that time of her passing. It was her love, stronger than life itself, able to travel through space and time to lift the veil of conscious sleep, to awaken me momentarily to all that is. She had come to me, in her perfection, to remind me of our pact.

In writing I did not have to search for the words. They were already there, emerging from my fingertips. I cannot even take credit for having the "idea," for it was really Mother's idea, or perhaps it was God's idea, in action within us. Still, it was her unerring belief in me that compelled me to do what was no more than my duty ~ to tell the story of my journey ~ from Hollywood to Calcutta, from make-believe to reality, uncertainty to faith, from death to life, and from fear to our final destination ~ for what she gifted me in life, she bequeathed in death: love.

Wednesday, September 10, 1997

Calcutta was a hive of bowed heads and hushed whispers as honored guests took their seats for Mother Teresa's memorial service. Across the airwaves, Tom Brokaw quietly recounted highlights of her life.

"She was a frail nun. Known to faint even while lighting the candles for celebrations. Indeed, she suffered throughout her life from recurring bouts of malaria. Quite remarkable then that she would have a vision in which she believed God came to her and called her to leave her post in the Church and dedicate her life tending to the poorest of the poor. She took to the streets of Calcutta, alone and without funding, an arduous task for even the strongest of people. Quite by chance, today, September tenth, the day of her memorial, is what is known throughout her Missionaries of Charity as Inspiration Day, the anniversary of Mother Teresa's vision of God and what she referred to as her 'call within a call.'"

Cameras caressed Mother's prone image where she lay for her final farewell. I strained into the TV to see Sisters I recognized, sitting front row, side by side with kings and queens, presidents and religious leaders. *What would become of these gentle nuns of the Missionaries of Charity without their fearless leader?* I wondered, though certain she would be looking out for them all. One lone tear trickled down my cheek. The service ended and dignitaries dispersed.

Petals languidly wafted from overhanging verandas as Mother Teresa's body, not closed inside a casket but laying there for the world to see, clad simply in her white sari with its three distinctive blue bands, made its final journey through the flower-laden streets of Calcutta, to her final resting place in the Motherhouse. She lay atop the same gun carriage that had borne the body of Mahatma Gandhi almost 50 years earlier.

When she disappeared inside her Calcutta home, I knew she was gone forever from the screen of this life.

I gave in to another tear, but my heart was neither heavy with grief nor forlorn with loss. She had passed beyond our reach, and she had left us all with a gift ~ the memory of who she was, what she believed, and what she had accomplished.

This one frail, diminutive woman was at the heart of a revolution, not born of anger, or fear, or greed, or violence, but a revolution greater and more profoundly far-reaching than we could imagine, because it was born of love.

This was her legacy.

With Mother Teresa I discovered time is not linear, nor can it be held up to measure our growth. Indeed, a lifetime in the unseen world is the blink of an eye in this. Life is not a pass-or-fail test or a race to a finish line. It is a wondrous holographic journey through an endless, many splendid thing. We make our plans and embark upon our journey as one. We separate and live inside a body and experience a life, for a while. In time, we go home to become one again.

If we are to bring heaven to earth, the challenge now falls to each of us, if we so choose, to be the one. In the here and now. To stand up for our dreams for they are seeded in the godlike aspect that is us.

I pray on this adventure you have met and aligned yourself with the One. The One who is the most authentic part of you. The One whom no one else can touch. The One who will take you into your fear and bring you healing, by the supreme gift you find there. The One who is your creator, who is God as you. The One who is setting fire to your passion, so you may embark on your own *revolution of love,* for when we are unified in body, mind, and soul, we can and will bring an end to poverty, anger, hatred, and war.

I believe this is possible, because there was her, and there is me, and now there is you. For with our melted hearts, our love can spread like a burning fire . . .

"Let us begin a revolution of Love.
The joy of loving is in the joy of sharing.
When my poor people are hungry for bread,
I give them the piece of bread and I have solved that difficulty.
But when they're hungry for love ~ lonely, unwanted, unloved ~
it takes very tender compassion, understanding, and love.
And where does this love begin?
In our own family.
And it's something so beautiful that love begins at home and
it can spread like a burning fire from house to house.
And by loving one another, we can spread throughout the world ~
peace, joy, unity, and love.
I call it a revolution. A revolution of love."

   Revolution of Love, the first global public service announcement featuring Mother Teresa, aired on more than 1,234 network and cable stations in the United States, on CNN worldwide ~ especially in troubled parts of the world ~ and by request at special humanitarian events.

   On the anniversary of Mother Teresa's 100th birthday in Rome, this personal message was chosen by the Missionaries of Charity to open the celebrations. It went on to garner what we assess to be around $20 million of gifted airtime and an International Broadcasting Award. It was sent always free of charge.

ONE LAST THING

Naomi Mann

Easter Sunday, April 20, 2014
Atlanta, Georgia

Love. It swells from your heart, explodes in your throat, and rockets from your eyes. In that piercing moment of clarity, you are bigger than the sky, greater than the earth, and more powerful than the galaxy itself. So powerful nothing can touch you. This is what I feel as I mention everyone here. This is the part where I bow down in gratitude ~ the most transformative of all human expressions.

To begin I must take you back to before this story was a blip on the screen.

love

For the very fact that I was even able to see or hear Mother Teresa calling me, or trust that I may write with a whisper of divinity, I owe recognition of those intuitive abilities to my first master teacher. This teacher was no longer in the body ~ yet he was fully alive in consciousness ~ for consciousness does not need the physical to be felt or heard. Had he been in his recognizable life form of an actor, I would have preferred to play tiddlywinks. As it was I went kicking and screaming into my lessons.

Love unfolded while I was living in his last home in Santa Paula, California. I owned it from 1983 to 2004, and during that time, he became my rather intense and relentless spiritual instructor. His influence upon me was holistic. While I owned that property, I learned, firsthand, of the effects of environmental impact, climate change, government influence, and corporate persuasion in our world today. I owe him my forever, undying love and appreciation for setting me straight, on what he called my "life path."

Twenty-one years have passed since I made that first journey to India ~ they flew by in a minute and somewhere in the middle we crossed over into a new century. Over that time our earth's vital functions have moved closer to flatline. By 2040, the world's finest scientists estimate planet earth will be in resuscitation mode. They say we will be fighting to save our home.

I, on the other hand, see our future through rosier glasses. Mother Nature is one powerful force, and she will bring balance and realignment to what ails her, but not without our help. With this memoir and over the years, I turned down publishing contracts, changed titles, and dug deeper while I watched and waited for its ending to reveal itself to me. Eventually I think, in my world-weariness, I may have fallen asleep.

Late in 2012, an angel must have tapped me on the shoulder and woke me, for I became strangely consumed by panic ~ writing like there was no tomorrow with naught publisher nor deadline in my sights. I thought I had been waiting for an ending. No. It was simply for me to realize what Mother Teresa meant, when she told me to write. It was simply for me to find my trust in the God she spoke of when she gave me that ring. For the words were already there. And yet there was something greater working with me.

What was it Mother Teresa said to me? "God speaks in the silence of the heart . . ."

I was privileged to be encouraged and supported by many, and it's my duty, my pleasure, my unbridled passion to add their names to those I have mentioned inside the narrative.

My dear best buddy, Belle Zwerdling, who dothed me with her magic wand, never stopped pushing me to keep it real, insisting I find the courage to go deeper. And who "saw" the subtitle. What a doll!

Rev. Michael Beckwith, and his wife, Ricki Byers Beckwith, who with hearts open wide befriended me at a crucial moment, allowing me to once again, find my joy in singing; and who continue to draw in thousands every week, opening them up to themselves to remind us all ~ we are not alone.

Those who stepped forth and were instrumental in helping me make the film: Robert Black, my one-time business partner and my all-time true supporter and friend. My editor Bobby Volpe and his boss, Rye Dahlman, who continue to be a shining light in the deep abyss of an edit bay. Skip Short, the late Alberta Kennedy, and everyone at the former GMS who did not miss a beat when encouraging me on and applauding me upon my return. DPs John Toll and the late Connie Hall, the illustrious costume designer Betsy Heiman, and those who in the trenches of film production, became family. And when we wrap, they are still there. Forever family.

Rachel and Alan Roderick-Jones, for their "knowledge" and friendship ~ both at the onset of my journey to India and every day since.

Grant Baird, his family and everyone in Salt Lake City and the Church of Latter-day Saints, who took one look at the film, understood the mission, and were so moved to freely give of their time and talent to distribute *Revolution of Love.* Would that we should all be so lucky to find that kind of nondenominational, unconditional generosity.

When a book wanted to emerge, there were those whom I chose as family, who cannot be left out of the love. My father, who with his understanding allowed me to reveal . . . well, not his most glowing moments. My mother, whose sublime mothers' love also granted me that privilege, albeit while little Baby Peggy tripped the light fantastic. Rosie and her children, Alexandra, Sophie, James, and Jessica, for whom this story tells of a loss they carry throughout their lives, yet who show me every time we meet, that love wears a courageous face and a coat of happy colors. And my cousins, Sue and her husband, Graham, and John, and Sally, and their slew of beautiful offspring, who dubbed me Auntie Rockstar. All of them reminding me that the scars of childhood are actually precious jewels, to be set in a crown and worn proudly when we grow beyond them.

Then there are friends, who epitomize the word *friend* by always having your back and always giving you their truth. Though I mentioned him in my narrative in an impartial manner because at that time we had never met, we have since come to be extremely good friends, so I must thank my deep love Ted Turner, for whom so many of us on planet earth should bless and say thank you. Thank you to him and his five children for giving me the space to bring this to completion. I echo that to my brilliant cohort, his first-born daughter, Laura Turner Seydel, for her golden heart. Likewise, to my dear friend Debbie Masterson, without whose true light I may have lost my way.

Blessings to my surrogate mothers, fathers, and children, though few know one another, their names are written upon my soul, for they gave me unconditional loving when they didn't even know I needed it: Dee Alvarado; Jean and Joan Black; Deborah Bodelson; Sam Bottoms, who left us way too soon; Steve Carroll; Jayni Chase; Jill Delvalle; Richie and Jacqueline Druz; Gail Foster; Valerie Gamache; Marilyn Mosley Gordanier; Christopher Hassel; Sean, Bridget, and Brooke Howard; Julie Hunter; Richard James; Sister Josma, who after 21 years, when I called her out of the blue at five in the morning, said, without hesitation and with a big smile, "Of course, I remember you"; Margo LaZaro; Amanda Leesburg; Naomi Mann; Elizabeth Meuer; the late Alan Morris; Lissa Morris; Landria Onkka; Jim Procter and his father, the late Bob Proctor; Josette Roe; Dr. Randy Rudderman; Vasser and Elli Seydel; John Singleton; Brian Sisco; Cary Spier; my dear pal

Leonardo Uribe, who holds up my sky; and my ever loving, the late, Christine Wetzel-Procter. To my fellow revolutionaries from Upper Montague Street for laying the foundation of my social conscience, and my Agape family for crowning it.

Timeless thank-yous to the visionary family at Hay House who sit on the leading edge of this great unfolding we are experiencing and who in their valiant way have weathered my first foray into publishing. Sally Mason, for her intuitive and brave curiosity. For our soon-mother-to-be, Laura Gray, who has been my midwife, every final step of the way, I thank you. Stacey Smith for her sweet energy and friendship and power, to Christy Salinas and Pam Homan, and their coterie of designers. And, my heartfelt appreciation to Louise Hay, whose first little paperback became my dog-eared reference guide and who was my hero long before I ever thought I would write.

With humility, I must acknowledge one woman who is not mentioned in *Love,* yet whose imprint is on every page. Bannye Marie has been my spiritual rock. Making sure I do the work so that I grasp and process every lesson that arises. Rare is the being who can communicate with our inner consciousness and any energies we may have interacted with on our journey and then, like an army drill sergeant pull us out of the stories, so that we may reprogram our matrix every step of the invisible way. When Bannye and I began working together we were at the foothills of the Aquarian age ~ now, we are in the thick of it. Now there are no borders nor boundaries to hold us back. Having passed 2012, we are walking upon brave new territory. Everything is possible.

I cannot conclude without acknowledging my four-legged friends who are there when things go wrong and there when things go right. They are there when we leave and there, faithfully, awaiting our return. They understand everything that flows through we two-leggeds, because they, who mirror our essence, have the uncanny ability to read our energy. My Andalusian horses Lucina VI and Harmony, who now roam home on the range, in New Mexico. My dogs through time ~ Gracie, Maxi, Angel, Ketchum, Bella, and lastly Thunder, who, in that order, have all gone to heaven. It was Thunder's passage that requires a little more than an afterword.

♡♡♡

Love ended with Mother Teresa's passing in September 1997. As the rubber band of time stretched on, I traveled far and wide on my life adventure, working with brilliant scientists, religious gurus, and world deciders and doers, becoming deeply involved in global change and learning more about civilization than the eight-year-old ballerina who tossed her lovebeams out to the world, ever imagined. That was all impressive and good, but there were times when so focused and myopic to my global mission, I rarely came up for air, and when I did, I found I didn't have enough money to buy dog food. It was a case of my outer world revealing how hungry my inner world was for true sustenance.

I was a plodding turtle on my soul journey. I could talk a good game, but bobbing here and there on the high seas of passion and survival, my inner growth lay dormant, as did I. And God, not the God without me, but the God within me, who is me, would not allow me to move forward until I GOT IT! And so came the day the rubber band snapped back. And it stung.

My pretty world collapsed, in the guise of my seven-year-old pup Thunder. Young, ridiculously playful, happy Thunder, my longhaired German Shepherd, whose chosen song to howl along with ~ in perfect tune and perfect timing I might add ~ was "No More I Love Yous" by Annie Lennox. Thunder, my fearless protector who intimidated anyone who came near me, and who from a cuddly, hairy handful never took his adoring eyes off me and who had literally saved my life more than once ~ challenged me to save his.

In January 2013, I was taken to Myanmar (née Burma) by renowned gemologist Henry Ho, whom I had befriended years earlier in the Himalayas while attending the Coronation of the 5th King of Bhutan. We were to meet with high-level ministers and corporate leaders to explore with them the pillars of Bhutan's Gross National Happiness and how they may help inspire and guide this beautiful nation in its momentous time of rebirth and reentry into the larger world.

I took off for Asia unwell, recovering from a fierce bout of flu, whose consequence was two broken ribs. While traveling overland from Rangoon to Naypyidaw, Myanmar's new capital, a friend of Henry's took us on a tour of his bountiful teak farm. Riding mirthfully atop water buffalo through waterways and dusty trails, where elephants ran wild and people had never before laid eyes upon a western woman, I contracted some kind of primordial fungal disease. By the time I made it to Naypyidaw, I had walking pneumonia. In meetings, I conducted myself as if I were a towering Amazonian from the western world, when in truth, I was walking dead.

On my return home, I found a tumor had wrapped itself around Thunder's rib cage ~ exact same spot as my broken ribs. For him, it was malignant and inoperable.

This is how connected we were.

Helpless and almost unable to get out of bed, I shuffled through two months with Thunder, matching me step by slow step. On the days when I couldn't rise, he lay down beside the bed so that I could run my fingers through his long thick coat and cup my hands around his tumor. I thought my quantum healing touch could shrink it, but a miracle was not forthcoming.

When I could begin to put two words together again, I set out to complete this book.

Less than halfway through 2013, the tumor had completely wrapped itself around Thunder's torso and his legs were thick, swollen puffballs. Though concealed in yummy munchies, he spat out every chemo pill and painkiller I gave him. I asked him, "When it's time, do you want me to take you to the vet?" He was adamant. "No!" When I asked him if he wanted to be buried in the garden, he was firm and clear again, showing me a vision of him dancing into the fire. And when I buried my face in his, sobbing, telling him how much I loved him and how much I would miss him, he fair near snapped my head off! He was taking none of that sloppy nonsense. There was work to be done!

As I got stronger, he became weaker. He would drag his puffy little legs up the four stairs into my cabin and sit beside me as I wrote. He hobbled down to the lake and stood in the water, beaming a penetrating gaze at me with his giant brown eyes, while I wrote on the verandah.

When I felt it was "done" I looked into self-publishing, and noticed Hay House was holding a nonfiction writing competition. The submissions deadline was a week away.

The day I woke to news that my story won the Grand Prize and Hay House would be publishing it, I didn't jump up and down. Perhaps it's my pilot training, but when a gust of wind blows into my world and I see change up ahead, I become very still and collected. I simply thought, *Oh, this must be what Thunder has been holding on for.*

When I told Thunder our book was to be published, his face lit up like a Christmas tree. In the next moment I watched in complete expectation that he would breathe a giant sigh, lay his head down, close his eyes and say, "All is well, I can go now. Good-bye."

"No," he said. "There's one last thing!"

The spring storms in Atlanta were fierce in 2013. As if Thunder was marking coordinates from on high, each day, rain or shine, I would find him resting in unusual and different spots around my cabin, in what appeared to be a mathematically measured configuration. (I am still trying to figure this one out.)

The storms hit at night. The sound of thunder always frightened him. It was how he got his name. Literally fell out of his mother on a clap of thunder during a storm in Los Angeles. Two hours later, his three brothers and two sisters followed. As bold and brave as he was ~ and he was ~ he would scurry to hide under the bed at first rumble.

When I tried to coax him up the steps into the house, he would stumble and fall. Even with friends' help, we couldn't lift him. He was like a dead weight. But each evening, miraculously, without a sound, he'd appear, looking the picture of health, on the verandah, eager to come inside, or simply sitting on his bison rug in the living room, panting happily and smiling. I didn't know what to make of it.

Equally perplexing, was the fact that there was this one last thing.

With all his shenanigans I hoped a miraculous healing was in order, and indeed, were I more adept or a greater magician, that may have been the case. He had stopped eating and though it never showed on his thick shiny coat and smiling face, I spotted him one time sleeping with his eyes rolled back and his lips completely shriveled inward. It seemed he had a paw in both worlds, heroically fighting to stay with me, yet equally "at home" in another place ~ but stay he would, until he was certain that I got it! That one last thing.

I refused to leave his side. Everything I needed was delivered and anyone who wanted to see me had to visit. And then came an invitation I knew I should accept. It was nothing special, an evening out with girlfriends. Thunder and I agreed ~ if I could go and not regret it, not feel guilty or torn that I should be home with him ~ if I could be 100 percent present with my friends, then I would go. An hour before I was to leave, I found him standing in the lake. When I tried to beckon him out he turned his back to me, still watching me, but clearly not inviting me to him.

I came home at midnight and he was there in the same spot, his eyes beaming like two red lights, from the lake. I wrapped myself in a blanket and drifted off to sleep on the water's edge. I woke with the sun and he was still standing, eyes focused on me. His head was wet and I could see he had submerged himself. But he was still standing, though dropping off to sleep, with his tired eyes still on me. I went into my house and showered. I dithered around for a bit for I knew it was time and I knew I could not have passively watched him take his own life. When I couldn't bear it any longer, I went out. There he was, floating motionless, face down. Peaceful. Geese were gliding nearby, and fish were swimming curiously around him.

It was Saturday morning. My friend and business partner, one of those brilliant scientists I mentioned, Dr. Randy Rudderman, just happened to call. "How is Thunder?" he asked.

"He's in the lake. He's gone," was all I could squeeze out. "I'll come over." We started up the boat and Randy helped me pull Thunder out and we built a pyre for him, in the fire pit on the lawn in front of the jetty.

"Goodnight, my sweet prince. May flights of angels see thee to thy rest." I don't know where I heard this or to whom I owe credit, but thank you. Those words roamed across my mind as I struck a match at sunset and sat with Thunder while he danced in the flames for the following 24 hours. When all that was left of him were glowing red embers, bells went off in my head.

One last thing!

I got it.

His adoring gaze, his love, was his great teaching. In his eyes I saw how magnificent I am, how perfect, how fantastic, how overwhelmingly captivating, how blessed and loved, truly loved, forever loved, I am. And how did it make me feel? Fearless. And powerful! So powerful nothing could touch me. It prodded me that right there was where I needed to ramp up my love, for myself.

To never forget that feeling.

He was showing me I needed to love and take care of myself 100 percent, all in, as we must do if we are to move upward in this time of universal mind, body, and soul reawakening. He showed me that this time of mankind's transmutation from polarity to unity consciousness was firstly about each of us, being unified unto ourselves. For how can the world become one, if we, each of us, are not that in our own right. It's the greatest gift we can give the world. For with that, everything less will simply fall away.

My story began and ended with Mother Teresa's passing over into the loving. I believe she wanted you to know what was on the other side and no longer fear losing a loved one or moving on yourself. However, and this is vital ~ I say this to myself daily when my feet touch the ground, "Thank you, God, for this life. This is where the real work is done. I will not wait until I have died and gone to heaven to ascend to my finest. I am already ascended."

"Love begins at home," Mother said. And where is home? Right here, right now, in your heart. Be love now.

With that, my final thanks goes to you. For having come this far on the journey with me.

A THANK-YOU GIFT
FOR YOU . . .

In appreciation, and in celebration that you made it this far, I would like to share with you my "unity process." A natural activity that takes less than ten minutes and can be done anywhere. I like to do it first thing in the morning, in the shower. But in fact, it is most effective when it can be done immediately. At those times when I must take a break and address an inner conflict the moment I feel it. Because any sort of confusion should be gone, as soon as we recognize it. Do you remember when I realized that Mother Teresa had this ability to process every negative emotion as soon as she felt it? This is why. So we may stay in the loving.

This process is something Bannye Marie has over the years drummed into me, but until I lost Thunder, I didn't quite understand why and how it worked and how to blend it into my rhythm so that it became a part of me, rather than something I reached for. It has come to be my daily exercise. Like working out muscles that each day build a purer, stronger, and more conscious and happier you. More transformative than any prayer, boot camp, mediation, or energetic practice I have experienced. Not that all these things are not valuable unto themselves. I am talking about a crisis-mode shift tool.

Daily we slip into crisis mode. A confrontation here, an unkind word from a loved one, a feeling of being less-than from a peer, a moment of sadness, anger, anxiety, disappointment, fear, worry ~ anything that takes you away from love now. Anything that interferes with your knowledge that you are perfect and in that perfection, you are love. That's a crisis.

With one simple, pragmatic process, you will be able to defend yourself from the crimes of the mind. To remove thought by thought, feeling by feeling, the negative habits that hold so many of us in limbo. You will access all the power and strength of heaven and earth, reenergize the "you" that has been allowing fear to act, shake up the Godlike that has been dormant in that part of you. You will realize that you are reawakening and taking charge of the life you have dreamed of and are daily transmuting it into your destiny. It is not about having details of your life mapped out, or bending the will of another to cooperate with your vision, or having wishes come true. This tool is about standing tall and true in who you are ~ nobody else. It will allow you to get out of your own way, feeling strong even with ambiguity of the future, knowing that as you step out onto the path of each new adventure you have whatever you need at your disposal and can add whatever strengths you require as you go along. I call it my "Seeker's Guide to Love." It's free to download from my website ~ christinastevens.co.

ABOUT THE AUTHOR

CHRISTINA STEVENS is an award-winning filmmaker, author, public speaker, and global environmental activist. Working at the intersection of cultural preservation, humanity, and media communications, she specializes in out-of-the-box problem solving. She speaks regularly at the United Nations on topics ranging from expanding consciousness to youth empowerment to solutions for global sustainability, well-being, and happiness.

Christina was born in Sydney, Australia ~ the fifth generation in a prominent theatrical family. She is the great-granddaughter of Randolph Bedford, MLA member of Parliament and publisher, who has been lauded as one of the most colorful personalities in Australian letters and politics; granddaughter of Madam Bedford-Young, acclaimed as Australia's first female writer/producer/director; and daughter of "Baby Peggy," beloved child star of the Australian theater. It was this heritage and her belief that storytelling inspires social change at a cellular level that impacted Christina's career.

From her early years in advertising, as creative troubleshooter for Young & Rubicam, and later as senior VP, creative director of Ogilvy & Mather, her team created breakthrough models of universal marketing and communications. Having lived and worked all over the world, her global foresight and innovation have led her to developing nations on the forefront of transformation ~ from the visionary Kingdom of Bhutan, with their roots in Gross National Happiness, to the culturally diverse nations of Indonesia and Myanmar.

Christina is recipient of the coveted Gold Lion, the highest award given by the Venice Film Festival, as well as numerous CLIOs, New

love

York Art Directors' and International Broadcasting Awards, including one for her series, *Voices from the Heart,* featuring Nobel Peace Prize winners His Holiness the Dalai Lama and Mother Teresa, M.C.

As a former board member of ECO, Earth Communications Office, and media consultant for Greenpeace and the American Council on Renewable Energy, she has worked alongside many of today's leading environmental scientists, activists, and political and religious leaders.

Christina presently serves on the Special Projects Committee of the Directors Guild of America and on the board of directors of Ted Turner's Captain Planet Foundation, whose mission is to empower the world's youth to work individually and collectively as environmental stewards, realizing their vital role in the transformation of life on earth today. To relax, Christina is a licensed pilot, and it's her love of antique planes that has brought her invitations from the US government to fly display, preceding the Blue Angels.

Hay House Titles of Related Interest

YOU CAN HEAL YOUR LIFE, the movie, starring Louise Hay & Friends
(available as a 1-DVD program and an expanded 2-DVD set)
Watch the trailer at www.LouiseHayMovie.com

THE SHIFT, the movie,
starring Dr. Wayne W. Dyer
(available as a 1-DVD program and an expanded 2-DVD set)
Watch the trailer at www.DyerMovie.com

♡

DYING TO BE ME: My Journey from Cancer,
to Near Death, to True Healing, by Anita Moorjani

MARRIED TO BHUTAN: How One Woman Got Lost,
Said "I Do," and Found Bliss, by Linda Leaming

THE ROSARY: The Prayer that Saved My Life,
by Immaculée Ilibagiza

STOP DRIFTING, START ROWING: One Woman's
Search for Happiness and Meaning Alone on the Pacific, by Roz Savage

All of the above are available at your local bookstore
or may be ordered by visiting:

Hay House USA: www.hayhouse.com®
Hay House Australia: www.hayhouse.com.au
Hay House UK: www.hayhouse.co.uk
Hay House South Africa: www.hayhouse.co.za
Hay House India: www.hayhouse.co.in

We hope you enjoyed this Hay House book. If you'd like to receive our online catalog featuring additional information on Hay House books and products, or if you'd like to find out more about the Hay Foundation, please contact:

Hay House, Inc., P.O. Box 5100, Carlsbad, CA 92018-5100
(760) 431-7695 or (800) 654-5126
(760) 431-6948 (fax) or (800) 650-5115 (fax)
www.hayhouse.com® • www.hayfoundation.org

Published and distributed in Australia by: Hay House Australia Pty. Ltd., 18/36 Ralph St., Alexandria NSW 2015
Phone: 612-9669-4299 • *Fax:* 612-9669-4144 • www.hayhouse.com.au

Published and distributed in the United Kingdom by: Hay House UK, Ltd., Astley House, 33 Notting Hill Gate, London W11 3JQ
Phone: 44-20-3675-2450 • *Fax:* 44-20-3675-2451 • www.hayhouse.co.uk

Published and distributed in the Republic of South Africa by: Hay House SA (Pty), Ltd., P.O. Box 990, Witkoppen 2068
Phone/Fax: 27-11-467-8904 • www.hayhouse.co.za

Published in India by: Hay House Publishers India, Muskaan Complex, Plot No. 3, B-2, Vasant Kunj, New Delhi 110 070
Phone: 91-11-4176-1620 • *Fax:* 91-11-4176-1630 • www.hayhouse.co.in

Distributed in Canada by: Raincoast Books, 2440 Viking Way, Richmond, B.C. V6V 1N2
Phone: 1-800-663-5714 • *Fax:* 1-800-565-3770 • www.raincoast.com

Take Your Soul on a Vacation

Visit www.HealYourLife.com® to regroup, recharge, and reconnect with your own magnificence. Featuring blogs, mind-body-spirit news, and life-changing wisdom from Louise Hay and friends.

Visit www.HealYourLife.com today!

NOTES

NOTES

NOTES

NOTES

NOTES

NOTES